Florida A&M University, Tallahassee
Florida Atlantic University, Boca Raton
Florida Gulf Coast University, Ft. Myers
Florida International University, Miami
Florida State University, Tallahassee
University of Central Florida, Orlando
University of Florida, Gainesville
University of North Florida, Jacksonville
University of South Florida, Tampa
University of West Florida, Pensacola

Mighty Peculiar Elections

The New South Gubernatorial Campaigns of 1970 and the Changing Politics of Race

Randy Sanders

University Press of Florida

Gainesville · Tallahassee · Tampa · Boca Raton

Pensacola · Orlando · Miami · Jacksonville · Ft. Myers

07 06 05 04 03 02   6 5 4 3 2 1

Library of Congress Cataloging-in-Publication Data
Sanders, Randy.
Mighty peculiar elections : the new South gubernatorial campaigns
of 1970 and the changing politics of race / Randy Sanders.
p. cm.
Includes bibliographical references and index.
ISBN 0-8130-2565-6 (cloth : alk. paper)
1. Elections—Southern States—Case studies. 2. Governors—Southern
States—Elections—Case studies. 3. Southern States—Politics and
government—1951—Case studies. 4. Southern States—Race
relations—Case studies. I. Title.
JK1965 .S26 2002
324.975'043—dc21   2002027135

The University Press of Florida is the scholarly publishing agency
for the State University System of Florida, comprising Florida A&M
University, Florida Atlantic University, Florida Gulf Coast University,
Florida International University, Florida State University, University
of Central Florida, University of Florida, University of North Florida,
University of South Florida, and University of West Florida.

University Press of Florida
15 Northwest 15th Street
Gainesville, FL 32611–2079
http://www.upf.com

For my mother and the memory of my father

Contents

Preface

I have always been fascinated by politics and especially southern politics; I got it honest. Some of my earliest recollections revolve around political discussions and debates among my father, grandfather, and uncles. Politics mattered to these small-town Georgians who sprang from populist farmers; they passed their passion on to me.

The seed for this book was planted as I observed Georgia's 1970 gubernatorial campaign firsthand. I was a high school senior and, like millions of other southerners, had been deeply moved by the civil rights struggles of recent years. That political contest, it seemed to me, reflected a diverse and ambivalent electorate coming to grips with profound changes in race relations. The sitting governor had years earlier gained notoriety when he prevented blacks from entering his chicken restaurant. His predecessor in the governor's office and the leading candidate for the 1970 Democratic nomination had been one of the South's most progressive and racially moderate chief executives. Another candidate in that campaign received a great deal of attention, although not many votes, because of a large rebel flag he wore in his breast pocket and the vile racial epithets he spewed at every opportunity. On the other end of the political spectrum, not to mention the scale of behavioral decorum, a black candidate, the first since Reconstruction, utilized his experience as a civil rights attorney and his dignified bearing to make himself a viable candidate. The eventual winner of that election ran a campaign employing subtle evasion of racially charged issues that appealed to a moderate electorate weary of upheaval. Other political contests across the South in the early 1970s reflected similar political ambiguities. By examining four of these political campaigns, I hope to reveal the character of the southern people by capturing a moment in their time of transition.

Acknowledgments

I began this work at the University of New Orleans, where I wrote a master's thesis on the 1970 Georgia gubernatorial campaign. I feel very fortunate that I began my graduate studies at an institution with so many fine and dedicated historians. Stephen Ambrose, Michael Lanza, Gerry Bodet, Arnold Hirsch, Warren Billings, Jack O'Connor, Richard Colin, and Raphael Cassimere all became good friends and contributed their knowledge and assistance throughout my stay at UNO. Jerah Johnson directed and probably did more work on my thesis than did I. Although his main academic interests fell centuries and continents away from southern politics, he was wonderfully adept at asking questions that readers needed to know and teaching me to write in a way that spoke to those questions.

The master's thesis expanded into a dissertation at Louisiana State University. The members of my committee all supplied invaluable assistance. William J. Cooper, Jr., besides reading the manuscript, imparted a great deal of sage advice and historical acumen while I served as his graduate assistant. Paul Paskoff offered insightful questions and comments on the work. Wayne Parent directed my political science minor and allowed me to tailor those studies to this project. The discussions Wayne and I had over numerous beers contributed immeasurably to my understanding of southern politics. Gaines Foster directed my dissertation. His unflagging efforts on rewrite after rewrite deserve whatever praise that may result from this work and more thanks than I can adequately express in such a small space. Gaines's ability to orchestrate harmony from cacophony often rescued this work.

Meredith Morris-Babb, editor in chief of the University Press of Florida, expressed enthusiastic support the first time she heard about this project and has continued to provide extensive encouragement. David Goldfield and Thad Beyle, who read the manuscript for the press, both supplied generous appraisals of the book's strengths and keen criticisms concerning its weaknesses. Their careful remarks made me more diligent in my observations and more precise in my assessments.

I am grateful to the staffs of the many research facilities I visited during my research. These keepers of documents make historians' work possible. Herb Hartsook, curator of the Modern Political Collections at the University of South Carolina, provided access to the archives for me on holiday weekends, steered me to important collections, and intervened personally with Governor John West to allow access to his papers pertaining to 1970 before the entire collection was made available to the public. His assistance certainly improved this work. Elizabeth Joffrion, with the Smithsonian Institution and a dear friend from graduate school, not only opened many archival doors but also her apartment door, giving me lodging during my many research trips to Washington, D.C.

I wrote the major portion of this work while teaching at Southeastern Louisiana University. The stalwart backing of my chairman, Roman Helleniak, helped me through some tough times during the long years it took to finish the dissertation and manuscript. When Roman retired, Bill Robison continued the departmental tradition of support. Many colleagues at Southeastern provided assistance. Michael Kurtz, Billy Wyche, Charles Elliot, and Jeff Bell read parts of this work and offered valuable suggestions and comments. Pete Petrakis gave unstintingly of his time and expertise. His deep understanding of southern politics and unerring sense of well-crafted sentences led me to interrupt his work repeatedly in an effort to improve my own. Pete, his wife, Angela, and young Tyler also opened up their home to me on many occasions when I needed a place to stay in Baton Rouge, and Dale and Bonnie Parent even provided my dog and me lodging and solace in Hammond when late night classes discouraged a long commute home.

Another colleague deserves special thanks. Sam Hyde, who shared my office at Louisiana State University, helped me find employment at Southeastern Louisiana University and offered me the benefits of his experience and advice on writing and publishing. He has made me feel like a member of his family. His parents, Sam and Allie, have often fed and entertained me. His wife, Robin, has furnished me with limitless computer advice and equipment. His sons, my godsons, Clay and Andrew, have comforted and sustained me through some very difficult times. They are a continuing source of joy.

Many friends who may not have contributed directly to my writing have provided the love and support that proved absolutely necessary in completing this project. My adopted family in New Orleans, Kelly and Taina Mechling, Jeff Struckoff, Ann Spoden, and Willie Parker supplied aid and comfort through innumerable acts of kindness. Kathy Oliver and all the people of Education for Living rescued me when I was drowning in a sea of angst. This project has also seen a wife and several girlfriends come and go. They have all suffered and contributed in some way to the completion of this work. I thank them all.

Finally, I must thank Speck, my border collie and the best dog in the world. Speck has dutifully spent days under my office desk at school and nights in my truck while we traveled around the South on research trips. She listened intently as I mulled over difficult passages of the book, and she ignored my rantings and bad temper when my creativity faltered.

All these individuals have contributed to whatever merit this work may warrant. The book, however, is mine, and I accept full responsibility for it.

1

Mighty Peculiar Elections

"Always before, you could tell right easy how somebody stood on the nigras," said a retired Georgia farmer, puzzled by the racial stance of the gubernatorial candidates during the 1970 campaign. "I don't say it isn't a good thing, but it does make for a mighty peculiar election."[1]

Such peculiar elections prevailed in several southern states at the dawn of that critical decade. In 1970 four racially moderate Democrats won the governors' chairs of Arkansas, Florida, South Carolina, and Georgia. The elections of Dale Bumpers, Reubin Askew, John West, and Jimmy Carter and their subsequent inaugural speeches signaled a change in the South. Each of these campaigns reflected unique aspects of its state's history, contemporary circumstances, and political idiosyncrasies. Taken together, however, the four races reveal a great deal about changing attitudes and the politics of race in the region as well as the nation. As southerners grappled with desegregation, they also elected a group of governors who reflected the electorate's newfound attitude of racial moderation. The winning candidates in each of the four gubernatorial campaigns eschewed the traditional politics of racial discord and demagoguery. These southern politicians were not, as the old saying goes, just whistling Dixie. Their tune had changed. Although their elections did not mark a total transformation of southern politics, they did suggest a subtle shift in the balance of power. Some whites in the region continued to roar the rhetoric of racism and resistance; most southerners, however, had come to realize the futility of overt opposition to federal civil rights policies and no longer wanted to hear political candidates singing the old refrains of white supremacy. Campaigns dominated by racial harangues played themselves out in 1970. Voters listened and, for the first time, rejected the din of pandering prejudices and chose the soothing sounds of unspecified solutions. The harmonious tone of moderation began to resonate in a region long attuned to the cacophony of racial discord.

The 1970 gubernatorial contests described herein do not demonstrate an overt departure from racial politics of the past so much as a subtle transition. All the successful candidates developed new approaches to the old politics of race that reflected the changing attitudes of their electorates. The southern gubernatorial campaigns of 1970 and the subsequent inaugural speeches signaled an emerging transformation of racial politics for the region even as the pace of integration and court-ordered busing of schoolchildren to achieve racial balances tempted many politicians to exploit these concerns. These elections demonstrated that most southerners had finally decided to obey the law. The electorate may have come to this decision with varying degrees of enthusiasm, but the successful candidates carefully shaped their campaigns to reflect their constituents' ambivalence, rejecting the rhetoric of resistance without uttering strong words in favor of desegregation and particularly busing. Noisy challengers conducting hackneyed campaigns of the past allowed most of the eventual winners to conduct quiet campaigns that included few overt gestures to gain the support of black voters.

None of the candidates who would ultimately achieve success in 1970 talked much about civil rights during their campaigns; they all downplayed, evaded, or finessed racial issues when those topics arose. When opposing candidates sought to gain political favor by playing on fears or resentments surrounding desegregation, however, these men refused to participate in the political pandering of race. This election marked a departure in southern gubernatorial campaigns and indicated an ambivalent electorate coming to grips with integration.

Moderate governors had served in southern states before 1970. Winthrop Rockefeller of Arkansas, LeRoy Collins of Florida, Ernest Hollings and Robert McNair of South Carolina, and Ellis Arnall and Carl Sanders of Georgia had all departed from the racism of their political peers and prepared the ground for the New South governors discussed in this work. But it should be noted that these men took actions while they exercised power, and even these governors had campaigned as segregationists. The only exception involved Winthrop Rockefeller in Arkansas, and he represents unique peculiarities. Not only was Rockefeller not a southerner, but he sprang from one of America's wealthiest and most philanthropic families. Rockefeller almost single-handedly built the Republican Party in Arkansas and openly sought to include blacks in his political coalition. Bumpers, Askew, West, and Carter, therefore, do not represent the first southern governors who took significant steps toward racial justice in their administrations. They do, however, constitute the first group of candidates who shunned racial pandering at election time.

The New South governors refused to play on racial fears or affirm support of segregation. The importance of the elimination of race as a campaign issue should not be underestimated. These men sensed the growing moderation in the region and reflected the wishes of most southerners. They did this with promises of unspecified solutions and the conveyance of an image of trust. These men realized the importance of media-driven campaigns. Television consultants worried more about style than substance. The cool images of reasoned calm played well on television and prevailed over the hot pictures of frenzied defiance. The region was in the process of change; these men recognized the political dynamic and, once elected, took actions to facilitate the positive changes in progress, but first they had to win their elections.

Several aspects of the South's culture, history, and politics will not be explored in the following pages. This study does not attempt to investigate every campaign in every state of the South. Instead, it focuses on four "peculiar elections" in order to provide a clearer picture of the evolving character of the region. The changes described herein also took place in years other than 1970, but by focusing on a moment in the midst of change, perhaps we can better understand the momentum of the metamorphosis.

This work concentrates on elections, not administrations. Several reasons militate in favor of this approach. Gubernatorial powers depend on a wide variety of factors that vary from one state to another. Budgetary considerations, veto powers, demographic pressures, and tenure limitations, to name just a few, all affect how a state's chief executive governs. These administrative variations obscure rather than clarify the phenomena examined herein. All four governors promised, in their inaugural addresses, an end to state-sponsored racial discrimination, and all made dramatic displays during their tenures to fulfill their promises, but these actions did not necessarily represent a majority opinion of their constituents. These four campaigns, on the other hand, conducted under intense public scrutiny and determined by direct voter participation, provide a more reliable portrayal of the ambivalence of the southern electorate in the process of coming to grips with integration than do the deeds of elected officials.

This study will consider only elections in 1970 and only four of the six southern gubernatorial contests in that year. Political observers have long subdivided the region into peripheral and Deep South states in order to gauge a state's white solidarity and resistance to civil rights. Elections of that year occurred in an even number of Deep and peripheral states. This work employs Arkansas and Florida from the peripheral South and South Carolina and Georgia from the Deep South. The combination contributes to the balance needed in an examination that hopes to discover changes in the region as a whole. Two 1970 gubernatorial elections will not be examined here, one from the peripheral and one from the Deep South. The campaigns of Winfield Dunn of Tennessee and Alabama's George Wallace did not embody the changing politics of race emerging in the South at that time.

The Tennessee campaign had little to do with racial politics or partisan change in the South. That contest pitted a Republican dentist, Dr. Winfield Dunn of Memphis, against the Democratic nominee, Nashville attorney John Jay Hooker. As the general election campaign began, Hooker's involvement in the speculative collapse of a fried chicken franchise business led to his political demise. The campaign's outcome resulted primarily from the taint of scandal and does not reflect the racial attitudes of the electorate or the politicians who sought their votes.[2]

George Wallace, an old stalwart of racial politics, ran true to form in 1970, warning of his opponent's dependence on the "black bloc vote." Only after staging a narrow come-from-behind victory did Wallace realize that the old-style politics he had mastered had changed. At his inauguration he made no mention of segregation and even sought to include blacks in the inaugural festivities. Although Wallace made his familiar complaint about the "despotic tyranny" of the federal government, one liberal southern newspaper, the *Louisville Courier-Journal*, observed that "his heart didn't seem to be in it this time." The content and tone of his speech clearly indicated, according to the paper, that Wallace recognized "a shift toward moderation on the part of the white electorate in the South, a reluctant acceptance of change, a disillusion with the old politics of race."[3]

In 1970, Wallace had narrowly escaped defeat. Even though this near-loss clearly impacted his political posturing, he cannot be included in the group examined in this work. Distance from the racial politics of the past distinguishes this new kind of politician. Wallace represents a figure from the demagogic past who recognized changes in the South and felt compelled to moderate his position. In contrast, the New South governors of 1970 embodied the transformation.

The elections of these New South governors did indeed signal a region in change. South Carolina Governor John West believed that 1970 marked the first southern election with "racial overtones where the moderates won." Florida Governor Reubin Askew saw the election of moderates across the South as "a departure from the custom wherein the person who took the hard racial line always won." Arkansas Governor Dale Bumpers asserted that his election and the victories of Jimmy Carter, John West, and Reubin Askew were not coincidences, but the result of "a cry for new leadership in the South." These elections prompted much of the southern and the national media to herald a new South. *Time* magazine put Jimmy Carter on its cover and wrote of a "New Day A'Coming in the South" in the accompanying story, which also included Bumpers, Askew, and West. "Something remarkable and significant is happening in this part of the country," wrote James Reston in the *New York Times*. "The men who have been appealing to regional and racial prejudice are declining." The elections of 1970 signaled the arrival of "a new market of southern governors," observed southern journalist Edwin Yoder, "all young, all anxious to put the slogans, the fears, the divisions, the despairs of the sixties behind them." Even a left-wing journal, the *Progressive*, joined in the celebration: "The coming of a 'New South' that will reject race and regional prejudice has been heralded prematurely a number of times, but now, at last, it may be nearing a reality—if some new Southern governors keep the pledges they made at their inaugurals."[4]

Dale Bumpers won Arkansas's Democratic primary over former Governor Orval Faubus, who had symbolized southern intransigence since 1957 when he ordered the state militia to prevent school integration at Central High School in Little Rock. Bumpers downplayed desegregation while Faubus sought to make it the centerpiece of his 1970 campaign. Bumpers took office promoting a vision of a future that "must be shaped and shared by all Arkansans: old and young, black and white, rich and poor."[5]

Reubin Askew of Florida defeated the Republican incumbent governor, Claude Kirk, who seized a school district during the campaign in order to thwart a court-ordered school desegregation plan. Askew pledged to his new constituents "equal rights for all of our people . . . black as well as white."[6]

In South Carolina, the Democratic incumbent lieutenant governor, John West, ran against a Republican who spewed fiery anti-integration rhetoric. "The politics of race and divisiveness," West pronounced in his inaugural address, "have been soundly repudiated in South Carolina," and he promised to run a "color blind" administration that would eliminate "any vestige of discrimination because of race, creed, sex, religion or any other barrier to fairness for all citizens."[7]

Jimmy Carter, a Georgia peanut farmer and former nuclear submarine officer, succeeded Lester Maddox. Maddox, known for his virulent anti-integration rhetoric, had established and maintained his hard-line segregationist reputation by autographing ax handles, mementos of the weapon he used years earlier to prevent blacks from entering his restaurant. As Carter took office he declared that "the time for racial discrimination is over."[8]

All four of the newly elected governors had proclaimed in their inaugural addresses that their states would no longer perpetuate racism, and each demonstrated the sincerity of their promises by taking constructive steps toward establishing better race relations during their administrations. The elections of these men reflected a people in transition. Southerners moved away from white solidarity and toward a more inclusive political modus operandi.

Bumpers, Askew, West, and Carter shared several common characteristics. A campaign strategy emerged among these candidates that some observers have called "new populism." Like its antecedent of the 1890s, new populism promoted the interests of common folk, but relied primarily on image and style rather than issues to attract support. Candidates tapped into the pervasive alienation within the electorate and portrayed themselves as good men who understood the problems of the average voter. Employing this strategy, political outsiders escaped association with the ills of the past while sidestepping controversial issues of the present. These candidates could demonstrate their knowledge of the issues, avoid controversial stands, and convince voters to trust them to do the right thing. Issues became subservient to style.[9]

By portraying themselves in a populist manner, the successful candidates effectively employed a relatively new and powerful political tool. Each of these men came of age as television began to exert a pervasive influence on society and culture. The presidential elections of 1960, 1964, and 1968 demonstrated the efficacy of the new medium; from the Kennedy-Nixon debates, to Lyndon Johnson's devastating nuclear explosion advertisement employed against Goldwater, to the spectacle of the 1968 Democratic convention, televised images demonstrated the ability to sway voters. By 1970 the impact of television on American politics could not be ignored. As southerners, these men had a special appreciation of the power of pictures beamed into people's living rooms. Civil rights struggles produced poignant pictures of African Americans seeking remedies to persecution while southern demagogues spawned reflections of immorality and backwardness manifested by their violent repression of peaceful demonstrations. The power of the new medium was not lost on these astute new southern politicians. In their campaigns they employed effective television strategies that emphasized their best qualities or planted seeds of doubt about their adversaries in voters' minds. All of the media-savvy candidates benefited to some degree from their opponents' lack of understanding of this powerful political tool. A little of the losing candidates' own televised advertising accentuated their political liabilities or confirmed the faults that their adversaries had charged. Some took actions that appeared on-screen to create or perpetuate racial problems that most southerners wanted to mollify. Others, employing demagogic practices of yore, yelled and screamed on the air the way they had at outdoor rallies of the distant past. Successful candidates perceived the diminishing power of party loyalty, political machines, and power brokers that controlled large groups of voters, and began to appeal directly to the electorate through television.

The four southern candidates of 1970 also shared political ambitions that stretched beyond their home states. Dale Bumpers would leave the governor's office and serve twenty-four years in the U.S. Senate. Reubin Askew twice campaigned for the presidency. John West became America's ambassador to Saudi Arabia. Jimmy Carter began planning his successful run for the presidency while still sitting in the Georgia governor's chair.

The wider political ambitions of these four men dovetailed with the changing perceptions of many Americans toward the South. Once black southerners gained the rights of citizenship and joined the body politic, the region rejoined the mainstream of the national political consensus. During the late sixties and early seventies America embraced the South as a prodigal son returning home. The demise of de jure segregation and disfranchisement transformed southern politicians into viable national candidates. Racial problems afflicted all parts of the nation, and many

Americans shared the ambivalent racial attitudes of southerners. States outside the South, long accustomed to de facto segregation, seemed unable to cope with the difficulties spurred by that pattern of segregation. Several northern states challenged busing plans in the courts, while their citizens took to the streets in dozens of urban riots. These actions seemed to confirm the declaration of the 1968 National Advisory Commission on Civil Disorders that the United States "was moving toward two societies, one white, one black—separate and unequal." Many southern leaders recognized that they had more experience and, at that moment in history, more success in dealing with racial integration than northerners. The four ambitious men who moved into the governor's mansions of Arkansas, Florida, South Carolina, and Georgia surely realized that development of palatable measures could garner national political appeal. Suddenly, southern politicians who could transcend the race issue, or at least avoid the stereotype of racial demagoguery associated with southern politicians of the past, possessed viable credentials to compete in the national political arena.[10]

The subsequent elections of 1970 not only featured a new type of candidate, they also took place in a drastically changed political context. During the sixties the South flirted with two-party politics for the first time since Reconstruction and even elected several Republicans to various offices. Beginning with the 1964 presidential candidacy of Barry Goldwater, the GOP sought to play on the desegregation anxiety of white southerners. This so-called "southern strategy" attracted many conservative voters, but in doing so, the Republicans relinquished a golden opportunity to curry favor from black voters who might serve as a potential swing vote. Once in motion, the wheels of American justice began to turn inexorably, and federal enforcement of desegregation measures continued with Richard Nixon's administration. Even the most recalcitrant white southerners realized that federal insistence on integration had moved beyond politics and that the law would be enforced regardless of which party held office. Politicians no longer found it necessary to demonstrate a devotion to white supremacy and segregation in order to gain office in the region. The implications of this tolerance of integration affected the gubernatorial campaigns and the candidates who participated in them.[11]

The hundreds of thousands of southern black voters who registered after the Voting Rights Act of 1965 also militated against pandering to racism in political contests. While black voters constituted only between 10 and 25 percent of the electorate in the four states examined in this work, the cohesion of black voters combined with the growing number of white moderates often represented the margin of victory in statewide elections. Because of Democratic efforts to pass federal civil rights legislation and national appeals by the party, the black vote moved solidly into the Democratic camp in the South.

While many southern Democrats, aware of the power of the civil rights movement and changing notions of racial justice, shunned the use of racial shibboleths that would alienate blacks, they still stopped short of addressing issues of racial justice in their campaigns. Partly this restraint resulted from the knowledge that black voters had nowhere else to go in the face of the Republicans' southern strategy. Although not catering to racial fears, the candidates who won in 1970 at least gave a nod to those apprehensions by neglecting to reach out to black voters.

All the successful candidates diverted attention from the racial issue by attempting to downplay dissension and emphasizing more positive approaches. This refusal to play the race card, in itself, indicated a change in the manner in which southern politicians approached campaigns. Instead of voicing the well-rehearsed refrains of racial antagonisms, these candidates sought to speak in the soothing tones of racial moderation.

Dale Bumpers could calmly respond to Orval Faubus's frenzied attempts to make busing the main issue of the Arkansas campaign by simply saying that all the candidates opposed busing. Florida's Reubin Askew could ignore desegregation and emphasize an issue with economic appeal after Claude Kirk unsuccessfully challenged federal authority over a court-ordered desegregation plan. Similarly, in South Carolina, John West promised little more than compliance with the law after his Republican opponent drew unfavorable national attention when his fiery anti-busing rhetoric seemed to foment an ugly incident in which angry whites overturned a bus that had carried black schoolchildren. Jimmy Carter faced a difficult campaign in Georgia because his main adversary had already established his place at the middle of the political spectrum. Running against a moderate former governor, Carter had to stake out a position that would appeal to those on the right of the political spectrum without alienating the growing numbers of black and moderate voters; he succeeded in running a campaign of subterfuge, diverting attention from racial prejudice without actually condemning it.

Taken together the elections of these four governors reveal a great deal about a pivotal period in the political history of the South. As Dale Bumpers asserted, his election and the victories of Askew, West, and

Carter had not come about by happenstance; they resulted from a cry for new leadership in the South. This appeal for guidance represents a people and a region in the midst of profound change. This work seeks to reveal transformation in process by focusing on the region's cultural mutations, the nation's altered perceptions of its other half, and the southern electorate's political metamorphosis as reflected by the gubernatorial campaigns of the New South governors of 1970.

The Other

By 1970 a New South characterized by a growing moderation and a desire to avoid racial conflict had altered the political pattern of the region. Not everyone had moderated their racial attitudes. Some southerners still clung to racism and wished that politicians would give voice to their rancor. These attitudes, however, no longer dominated the political contests of the region. The South had changed. Many of the changes, it must be confessed, had been forced on the South, but this does not lessen the magnitude of the alterations. With the inclusion of black southerners into the body politic, the South rejoined a nation that professed equality of opportunity for all its citizens as the foundation of its democratic form of government. No longer an island of white exclusivity, the elimination of de jure segregation and disfranchisement allowed the states of the former Confederacy to rejoin the American political mainstream. The region even seemed to have fewer racial problems than the rest of the country. The South had been castigated and ostracized, regarded as separate and somehow other. America now embraced its other half. Many outside the region began to look away down south to Dixie, and southern politics moved onto a national stage for the first time in generations.

Political campaigns do not initiate social change, rather they mirror the electorate that decides the election. The southern governors elected in 1970 won office because they convinced voters that they held the same beliefs and would, if elected, act on those issues important to voters. In other words, these politicians did not lead while campaigning, but followed the electorate from which they sought favor.

Writing at the time of the 1970 election of a "new mood in the South," Tom Wicker of the *New York Times* noted that these new governors described themselves as "products of a particular time and mood in the South, rather than as creators of a movement." Reubin Askew, the governor-elect of Florida, believed that southern whites had changed their attitude on the race question. "That question, is, I believe," said Askew, "fading away as an overriding political consideration." Jimmy Carter, Georgia's newly elected chief executive, asserted that it would be a serious mistake for a candidate to revive racism as a campaign theme. "I know my people, and I am saying what they are thinking," Carter told *Time*. "We have a lot of problems still left concerning race, but we are no longer preoccupied with this problem to the exclusion of others. There is a new dynamic, a new freedom that exists throughout the South."[1]

Many things did seem new in the South of 1970, although to herald change in the region was not new at all. "New Souths" had been proclaimed since the 1880s when Henry W. Grady and other optimistic southerners envisioned a region rising out of the ashes of Civil War and Reconstruction. The term "New South," according to historian Paul Gaston, "bespoke harmonious reconciliation of sectional differences, racial peace, and a new economic and social order based on industry and scientific, diversified agriculture—all of which would lead, eventually, to the South's dominance in the reunited nation." During the 1920s an infusion of new and expanding industries in the region prompted Richard Edmonds, the patriarch of southern boosterism, to claim that the region was "writing an Epic of Progress and Prosperity in Letters of Gold." During World War II the South benefited from the increased presence of defense industries. The region emerged from the conflict, claimed contemporary political scientist H. C. Nixon, with "a standard of living for the common man that was undreamt of in its prewar philosophy." Although the postwar South held promise, the region could not adjust to the onslaught of social change brought on by economic and racial adjustments. Over and over, southerners had sought redemption from the past with sanguine proclamations for the future—while refusing to deal with the problems of the present.[2]

The Good South

By 1970 there seemed little doubt that the South had changed for the better. Some even called the region the "Good South" to communicate the positive changes occurring. Evidence of a good South abounded. The census figures of that year reflected significant regional gains in education, wealth, and population. The number of people moving into the South exceeded out-migration for the first time since Reconstruction.

Many northern blacks returned to the land of their ancestral roots, feeling more comfortable there than in other parts of the nation. The South had moved closer, albeit reluctantly, to a new society that most found better than the old one they had been forced to leave behind. "By accepting the legal direction to obey the Constitution and do what was morally right," Atlanta journalist Ralph McGill observed in 1968, "the Southern white man was freed to advance his economy, to remove his political system from bondage, and to begin improving the quality of his education so that it would give Southern children equal opportunity . . . with children in the rest of the nation."[3]

Many southerners exhibited attitudes that suggested less rigid, more accommodating race relations. The fact that these new more agreeable relations came about after years of civil rights struggles and federal pressure to alleviate de jure segregation did not diminish the transformation. In the fall of 1970, sixteen years after the Supreme Court's *Brown v. Board of Education* decision ended legal school segregation, southern schools became the most thoroughly integrated in the nation.

Although significant integration came about primarily through federal coercion, individuals across the South displayed a growing desire to avoid racial strife. Deeply held notions concerning the impropriety of integration did not disappear easily. Many southerners required prodding before stepping outside the circle of racial segregation that had surrounded them all their lives. Jerris Leonard, assistant attorney general for civil rights, found that many school superintendents in the South had desegregation plans in their bottom desk drawers, but were unwilling to use them unless court orders required implementation. "Often they would tell us, 'You must make us do it if you want us to do it.'" Pat Watters, of the Southern Regional Council, made a similar point: "Many white southerners still need the excuse that they are being forced to do what they know is right about race."[4]

The changes in southern politics and race relations that shaped the electoral battles of 1970 came about for several reasons. The civil rights movement awoke a sense of guilt over the costs of segregation in some white southerners who now accepted integration without question. Many worried that the region suffered from the stigma of segregation. The taint of racism distorted how some southerners pictured themselves, while others feared that rancorous race relations threatened the prosperity brought on by urbanization and industrialization. Still other southerners realized that they could not stop change and altered their racial attitudes accordingly. The factors mentioned above influenced southerners in various degrees; several may have been affected to an extent by all of them, others by one or a few. Many southerners became true converts, while some moved grudgingly toward accommodation. But little doubt remained that most southerners, aside from those few who held firm to the old notion of maintaining a strict caste system, modified their racial attitudes.

By 1970 many white southerners had come to appreciate the injustice of segregation. R. A. Fennell, school superintendent in Williamsburg County, South Carolina, found himself faced with the inequities of a social system he had helped perpetuate. After Fennell's mostly black school district desegregated, teachers tested 160 black seventh graders and learned that one out of three could not read. "They're my product," lamented Fennell, recounting that all those children had started school while he had been superintendent. "I think that, as educators, we have to level with the people and be frank about the kind of education we've provided for the Negro children in the past. We haven't been candid in the past." The civil rights movement also stirred a deep-seated sense of guilt that lay just beneath the surface of the southern experience. The media images of brutal repression toward peaceful blacks seeking simple justice awoke many white southerners to the injustices of a social system that most had never questioned. Richard E. Yates spoke for many whites when he wrote of the shame he felt about the system of segregation in which he had grown up, and to which he "gave unthinking approval to until demagogues like Wallace and Faubus, without intending, taught me the errors of my ways."[5]

Many southerners altered their thinking about race relations due to the stigmas or the costs associated with segregation. Ironically, southern leaders who demanded defiance of desegregation changed racial attitudes in ways that no one would have suspected. Elected officials had presided over efforts to prevent black children from entering schools, condoned the use of fire hoses and attack dogs to thwart peaceful demonstrators, promoted agitation that resulted in violence, and defied civil authority while denying basic rights to black citizens. The incongruent behavior of their own public officials swayed many southerners disgusted by the lawlessness of urban rioters and student protests and embarrassed a people long convinced of the appropriateness of polite behavior. Even individuals steeped in segregation who believed that any change in the racial caste system would produce devastating results began to alter their thinking.

Some very practical costs and benefits also induced changes in the attitudes of leaders as well as rank-and-file members of the New South. Boosters who sought to paint the South in hues of progress found their efforts diminished by the patina of racism. During the 1950s, leaders who sought to entice industry below the Mason-Dixon line began to discourage resistance that might lead to racial turmoil. In 1956 Winthrop Rockefeller, chairman of Arkansas's Industrial Development Commission, warned that an "unhealthy reputation" in regard to race relations would scare industry away. The most outspoken proponents of moderation at the 1957 Southern Governors Conference were two governors known for their efforts to promote industrial development in their states, North Carolina Governor Luther Hodges and Florida Governor Leroy Collins. A growing body of middle-class, commerce-oriented whites in the region realized that racial turmoil stymied efforts to invigorate the business community, discouraged northern investment, and impeded the economic progress that accompanied urban growth. The Southern Regional Council, an Atlanta-based organization committed to social progress in the region, encouraged businessmen to work toward ending segregation in their cities. Between 1959 and 1961, the Southern Regional Council's Southern Leadership Project periodically distributed thousands of Leadership Reports to business leaders across the South. The "L Reports" employed negative as well as positive persuasion. They would point to areas in which racial disturbances had damaged industrial growth and juxtapose those against glowing success stories of prominent business groups that had promoted moderate race relations to the economic benefit of their communities. The reports sought to convince the boosters of the region that helping their cities desegregate peacefully would provide honorable leadership as well as financial rewards. One L Report included, for example, a statement circulated by the Knoxville Chamber of Commerce contending that "what is morally right is economically sound." The council also sent representatives to offer advice and encouragement to officials and community leaders across the South. Accounts of these activities depict a great many southern businessmen working behind the scenes to moderate their city's desegregation transition.[6]

Blacks also recognized the economic consequences of racial disturbances. Bayard Rustin, widely regarded as one of the leading tacticians of the civil rights movement, developed a strategy of actions designed to portray segregation as anachronistic. By attacking urban focal points such as hotels, lunch counters, transportation terminals, libraries, and swimming pools, black protestors demonstrated the glaring contradiction of segregation in a modern, industrialized region. Jim Crow, Rustin contended, impeded the flow of commerce in the broadest sense: "it is a nuisance in a society on the move (and on the make)." Business leaders across the South reordered their priorities when they realized they could not maintain traditional race relations and at the same time pursue economic revitalization.[7]

The new concern with the southern image became acute during the process of urbanization. A pattern of adjustment in the cities of the South preceded the newfound moderation throughout the region in the early 1970s. Those governors elected in 1970 often repeated scenes played out by mayors of southern cities during the previous decade. Atlanta led the way. While other southern cities received negative national media coverage of racial incidents, Atlanta businessmen, journalists, and civic leaders led by longtime mayor William Hartsfield sought to avoid confrontation and called the Georgia capital "the city too busy to hate." Their decision to accommodate rather than resist social change contributed to the revitalization of the city and region. During the 1960s, Atlanta Mayor Ivan Allen, Jr. continued Hartsfield's example and rallied a black-white coalition that sought to improve the city's image. Allen also became the first southern politician to testify before Congress in favor of passage of the 1964 Civil Rights Act. City officials across the South eventually sought cooperation from black leaders. Some acquiesced after defiance produced negative publicity for their cities; others sought out black cooperation before harmful consequences could be brought about by racial incidents and federal pressure. Thus the urbanization of the South played a major role in racial accommodation. Southern cities, as Blaine Brownell and David Goldfield have argued, always served as "links between the traditional South and the contrary influences of northern capitalism and the American 'mainstream.'"[8]

Some southerners, even if they were not truly converted, grasped the inevitability of racial change. By the early 1970s, even the most adamant segregationists realized that school desegregation and black voting could not be reversed. As Georgia Governor Lester Maddox ended his term in 1971, liberals and moderates conceded that their fears of four years earlier had not materialized. Although Maddox noisily protested federal interference with desegregation during his administration, he presided over more integration than in any previous period in the state's history and appointed blacks to state boards for the first time. "He did not practice what he preached," said Charles Weltner, an Atlanta lawyer who gave up a seat in Congress rather than run for reelection on the same ballot with Maddox.[9]

In August 1971, *Ebony*, a magazine with a predominantly black readership, ran a special edition on conditions in the South. It included interviews with several prominent political leaders, including George Wallace. The very fact that *Ebony* would ask for an interview, or that Wallace would agree, spoke volumes about the changing attitudes of the South. Wallace told the magazine that the South had "fewer problems in regard to race than does the rest of the nation. The federal government can use the South as an example for other states to emulate in years to come." In 1971 Senator Strom Thurmond, the Dixiecrat presidential candidate of 1948 turned southern strategy Republican, appointed a black staff assistant. Thurmond also spoke to *Ebony* and asserted that "we have more in common as Southerners than we have reason to oppose each other because of race."[10]

Indeed, it seemed something united the South's inhabitants, whatever their color or background. Some whites saw themselves as having more in common with southern blacks than with the outsiders who flooded into the region. George Brown Tindall, in his 1973 presidential address to the Southern Historical Association, described a "southern ethnicity" that joined black and white southerners who "share the bonds of a common heritage, indeed a common tragedy, and often speak a common language, however seldom they may acknowledge it." Pat Watters described a distinct southern culture belonging to black and white alike, which "gave the most promise of achievement finally of a real interracial society." And sociologists Leonard Broom and Norval Glenn, using thirty-two questions from ten national public opinion surveys, concluded that "Negro-white differences are smaller than the differences between Southern and non-Southern whites." The South had somehow maintained its unique culture. Once the onus of a segregated social system had been removed, the South offered hope of an integrated society that might actually work.[11]

Many southerners hoped that their region, long despised, ridiculed, and pitied by the rest of the nation, might somehow attain redemption by leading the way toward a more just society. A letter to the *New York Times* from Baton Rouge, Louisiana, suggested that the South, "despite its record of documented social injustices, has a great opportunity to lead this country in the resolution of racial conflict." Jimmy Carter spoke of a feeling that southerners had "been afflicted both personally and in the national press with . . . unfair criticism because of the racial problems in the

South. . . . With the alleviation of this particular aspect of the South's problem—which is now a nationwide problem—we have been brought along with some moderation toward the center and into a feeling that the South is now truly representative of the finer characteristics of all Americans." Many believed that since the problems of integration extended to many other parts of the nation, the South, with more experience, more practical and realistic solutions, could lead the way toward better race relations in America. "Racial division is the sickness of the nation, and the region longest and most sharply afflicted has surely undergone the most drastic treatment," observed southerner Tom Wicker, a *New York Times* columnist. "Perhaps, therefore, Southerners—slowly but surely dealing with their racial ills while other Americans only begin to face theirs—have found their energies more nearly freed, their spirits more nearly lifted, than anyone else."[12]

Hope that the South might lead the nation toward a racial reconciliation sprang from outsiders as well as from Southerners. Jon Nordheimer wrote in the *New York Times* of a vastly improved region with a promising opportunity to help salvage the Union. Richard N. Goodwin, a member of the Kennedy and Johnson administrations, speaking in 1970 before a meeting of the L.Q.C. Lamar Society, a group of liberal southerners, said he believed that the South was capable of not only solving its own problems, but of imparting its values to an America that was "confused, divided and in turmoil."[13]

The chance seemed to have arrived. A new South emerged in many facets of the southern experience. The 1970 Southern Baptist Convention meeting in Denver displayed a general desire for accommodating policies within the organization. The members selected a new president regarded as a moderate and, more significantly, allowed an unscheduled appearance by a group of black students who lectured the Baptists on following the principles of Jesus in regard to race relations. In one Mississippi town, school board members could not decide whether to desegregate on their own or take their case to court. The chairman decided to take a secret vote in the town's service clubs. The service club members—all white, middle-class businessmen—voted against challenging integration. The school board took this as the mandate they needed to implement a plan.[14]

Busing

By 1970, most southerners had accepted integration in principle and in fact. But a decided ambivalence concerning race relations lingered in the South. Uncertainty resulted largely from decisions by the federal judiciary. "The protests being heard throughout the Southland," wrote Hank Drane, political editor of Jacksonville's *Florida Times Union*, "come not from the arch-segregationists or the Klan element who in past years have violently opposed equal educational opportunities for blacks. They come instead from parents who are sympathetic or have resigned themselves to neighborhood integration of schools but not to integration by gerrymandering or a federal mathematical formula." A small number within the southern electorate held fast to the segregation of the past and detested federal intervention in race relations. A great many southerners who had accepted integration shared with those few hard-line segregationists a deep indignation over what was being called "forced busing." These beliefs and resentments were gaining adherents outside the region where incidents of resistance to busing made matters even worse.[15]

What many deemed federal interference seemed to go beyond affording all citizens equal opportunity and moved into social engineering. "Freedom of choice" plans, in the minds of most southerners, symbolized the notion of equality for all races and demonstrated southern acceptance of integrated schools. In 1968 the Supreme Court, however, concluded in *Green v. School Board of New Kent County* that "freedom of choice" plans failed to produce significant school integration and rejected those plans as an acceptable remedy. Several southerners expressed consternation at the ruling. Until the *Green* decision state-segregated school systems satisfied the courts by removing legally imposed attendance assignments based on race. Previously even the National Association for the Advancement of Colored People had urged southern schools to follow "freedom of choice" plans. With *Green*, however, the federal courts required what *Brown* had condemned: racially based pupil assignments.[16]

In August 1969 Georgia Governor Lester Maddox hosted a conference to challenge federal guidelines on ending dual school systems in the region. Participants in the conference included the governor of Mississippi, five southern congressmen, and school authorities from nine southern states. Maddox called on the gathering to defend the South's "freedom of choice" in school desegregation. The 120 delegates adopted a resolution by Mississippi Governor John Bell Williams urging President Nixon to substitute maximum individual freedom for bureaucratic directives."[17]

Some parents, frustrated by the Court, withdrew their children from public schools and placed them in private segregated academies springing up around the South. By August 1969 these schools contained 300,000 white students. As white flight increased, only busing could achieve *Green*'s objective. However, the advent of court-ordered busing for the purpose of desegregating schools adversely affected not only working-class whites who had always borne the brunt of integration, but also sub-urban, middle-class whites who had led the movement toward racial accommodation. More than a few southerners saw busing as an issue that transcended race. Once the South accepted integration, it seemed to many that the Court intended to force on the South a social system that did not exist in other parts of the nation. Busing represented a loss of parental control over the education of their children. In some areas parents feared for the safety of their children being bused into dangerous neighborhoods. In short, busing represented an issue that could potentially galvanize a coalition that cut across party and class lines. Southern politicians seeking to embrace the more moderate climate of the region also had to consider very strong feelings of voters who saw their children's lives disrupted by busing plans.[18]

Although the large majority of white southerners disapproved of busing, some believed that the resistance to busing was merely an attempt to maintain the duplicity of segregated school systems. In January 1970 G. Holmes Braddock, chairman of the Dade County school board, called his fellow southerners "hypocrites" and criticized their complaints. "We cross-bused in Dade until three years ago," said Braddock, "and I never heard a white family complain, because we were busing to maintain segregated schools." Whites who shared the views of Braddock, however, remained a minority.[19]

Early in 1970, a dozen southern senators demanded a busing ban and attached an amendment to an education bill pending in the senate that would prohibit busing to "alter racial composition." In January 1970 the chief executives of Georgia, Louisiana, Alabama, and Florida promised to defy federally designed student busing plans in their home states. Louisiana governor John McKeithen vowed that his own children would not participate in busing to achieve racial balance. McKeithen described himself as a person standing firm and "drawing a line in the dust." Governor Albert Brewer declared that the Supreme Court did not have the constitutional authority to order busing in Alabama. Governor Claude Kirk said he would order Florida school boards to defy the Supreme Court even if it meant "going to jail." Governor Lester Maddox called on the Georgia legislature to abolish the compulsory school attendance law in order to defy the federal busing mandates.[20]

School Desegregation

The desegregation of southern schools best illustrated the ways in which the South had changed, why it had changed, and perhaps ultimately how it had not changed. By 1970, in spite of dissatisfaction over busing, desegregation of southern schools seemed to work in the places where it had taken hold. In general, once exposed to school integration, most people seemed to favor it. In the spring of 1969 the U.S. Department of Health, Education and Welfare conducted a survey in thirteen southeastern school districts that had experienced substantial desegregation over a two-year period or longer. Teachers, parents, and high school students answered questions concerning their feelings about desegregation. Almost every person interviewed stated that the process had gone better than expected. Seven out of ten black high school students interviewed believed that they received a better education in integrated schools. More than nine out of ten white students saw no difference in the education they received. Both black and white students expressed satisfaction with teacher desegregation. The great majority of students felt that the race of the teacher made no difference in the quality of teaching and that the teachers generally taught without racial favor.[21]

White southerners had indeed adjusted their attitudes toward school desegregation. Studying the period between 1961 and 1976, political scientists Earl Black and Merle Black saw a marked transformation. "The magnitude of cleavage separating the races had moderated, with most of the change concentrated among white southerners. No longer does an atmosphere of impending crisis pervade the region." A Gallup Poll indicated that white southern parental objection to sending their children to racially mixed schools had dropped from 61 percent in 1963 down to only 16 percent in 1970. This change led George Gallup to remark that this drastic reduction represented "one of the most dramatic shifts in the history of public opinion polling." By the end of 1970, a Harris Poll found that southerners believed that de jure school segregation was "wrong" by a 48 to 28 percent margin.[22]

Southerners had not arrived at acceptance of school desegregation easily. Numan Bartley argued in *The Rise of Massive Resistance* that southerners acquiesced in the interest of social stability. Continued federal pressure eliminated southern options until the only response to desegregation became school closures. "Such a policy of calculated anarchy assaulted public education and threatened the whole structure of southern society, the regions' economic future, and the vested interest of southern institutions." Thus, Bartley argued, the central issues changed from desegregation to the viability of public education, the creation of economic opportunity, and the stability of governmental process.[23]

Earl Black and Merle Black made much the same argument using the presidential election-year surveys of the Center for Political Studies of the University of Michigan (formerly the Survey Research Center), SRC-CPS. They found waning support for strict segregation after 1968, with most white southerners opting for something in between segregation and desegregation. The authors reasoned that this change in southern white attitudes resulted from the fact that "many whites appear to have decided that the price of maintaining complete segregation . . . was prohibitive. To insist on total segregation in the face of escalating black protest and increasing federal intervention meant that other valued goods—public schools, economic development, an orderly and peaceful society—might be denied white southerners."[24]

Most white southerners realized that if they did not share social benefits with blacks, they would compromise or lose those assets themselves. Despite widespread predictions of disorder, when the schools opened in the fall of 1970, a resigned acceptance prevailed throughout the South. Implementation of widespread desegregation of the region's schools proceeded smoothly and with amazingly little disruption.[25]

While many whites did not support school integration, those politicians who sought to exploit the situation received little support. George Wallace, a private citizen in September 1969, urged parents to ignore court orders and enter their children in the schools of their choice. Instead, compliance prevailed and schools receiving desegregation mandates opened without incident. The following year in Georgia, parents ignored a newly passed state law and the public urging of Governor Lester Maddox and sent their children to their assigned schools. And plans for school boycotts in Richmond, Virginia, and Augusta, Georgia, never materialized.[26]

For most parents, welfare of the schools outweighed any other considerations—even local control or the traditional culture of the South. Professor James H. Chubbuck, director of the Institute of Politics at Loyola University in New Orleans, Louisiana, saw a coalition of blacks and middle-class whites forming because of their concerns "about the needs of quality education and economic development." In an article entitled "The Schools Must Survive," the *Birmingham News* urged the people of Alabama to "avoid doing or saying anything which might endanger the physical or educational well-being of the children who will be attending the schools." In South Carolina state officials expressed relief and pleasure as integration plans proceeded smoothly after one observer labeled those efforts "the biggest social change to hit the South since the abolition of slavery." Virginia Governor Lynwood Holton set an example of southern resolve not to disrupt schools when he escorted his thirteen-year-old daughter to a school where most of her classmates would be black, even though as governor he could have legally sent her to any school in the state. In an unusual tribute from a political foe, Virginia's Democratic lieutenant governor, J. Sargent Reynolds, issued a statement calling Governor Holton "a man of rare courage and deep dedication to do what is right for right's sake." The *Washington Post* described the mood over desegregation in Virginia as one of "passive resignation." Many southern state officials urged obedience to the court's edicts, even when challenging their validity in higher courts. In an article entitled "Making It Work," the *Winston-Salem Journal* praised the local school board for dealing with desegregation orders with "dignity, decorum and common sense."[27]

Black Southerners

The metamorphosis in southern white attitudes and the relatively successful desegregation of southern public schools did not escape the recognition of victims of past discriminations. African Americans provide the most convincing evidence of a change in the South. Sociologist John Shelton Reed and political scientist Merle Black studied southern public opinion and discovered that black attitudes toward the South had improved. Using the SRC-CPS presidential election studies between 1964 and 1976, Reed and Black evaluated a series of questions that asked respondents to rate several politically relevant groups on a "feeling thermometer." The data showed a steady rise among southern blacks in their feelings toward southerners. "Southern blacks were as likely as Southern whites—very likely—to express warmth toward Southerners." Reed and

Black attributed the rise to the social and political changes in the South since the mid-1960s. Historically blacks faced extensive discrimination, pervasive segregation, and widespread exclusion from the political system, which led many to cast aspersions on those values that seemed embedded in the traditional image of a southerner. Changes in the South after the civil rights movement enabled blacks to evaluate whites more favorably, claim full citizenship in their native region, and, as Reed and Black suggested, lay "claim to the label 'Southerner.'"[28]

Although generally pessimistic about American race relations in the early 1970s, Vernon Jordan, director of the United Negro College Fund, believed that "to the extent that there is a ray of hope, it doesn't come from Washington; it comes from the state capitols of the South." Jordan cited the recently elected "New South" governors' remarks made "not in the quiet before the election but from the inaugural platform . . . Perhaps a new day is dawning. I hope." Dr. Norman C. Francis, president of Xavier, a predominantly black Catholic university in New Orleans, Louisiana, saw in the South "the emergence of a just reconstruction which the nation as a whole might well emulate."[29]

Many northern blacks began to see the South as an agreeable place to live. Now that segregation no longer prevented educated and skilled black workers from taking advantage of employment opportunities, many favored living in the South. After decades of black flight out of the region, a reverse migration from the North back to the South had commenced. Economic opportunities now existed for blacks that had previously been impossible. Black movement in and out of the South now began to resemble migration patterns of the white population.[30]

John Lewis, a veteran of civil rights struggles and director of the Atlanta-based Voter Education Project, reported that his organization received fifteen to twenty letters a month from young blacks wanting to move South. Northern cities no longer held their previous promise for southern blacks. Lewis spoke of employment opportunities for young, trained blacks that had opened up in the South during the 1960s. "Segregation barriers are gone. And, more than in any other area, there has been a tremendous amount of progress in the political arena. I think we will see a complete drop-off in the next few years of migration out of the South by black youths."[31]

Many black Americans yearned to return to the land they had deserted and believed that the South offered them "the best potential for a better life," according to the *New York Times*. A black activist from Charleston, South Carolina, said that southern blacks were preparing "a refuge" for northern blacks who had grown tired of "beating their heads against the integration wall." One recent transplant, a public relations executive who had moved from Detroit to Atlanta, said: "The potential for success is simply so much greater here in the South where people, black and white are getting themselves together." Carol Hall, a Memphis television news reporter from New York, saw both economic and social changes in the South and attributed the improvements to more open communication between the races. After leaving Memphis when he was four years old, Larry Shaw, a vice president of Stax Record Company, characterized the region as "the promised land" upon his return. "I find that the things we blacks are anxious to have straightened out are more possible in the South. People are warmer no matter how caught up they are in their racial prejudices." Charles Scruggs moved to Memphis from Cincinnati in 1970. "I think white people in the South are more decent. They haven't changed enough, and the changes they made were not because they wanted to—they were forced to. But at least they're different from the average white in the North."[32]

Many of the blacks who returned seemed to share the belief that southern hospitality was no longer strictly for whites only. "Here, you go into a store, and people take time to say, 'How are you today?'" said Daniel Lane, who moved south from Boston, "and when you leave they say, 'Come back, you hear?' In the North, they act like they're mad because you even walked into the store." The Rev. C. T. Vivian, active in the civil rights movement throughout the South, moved to Chicago in the mid-1960s. He described blacks who migrated from the South to the North as being "homesick for just plain folk. There is more a sense of humanness in the South than in the North."[33]

James Meredith, the first black student to enter the University of Mississippi in 1962, left the South after he was shot during a march across that state in 1966. Five years later Meredith called a press conference announcing his and his family's plans to move from New York to Jackson, Mississippi. "On a person-to-person, day-to-day basis, the South is a more livable place for blacks than any other place in the nation." The Gallup Poll repeated Meredith's comment and asked people if they agreed. Blacks agreed by a margin of 48 to 30 percent. These improved opinions did not mean that prejudices had disappeared. The South did not become the promised land for northern blacks. By the early 1970s, however, many blacks felt more comfortable in that region than in other parts of the United States.[34]

Political Moderation

By 1970 southerners, both black and white, had altered their perceptions and accommodations in regard to race relations. Several factors contributed to changes in the electorate. But what motivated the moderation in the politicians who sought to represent this changing electorate? The demographics of the electorate presented the most obvious drawback to the use of racial shibboleths. Although blacks controlled no state they did represent a powerful portion of the electorate, since the Voting Rights Act of 1965 dramatically increased the numbers of black voters in the South. Most southern politicians knew how to count, and the political numbers added up. Southern Regional Council figures showed that between 1968 and 1970 alone, black registration jumped by 212,000 to a regional total of 3,357,000. The increased numbers, coupled with black voting solidarity, compelled political candidates to at least consider the needs and desires of African Americans.[35]

In the 1960s southern politics opened up in other ways as well. The abolition of the poll tax, court-ordered reapportionments, and redistricting of state and federal legislatures all led to a more broad-based electorate. More moderate groups of middle-class urban dwellers and the infusion of two-party competition upset the traditional mechanics of Democratic politics of the solid South. New coalitions began to form. The metamorphosis of the electoral system in the South led to the rise of what some called the "new face syndrome" in gubernatorial politics. Candidates such as Bumpers, Askew, West, and Carter drew little negative publicity. They carried no stigmas of a segregationist past; they had not been scarred by the battles of civil rights resistance. An important part of their appeal lay in their relative anonymity. Most voters did not know them or associate them with a discredited political system.[36]

By 1970, the economic, social, and political characteristics of the New South looked a great deal like the rest of the nation. Sophisticated and urbane candidates could appeal to a modern and diverse electorate no longer consumed with all things southern, including racial pandering at election time. All the successful New South gubernatorial candidates of 1970, according to political scientist William Havard, had a "middle

American presentability and a low-key manner," which made them "adaptable to the demands of television and capable of symbolically representing a considerable cross-section of their respective constituencies."[37]

To secure a winning margin a candidate still needed to appeal to some white voters who remained hostile to integration. Not all southern voters welcomed the zephyr of change, but the politics of blatant racism proved unacceptable in the South of 1970. The new temperate climate in the region made open appeals to racial prejudices costly, if not prohibitive.

The power of the black vote could not be ignored. The number of black elected officials in the region had increased dramatically. Some black candidates, such as Maynard Jackson and Andrew Young in Atlanta, had captured sizable segments of the white vote in their campaigns. This result suggested that nonracial appeals to the economic interest of both low-income whites and blacks might achieve success at the polls. A politician in Louisiana described the Democratic Party in the South as "evolving into a coalition of low-income whites, labor elements, some intellectuals and blacks—a new type of constituency." And Bill Welsh, the national Democratic Party's chief southern strategist, saw a real chance for a natural black-white coalition in the South.[38]

The South's newfound economic progress made biracial coalitions more palatable for working-class whites. "In prosperity, you don't need scapegoats," Emory University political scientist James Clotfelter explained: "You don't have to blame or apologize for giving blacks jobs if you have enough jobs to go around." Clotfelter and William Hamilton attributed the success of moderate southern politicians to a new populism that changed the dynamics of traditional campaign methods: "To meet his constituents' need for scapegoats, a nonracist candidate might identify new targets for attack . . . to replace blacks. The most appropriate targets would be powerful economic groups . . . that embody sharply contrasting class styles."[39]

Political Alienation

Voters in the early 1970s displayed impatience, discontent, and anger toward political candidates as well as toward the entire political system. Vocal and often violent minorities had dominated the turbulent sixties. Citizens across America belonging to what President Richard Nixon called the "silent majority" felt excluded and overwhelmed by a sense of powerlessness. Politicians who gave voice to the problems of the average man increased their chances of success. Candidates across the South began to voice appeals that transcended color lines and spoke to a pervasive alienation that permeated the electorate. Many political observers have attributed southern voter discontent solely to resentments concerning desegregation, but that assessment overstates and oversimplifies a sentiment that ran deep and wide throughout America. In the South this broad sense of disaffection formed into a pattern of populism that defended the little man and attacked the Establishment. Polls in several southern states demonstrated widespread exasperation among both whites and blacks who strongly endorsed statements that the average man was neglected or abused by politicians and public officials. So while voter discontent may have included those who held racial antagonisms, it also contained many who simply found government distant and unresponsive to their hopes and desires, as well as to their needs.[40]

Any discussion of political alienation must include George Wallace, who, more than any other person of that era, represented the rancor of estranged Americans, both in and outside the South. In a book describing the shift of national power toward the South, Kirkpatrick Sale exposes the core of the Wallace appeal:

> He plumbs to, rubs, and inflames the fears of those uneasy with the present and wistful for the past—or, at least, some imagined past— the uncertain few who see themselves as the little against the big, the white against the black, the uneducated against the intellectual, the powerless against the powerful, the frightened against the secure, the looked-down-on against the lookers-down. Racism is part of it, though somewhat muted in recent days and spoken of largely in such code words as 'bussing,' 'federal interference,' and 'law and order,' but more potent still is a broader *adversarianism*, a being-against. Wallace has no real policies, plans, or platforms, and no one expects them of him; it is sufficient that he is *agin* and gathers unto him others who are *agin*.[41]

Even though Wallace had used blacks as scapegoats, his campaigns also included a populist, antiestablishment rhetoric that lay at the core of his political appeal. Wallace's attacks on powerful economic groups such as the "big newspapers, banks and utilities," Stewart Alsop keenly observed in 1970, "account for that electric current in his shirt-sleeve crowds at least as much as the race issue." Southern politicians learned, in the words of historian David Goldfield, "that hollering 'class' was as effective as hollering 'nigger' once had been."[42]

The men who would represent the New South did not ignore George Wallace. After his third-party run at the presidency in 1968, Wallace remained a wild card in the deck of southern politics. Political observers could not quite figure out how the Wallace phenomenon would play out. Those who donned the cloak of the American Independent Party discovered that Wallace extended very short coattails when they ran unsuccessfully for offices across the South. And yet, to ignore the impact of Wallace on the psyche of voters could have grave political consequences. Some aspects of Wallace's style and populist themes could be gleaned in all of the successful candidacies examined in this work. Dale Bumpers spoke the language of the common man. Roy Reed, a native Arkansan who covered the South for the *New York Times*, described Bumpers on the campaign trail as relating his concern over the economic problems of working people "not in theory and statistics but in anecdotes. The problems become drama in everyday life. . . . there is passion in his voice, as if his blood remembered the ancestral poverty of the hills." Reubin Askew aimed the main thrust of his campaign at exacting a corporate tax in Florida. John West told South Carolinians that the integration efforts of the U.S. Department of Health, Education and Welfare amounted to "social experimentation." Jimmy Carter claimed that the real issue in Georgia's gubernatorial campaign was "who will control the government—the people or a small band of men?" And Carter left no doubt about the kind of men in that small band when he characterized the former governor as a rich, citified liberal who could not understand the problems of common folk.[43]

All of these men employed themes and tactics, it must be admitted, that mirrored the image of George Wallace. The successful candidates of 1970 relied on populist appeals similar to those perfected by the Alabama master, but they made these appeals in a manner that avoided, or at worst muted, racial pandering. Bumpers, Askew, West, and Carter may have mimicked Wallace, but their messages also differed from the defiant governor in one crucial aspect. The men who would lead the New South into the seventies replaced fears of the present with hopes for the future. They may not have supplied much in the way of specific solutions, but they did project an image of trust that they would do the right thing. They realized that Wallace appealed to the common citizen's feelings of exclusion from the political process, but they also realized that the South was changing and that the antagonisms implicit in Wallace's message would not serve the region in the future. Bumpers' language in talking with common folk did not elicit resentment, but offered understanding. When Askew laid out his proposal for corporate taxes, he presented the tax as equitable and progressive without seeking to engender vindictiveness or animosity toward big business. John West's campaign slogan urged voters to elect a good man and offered calm assurances that the state would project a positive image under his administration. His opponent patterned himself after the old demagogic example Wallace set in the early sixties and spewed venomous threats that struck most voters as crude and disruptive to the peace and progress the state had attained. West carried ten of twelve counties that had given Wallace a majority or plurality in 1968. Even Jimmy Carter, the most blatant example of Wallace-posturing in this successful group of southern governors, had begun to fashion a strategy that moved beyond the *adversarianism* of the Alabamian. Carter cast himself as a man people could trust. His campaign slogan asked: "Isn't it time someone spoke up for YOU?" Carter's appeal, he claimed, would be to "average working people" who wanted "someone in the governor's office who understands their problems." He delivered his message of class resentment through subtle and ambiguous methods without making overt references to the racial animosities harbored by many of the "redneck" voters he identified with.[44]

Southern Democrats thereby practiced a new brand of politics that allowed a discreet appeal to blacks while maintaining a large portion of the rural white vote, heretofore the mainstay of the party. Democratic candidates now tried to perch between two difficult and conflicting elements of the electorate. Candidates such as Bumpers, Askew, West, and Carter benefited from this new brand of politics. Blacks could not associate them with traditional white supremacy politics or defiance of desegregation measures, and yet, as David Goldfield observed, their "populist rhetoric and modest background appealed to the traditional element of the party. This was a facile merger of class and race, and it became the standard of Southern Democratic strategy of the 1970s."[45]

Partisan Change

Candidates in 1970 who sought to exploit resistance to desegregation, such as Orval Faubus in Arkansas, Claude Kirk in Florida, Albert Watson in South Carolina, and Jimmy Bentley in Georgia, found voters unsympathetic to their ploys. The willingness of white southerners to vote for moderate Democrats in 1970 contradicts the theory that most southerners did not change their hearts and minds but their partisan loyalties in the 1960s. The interpretation that a white backlash against Democratic support of civil rights created gains for the Republican Party in the South has come to enjoy widespread acceptance. For its adherents, the 1964 election marks the point at which southern Democratic loyalties began to wane. Before the early 1960s, the public did not see much difference between the two parties on race relations. The image presented by both parties reflected sufficiently ambiguous records to permit voters to come to whatever conclusion they chose. Supporters of segregation or integration had little trouble squaring their racial attitudes with party loyalties regardless of which party they supported. The Civil Rights Bill of 1964 and the subsequent presidential campaign changed that. A Democratic president proposed the bill, a Democratic Congress enacted it, and another Democratic president signed the bill into law. Whatever identification with civil rights Republicans in Congress may have acquired by their role in passing the legislation was quickly lost by the presidential nomination of Barry Goldwater, who made no secret of his intention to ignore the black vote in the South and go hunting "where the ducks are." The popular impressions of the two parties' civil rights positions changed dramatically. The Democrats assumed a liberal image on racial issues, and the Republicans a conservative one. Among southern whites who perceived any difference between the parties on these issues, the percentage viewing the Democrats as the more liberal rose from 35 percent in the early 1960s to almost 80 percent by the end of the decade.[46]

The differentiation in parties' perceived support for racial change, however, did not necessarily determine how people voted. "Greater voter awareness of party differences does not in itself create a mandating election system," cautioned Gerald Pomper in a study of party image. "It would also be necessary to show that votes are actually cast *because* of issue preferences." Common perceptions of the Democratic Party as pro-integration, it has been widely assumed, caused widespread defections among a largely segregationist electorate. But, as Paul Beck points out, "aggregate relationships only imply individual ones, they do not prove them."[47]

Analysis of aggregate voting patterns through 1968 led Kevin Phillips, in his *Emerging Republican Majority*, to conclude that a white backlash had contributed substantially to Republican growth. Other more detailed analyses of survey data, however, suggest that civil rights had little to do

with partisan change in the South. In a study of native white conservatives, Paul Beck found racial issue partisanship in the South surprisingly
low. Beck saw the high number of Democratic loyalties as a major con-
straint. "That no more than one in ten," Beck said, "have brought their
partisan loyalties into line with their racial attitudes and party images be-
lies the popular image of whites motivated largely by their racial prejudices in establishing their long-term loyalties." While Beck conceded that
a significant portion of the partisan change within the native white electorate may have deserted the Democratic party because of its racial policies, he argued that an even larger share could not be traced to the racial
question, which Beck saw "losing its position as an important issue to
southern voters."[48]

Bruce Campbell, in another study of southern voting patterns, saw the
civil rights struggles, which so profoundly affected blacks, as having only a
passing influence on white partisanship in 1964 and 1968. Similarly,
Raymond Wolfinger and Robert Arseneau, examining the SRC-CPS
election-year "likes and dislikes" questions concerning parties, found that
few native white southerners ever mention civil rights or racial issues as
reasons for liking either party. Racial matters became less important after
1968 and by 1970 had almost disappeared as a component of either party's
image. Democrats continued commanding the loyalty of native segregationists, and although Republican strength grew at the expense of Democratic declines, in the 1970s racial issues faded in importance. One South
Carolina political authority asserted in 1971 that the time when the Republican Party could expect large gains merely on a protest vote against
the Democrats was over. "As a live issue, integration is fast losing its potency. Translated into politics, this means the momentum of the Republican Party is slowing down."[49]

When the partisan loyalties of the South are compared to the rest of
the country, the supposition that a partisan shift in the South occurred
because of the racial policies of political parties loses more of its persua-
siveness. For many voters, the Democratic Party represented the turmoil,
dissension, and pain suffered by the nation during the 1960s. Wounded,
the Democrats spilled blood not only in the South, but all over America.
According to a Harris Survey in February 1970, the Democrats lost their
position as the nation's majority political party for the first time in the
modern political era. Among the national electorate, those who called
themselves Democrats slipped to 48 percent, down from 52 percent in
1968. The South, with 64 percent of the electorate calling themselves

Democrats, remained the most loyal region in the nation. Even considering the strength of black Democratic partisanship in the South, continued Democratic strength in the region suggested that the indications of a national weakening of its strength more accurately explained Republican gains in the South than assumptions of a white backlash. Jimmy Carter saw the South as a reservoir of support for the Democratic Party. A national Democratic candidate, Carter believed, no longer needed to devise a special appeal on the race question because the southern voter had become "just like the voters in the rest of the nation."[50]

National Politics

Since southerners no longer voted in accordance with segregationist tendencies, and since the region's electorate had become more diversified and less provincial, southern politicians began thinking national thoughts. Charles Morgan, a southerner who led the American Civil Liberties Union in the South, saw positive changes in the country originating in the South. He pointed to the "new South" rhetoric of the newly elected southern governors' stance on civil rights. Morgan believed these politicians harbored national ambitions, and that a southern governor who reflected a segregationist line did not stand a chance of being tapped for vice president. Lawrence O'Brien, chairman of the national Democratic Party, said that the South had "finally resumed its place in the national Democratic Party."[51]

Southern politicians saw themselves playing to a national audience. They also viewed maintaining the improved status of southern race relations as an opportunity to offer leadership on the racial problems raging in the rest of America. Just as outside pressure on the South had helped cure their racial ills, maybe an outsider to national politics could guide the North toward better racial relations. Ghetto riots had rocked urban centers across the North beginning with Watts in 1965 and erupting at frequent intervals throughout the rest of the decade. Perhaps a politician from the region long beset by racial difficulties who demonstrated success in dealing with racial turmoil might offer true leadership in a country that the National Advisory Commission on Civil Disorders concluded in 1968 was "moving toward two societies, one black, one white—separate and unequal."[52]

A southern politician who renounced the bad old days of segregation represented the prospect of a more viable practitioner of political equality than a glib northern liberal who had never dealt with the problems of integration. Having taken that most difficult step of publicly repudiating a social system that had been a part of white southerners' upbringing, these politicians achieved a sort of redemption in the eyes of black southerners as well as the rest of the nation. After his election John West spoke candidly about the evolution of his attitudes: "I won't say that I'm completely free of any racial prejudice. Anybody raised in the South has been exposed to that and a certain amount is bound to rub off. But I've watched here in South Carolina some great leadership during this period of transition, and I've watched what happened in other states where governors defied federal court orders on desegregation. I've watched and I think I've learned a great deal."[53]

West was not the only politician who had grasped these lessons. Several southern governors attracted a national audience. The civil rights movement isolated the white South. To the rest of the nation the South seemed different, somehow "other." Most citizens outside the South saw the practice of legal segregation as different from their racial attitudes, anathema to accepted norms of behavior in America. The brutal scenes played out in the national media of southern whites attacking peaceful black demonstrators convinced many that white southerners behaved not only differently, but unjustly. These actions reinforced and intensified the image of the South as outside the mainstream of American thought and behavior. The South became a pariah. Racked by racial turmoil and violence, however, the nation began to look away toward Dixie. After years of ostracism and scorn, America embraced the South.

Embrace of the South

By 1970 several factors came to bear on the racial attitudes of the nation as a whole. Most southerners had joined the majority of northerners in viewing legal segregation as unjust. Many Americans had deemed a repudiation of de jure segregation as necessary for the South to rejoin the Union. It had taken more than a century, but now the North welcomed the return of its prodigal son. The South was "in." America had "always loved the ideal of the South, even as it hated the region," according to David Goldfield. "Like an errant though beloved child, the South's periodic tantrums evoked national reproach; but after 1965, when Southerners had seemingly adjusted to new race relationships, and racial harmony and peace prevailed where everywhere else there existed only turmoil, the South could be taken to the nation's heart again."[54]

Literature of Southern Renascence writers such as William Faulkner, Thomas Wolfe, and Robert Penn Warren had become required reading throughout the country. Modern southern writers such as William Styron, Flannery O'Connor, James Dickey, and Eudora Welty had become enormously popular outside their native region. The long-running television show the *Beverly Hillbillies* continued with ever-increasing popularity. *Hee-Haw*, a vaudevillian send-up of southern culture, became the prime-time prize of Sunday night. *The Waltons* television show achieved tremendous popularity, attracting forty million viewers a week. Based on the novel *Spencer's Mountain* and set in the Blue Ridge mountains, the tales of this rural southern family reflected a southern sort of conservative stability that appealed to a country racked by the civil strife of the 1960s. Southern cooking also became the fad across America as the Kentucky Fried Chicken chain swept the country with astounding success.[55]

Country music—the music of the South—swept across America. The nation had gone "country-crazy," according to a *New York Times Magazine* feature story on country singer Johnny Cash. George Wallace made country music a part of his 1968 presidential campaign. President Nixon ordered his chief of staff to invite country music stars to perform at the White House. Country music seemed a welcome alternative to rock music that reeked of student protests and black music that reminded many of race riots. Country singers Glen Campbell and Johnny Cash hosted popular prime-time network television shows. By 1970, 650 "all country" radio stations had spread across the United States and Canada, appealing to northern whites who identified with the conservatism that characterized the southern value system. These forgotten Americans made up the core of Richard Nixon's "silent majority": they were the working-class Americans most directly affected by integrated schools and neighborhoods, who approved of Spiro Agnew's stinging criticism of the media, of young protestors, and of race rioters who seemed to be shaking the moral foundation of America.[56]

So it would seem that the white non-South had embraced its other half. Statesmen below the Mason-Dixon line must have welcomed the region's newfound acceptance. Having seen the frightening images of southern demagogues displayed in the national media, those who sought leadership roles in the early seventies tempered their actions lest they be portrayed in a similar fashion. Southern candidates could now aspire to a national political forum that had been denied them for generations. Political actions, therefore, must be guided by what would play in Peoria as well as Podunk.

Political Decisions

Southerners had to decide if they would cling to their newfound moderation or elect leaders who would return the region to defiance and resistance of federal pressures over integration. Could southern politicians resist taking advantage of the emotional furor associated with the busing issue? Would the issue of busing divert southern voters away from their newfound moderation back toward racial intolerance in an altered form?

In order to answer these questions, the next four chapters will take a closer look at the 1970 gubernatorial campaigns of Arkansas, Florida, South Carolina, and Georgia. The campaigns in these states represent various degrees of racial recidivism. Some candidates emulated demagogues of the past and sought to tap into the rancor associated with busing. New-style candidates appealed to disparate segments of the electorate with campaign subtleties. Those representative of the New South avoided overt racism that would insult the region's improved self-image, while at the same time they offered quiet assurances to those in the electorate who had not embraced the notion of total integration.

Arkansas

The gubernatorial campaign of 1970 presented the Arkansas electorate with a unique assortment of candidates representing the past, present, and future. Former governor Orval Faubus, attempting a political comeback, hoped that the rhetoric of the past would appeal to an electorate frightened by the uncertainties of the present. Winthrop Rockefeller, the Republican incumbent, after dragging Arkansas into the twentieth century, seemed incapable of escorting the state into the future. Dale Bumpers, a political novice, did not make promises or even say much about the issues, but sought to convince voters that an honest, principled approach to the problems of the day would serve to answer the difficulties of the morrow. Three very different men brought diverse backgrounds and visions to the same campaign.

Winthrop Rockefeller had almost single-handedly molded Arkansas Republicans into a viable opposition party and in 1966 won the governor's chair. He achieved electoral success by incorporating Republicans, black voters, and the growing body of disaffected moderate white Democrats into a winning coalition. Once in office he dispelled the legacy of the corrupt Faubus political machine, dedicated his administration to reform and equal opportunity, and brought business and industry into the state. Nevertheless, by 1970 the Republican governor had accumulated several political liabilities. Rockefeller's image, in the minds of many Arkansas voters, remained that of a rich Yankee playboy. He drank too much, divorced his first wife, and seemed to spend more time flying around in his private planes or at his mountaintop ranch than he did in the governor's office. On top of all this, Rockefeller's inability to work with the Democratic legislature had stifled many of his reform measures.

Sensing Rockefeller's vulnerability, eight candidates sought to capture the Democratic nomination to challenge him. The field of Democratic challengers included Attorney General Joe Purcell, former House Speaker Hayes McClerkin—both moderates—and arch-conservative Bill G. Wells. One candidate, however, led the field from the day he entered. Previously elected to six two-year terms, Orval Faubus remained the longest-serving governor in Arkansas history. After a self-imposed political exile, Faubus believed he could reclaim his political crown.

Faubus came from a desperately poor little place called Greasy Creek in the Ozark region of northwestern Arkansas. His father, Sam Faubus, scratched out a meager living as a hardscrabble farmer in order to support Orval and the six children that followed. While they may not have eaten sumptuously, Sam provided his children with a steady diet of political radicalism. The elder Faubus went to jail during World War I for antiwar activities, resented Wall Street, and supported Socialist causes. Sam named his oldest son Orval Eugene Faubus, the middle name in honor of Eugene Debs, a political hero of Sam Faubus.[1]

After completing eight grades in a one-room school, Orval walked to Huntsville, Arkansas, where he passed the teachers' examination. He began teaching and completed his formal education by taking night courses. During summer breaks he worked as an itinerant fruit picker, sawmill hand, farm laborer, and lumberjack, traveling from the Ozarks to the Midwest to the Pacific Northwest. At twenty-one Faubus married a minister's daughter named Alta Haskins. Faubus enlisted as a private in the army shortly after the Japanese attack on Pearl Harbor and rose to the rank of major, serving with distinction in General George Patton's Third Army. During his time in the army he wrote a column for his hometown paper, the Madison County *Record*. When Faubus returned home he became the county postmaster. With his first six months' salary he bought the *Record* and soon turned it into the third largest weekly newspaper in the state. Faubus actively supported Sidney McMath, another veteran who was running for governor by calling for a reform-minded political revolt. Faubus was attracted by McMath's moderate New South approach and backed the candidate in his newspaper. After McMath won he appointed Faubus to the Highway Commission, an agency Faubus went on to head. In 1954 Faubus captured the governor's chair by promising to bring roads, schools, and prosperity to rural Arkansas.[2]

During Faubus's bid for reelection in 1956, his opponent, Jim Johnson, accused Faubus of covertly supporting school integration by not resisting the federal government's assault on Arkansas's state rights. Johnson campaigned on a "mish-mash of distortions, half-truths, and deliberate lies," wrote the *Arkansas Gazette*, labeling the effort "demagogy, with the addition of racial overtones." The governor labeled his opponent a "purveyor of hate" and accused him of stirring up "strife and racial hatreds and tensions . . . to the detriment of the state as a whole." Faubus pointed to the accomplishments of his first term and promised more progress if reelected.[3]

Faubus easily won another gubernatorial term in 1956 and soon decided he would seek an unprecedented third term. To break the Arkansas mold of no more than two terms, Faubus would need a compelling issue. School integration seemed an unlikely choice. As governor, Faubus had given no indications in his first term or reelection campaign that he would employ the powers of his office to resist school integration. The University of Arkansas admitted black students even before the Supreme Court's 1954 ruling, and by 1955 five of the six state-supported white colleges had admitted blacks as well. Faubus's predecessor, Governor Francis Cherry, had promised compliance with the *Brown* decision and announced that Arkansas would "obey the law." In 1954 and 1955 ten school districts in the state began programs of gradual desegregation. When the Little Rock school board, in cooperation with the federal district court, began limited integration of Central High School by enrolling nine black students for the fall, no one expected significant opposition.[4]

As the date approached, rumors of trouble threatened to disturb the peace. Only hours before the opening of school Governor Faubus announced that bloodshed and violence might result if "forcible integration" ensued. Faubus called out 270 Arkansas National Guardsmen to maintain order. Claiming he had information that "caravans" of unruly whites were speeding toward Little Rock, Faubus decided to preserve the peace by ordering the guardsmen to prevent the nine black students from attending Central High. Harry Ashmore, editor of the *Arkansas Gazette*, described the day school opened: "Little Rock arose to gaze upon the incredible spectacle of an empty high school surrounded by National Guard troops called out by Governor Faubus to protect life and property against a mob that never materialized." But in the days that followed white mobs did form to heckle the black students.[5]

Governor Faubus had set up a confrontation between state and federal authority in which he and Arkansas would certainly lose. Winthrop Rockefeller, heading up state industrial development efforts at the time, spent two and a half hours trying to dissuade the governor from intervening in a local affair that was none of his business. "I reasoned with him, argued with him, almost pled with him," Rockefeller recalled years later. But Faubus told Rockefeller that he was already committed. "I'm going to run for a third term, and if I don't do this, Jim Johnson and Bruce Bennett [two segregationist politicians] will tear me to shreds."[6]

On September 13, Faubus met with President Eisenhower and seemed to acquiesce. "I have never expressed any personal opinion regarding the Supreme Court decision," Faubus announced after the meeting. "That decision is the law of the land and must be obeyed." But by then the confrontation had taken on a life of its own, and Faubus found he could not control the situation he had created. White mobs rioted in an orgy of defiance and anger. On September 23, President Eisenhower federalized the Arkansas National Guard and ordered in paratroopers to disperse the mob and to protect the nine black students. The soldiers would remain for the remainder of the school year. In response, Governor Faubus pushed a bill through the legislature that authorized him to close schools that he deemed had been integrated "by force" and then employed that power to close the Little Rock high school during the 1958–59 school year. In June 1959, the federal district court ruled the school closing unconstitutional and the schools reopened. Faubus continued his defiance in an unsuccessful drive to add a "close the schools" amendment to the Arkansas Constitution.[7]

In the Little Rock crisis Faubus latched onto racial politics as a means to improve his political fortunes. He believed that a failure to take a stand against integration would make him vulnerable in the next election. In an interview the year before his death, Faubus said of his actions in 1957: "It's true in politics as it is in life that survival is the first law." And he added: "One of my black friends came in during 1957 and said, 'Governor, if you hadn't done something, you'd have been a goner.' Voted out."[8]

Faubus had grasped an issue that would garner political favor in the state. He won a landslide victory in 1958 and three subsequent terms as well. The integration issue held great potential for political capital. Many white southerners believed that the federal government had overstepped its proper role, interfering with a social system deemed appropriate by the majority in the region. Further, a loss of local control over schools disturbed even moderate southerners. The act of defiance by a governor against federal authority touched most southerners. The governor's recalcitrance evoked states' rights rhetoric that permeated southern history and elicited the memory of defeat and subjugation. Many southerners, regardless of their political beliefs, admired seeing the representative of

the state fighting the intrusion of federal forces. But the governor's actions also carried consequences that many Arkansans would eventually
come to regret. On the day Faubus died, December 14, 1994, a Little
Rock KTHV television news commentator, Robert McCord, summed up
Faubus's legacy as having given Arkansas a "reputation of racism and
lawlessness throughout the world." Many in the state did not like this
reputation. A decided ambivalence lurked within white Arkansans; while
overwhelmingly opposed to integrated schools, most whites nonetheless
expressed a reluctant willingness to go along with court-ordered desegregation rather than see their schools closed and their reputations be-
smirched.

Faubus reaped tremendous immediate political benefits and seemed
politically invincible after the Central High incident, but he also came to
symbolize racial demagoguery and abuse of political power. An opposition faction quickly formed within the state's electorate. The *Arkansas
Gazette* led the way with critical editorials of Faubus's actions in the Central High affair that won it Pulitzer prizes. The Women's Emergency
Committee of Little Rock fought the governor over school policies.
Staunch segregation had a price that most Arkansans did not want to pay.
The center of the political spectrum began to grow and move toward tolerance, if not total acceptance, of integration. The racial card that Faubus
played so effectively in 1957 soon lost its political potency. According to a
1961 Arkansas poll, the public expected a candidate for governor to do the
impossible: "do not mix the races, keep the schools open, but do not go so
far as to disobey the law." Five years later a plurality of voters believed that
Arkansas had improved in terms of racial integration, even though a great
deal more of it existed. Only 18 percent wanted the governor to contest
federal desegregation guidelines. In 1966 two out of three Arkansas voters
attached primary importance to maintaining racial peace. Even if white
Arkansans did not enthusiastically support integration, they preferred it
to racial turmoil.[9]

In 1966 Faubus decided not to run for governor. After twelve years of
earning the governor's salary of $10,000 per year, Faubus moved into a
home valued at between $100,000 and $200,000. Faubus explained that
his Scottish heritage enabled him to marshal his resources wisely. He soon
divorced his wife of thirty-seven years and three weeks later married a
woman twenty-nine years his junior. After the divorce Faubus moved out
of his luxurious home and into a trailer, where he published a handful of
weekly newspapers until he became president of "Dogpatch USA," an

amusement park featuring Al Capp's cartoon characters. All the while, Faubus longed to return to the political limelight.[10]

Winthrop Rockefeller presented a tempting target for Democrats, but Faubus seemed an unlikely candidate to unseat the incumbent. The Republican ascendancy in the statehouse had come about because of voter resentment of the entrenched political power Faubus represented. Nevertheless, Faubus believed his political acumen could overcome these odds. The Democratic primary season began gearing up in early May for a vote in late August, and the old master believed he had time to reassemble the most powerful state political machine ever built. He planned to call in political favors and carry the crowded Democratic primary with his old backers while the other candidates cancelled out each other's support.

In early May Faubus purchased thirty minutes of television time to announce that he was ready to run for governor and asked for support. He began his speech by pointing out that most voters wanted Governor Rockefeller out of office, and the voters realized that not just any candidate could do that. It would take a man of experience. "Thus," Faubus said, "many people have turned to me and urged that I again seek the governor's office." Faubus then presented what would become the central theme of his campaign. While not directly contesting racial integration, Faubus focused a great deal of attention on that controversial topic. He opposed the busing of schoolchildren to achieve racial balance. Faubus said his administration would encourage the establishment of private schools like the ones springing up around the South to avoid desegregation.[11]

Faubus pointed to the latest racial incident in Arkansas and sought to make political hay by associating Governor Rockefeller with troublesome blacks. Faubus claimed that state officials had ordered state troopers to transport Lance "Sweet Willie Wine" Watson "and two of his girlfriends" from Little Rock to Memphis. Watson, a civil rights activist from Memphis, had led a march across east Arkansas to protest discrimination against blacks. Many saw Watson as an outside agitator who exacerbated an already tense racial situation in Forrest City, Arkansas. Faubus went on to point out that "Sweet Willie has a police record as long as your arm." Instead of catering to people like Watson, Faubus said, state officials should be concerned about "children of all races and creeds who need protection while getting an education," a thinly veiled reference to disturbances among students at several integrated schools. That point led Faubus into an embrace of the law-and-order theme that had garnered support in the 1968 presidential campaign for both Wallace, who carried the state, and Nixon, who eventually won the election. These concerns struck a resonating chord with voters. Even in a state where there had been very little campus unrest, 68 percent of voters polled that year answered affirmatively when asked, "Do you feel there is a serious need for more law and order on Arkansas campuses?" Tapping into these concerns, Faubus claimed lawlessness had reached an all-time high and cited as an example a recent demonstration by black college students at the state capitol. Faubus described the students "rudely" occupying the governor's office, burning holes in the carpet with cigarettes, taking over the House chamber, scattering files, swinging from the chandeliers, and shouting the "vilest obscenities." It mattered little to Faubus that his details of the behavior of the demonstrators embellished and contradicted those of newsmen who covered the event.[12]

Faubus's speech then reached a crescendo. Small lies amplified into bold, unsubstantiated attacks of outright innuendo. Faubus knew Rockefeller's political weaknesses. According to an Oliver Quayle poll done for the Democratic Committee of Arkansas in 1968, the state's voters thought Rockefeller seemed "strange, alien, and foreign." Many believed that he wanted too much power, that he drank too much, and that he did not spend enough time in his office, and a majority believed that Rockefeller could not understand the real problems of common people.[13]

Faubus, the ultimate Arkansas insider, sought to cast himself in the role of outsider. In his first term, the former governor claimed, he had been invited to a meeting at "the mountain." Although providing no details concerning this vague location, everyone in Arkansas knew that Winthrop Rockefeller had a large mountaintop farm home. Faubus went on to say that powerful people there said they should make plans for the state because the people were too dumb to be trusted. Faubus said he objected to this "hidden government" and as a result had lost financial contributions and suffered thereafter from bad publicity in the press. "I did not become a puppet," Faubus said. "I rejected the role with all its implications of power, wealth and popularity." Faubus ended his speech by reminding voters of Rockefeller's great wealth and urging supporters to help raise campaign money. "We cannot hope to match the Rockefeller millions in a campaign but there must be enough money to pay proper expenses."[14]

Faubus's television speech drew mixed reactions. One very negative response came from Faubus's former wife. "Oh, it's the same old story," said the woman Faubus divorced in 1969. "Just a lot of promises. They don't mean a thing to me. He promised to love, honor, and obey me and he broke all those promises." Faubus's speech fared somewhat better among other viewers of the telecast. A spokesman for the television station said that about sixty people had called after the speech. Thirty-four callers said they did not want Faubus to run again and twenty-five said they supported the former governor. The negative phone calls did not bother Faubus, who did not take long to make up his mind; he entered into the Democratic primary race as the clear front-runner. "I am not a perfect man nor the perfect candidate," Faubus humbly noted. "I will be glad to withdraw when one is found."[15]

The former political kingpin who had once controlled the Democratic organization in the state still had political friends in every county and meant to reclaim their loyalty. Faubus said he wanted to return to the governor's mansion in 1970 because he got tired of "watching Arkansas go to hell in a handbasket." Only a seasoned politician could defeat Rockefeller, Faubus told those who asked why he should be the party's nominee, and an experienced governor could quickly straighten out the state's affairs. The others would have to take time to learn what it was all about, Faubus added.[16]

Faubus wanted to take advantage of rising resentment over crime and racial disturbances without alienating the growing body of moderates who now disdained racist posturing. While never making overt racial connections, Faubus expressed alarm about the rising crime rate in the state and peppered his speeches with accounts of recent criminal attacks that happened to have been committed by blacks. Disorder in the schools became another favorite example of lawlessness. And with the now heavily integrated Central High School in Little Rock experiencing interracial student conflicts, Faubus even sought to capitalize on memories of his defiance of integration there in 1957.[17]

During the campaigning season leading up to the Democratic primary Faubus reserved most of his scorn for the Republican governor. Concentrating on the enormous wealth of Rockefeller, one of his campaign flyers asked the question: "Will you be bought or will you be free? Vote Faubus." The former governor acted as though the Democratic primary would serve as a mere formality. Faubus hesitated in attacking Democrats whose support he would need in the general election. Faubus held to this strategy until the week prior to the Democratic vote, when one of his opponents claimed an issue Faubus felt he could not relinquish.[18]

In the last week of the primary Democratic candidate Bill Wells gave a speech in which he advocated standing in front of any bus used to achieve racial balance in schools. In response, Faubus delivered a statewide televised address four days before the primary vote, claiming he had staked out the anti-busing issue first. The people "pushing such an idiotic policy as busing," vowed the former governor, would "not be permitted to prevail." When he returned to the governor's chair, Faubus promised his audience, he would introduce legislation requiring written parental consent before children could be transported to school by bus. If the federal courts and agencies continued to "destroy public education, forcing citizens to start private schools," Faubus promised tax breaks for both the parents and the schools.[19]

As the Democratic primary vote neared, newspapers from around the state published their own opinions on the campaign. The *Eagle Democrat* of Warren, Arkansas, pointed out that everybody seemed "to be getting on one side for massive potshots at former Governor Faubus." The *Paragould Daily Press* described a Democratic rally in their town. The crowd had obviously come to see Faubus "like a crowd waiting to see Jesse James." Faubus lived up to local expectations with "a rousing speech" concerning crime in Arkansas. The editorial pointed out that for a candidate so concerned about the rising crime in the state, Faubus had a poor record. "We all know how miserably he failed in carrying out the law of the land in 1957. It took the President of the United States plus the conscience of a nation to put Orval back on the straight and narrow path." The *Jacksonville News* wrote: "Faubus doesn't sound all that bad this year, it's just that we can't help thinking of the twelve dark years when the Huntsville king-maker was in the capitol. Those were the years when the state was embarrassed nationally and internationally over Central High School's integration."[20]

One of those Arkansans who had been embarrassed by Faubus was a forty-five-year-old Democrat named Dale Bumpers. The youngest of three children, Bumpers grew up in Charleston, Arkansas, a town with a population of less than 1,400 in the foothills of the Ouachita Mountains. Bumpers' father owned a hardware store and was active in the Methodist church and area politics. William Bumpers served in the state legislature for one year and passed on his love for politics to his youngest son. During the Depression Dale worked as a field hand and as a butcher in a local grocery store. In 1943 Bumpers graduated from high school and joined the marines. When he returned home in 1946 he entered the University of Arkansas at Fayetteville and graduated two years later with a degree in political science. From there he went on to Northwestern University in Evanston, Illinois, where he received a law degree in 1951. While he was away both his parents were killed in an automobile accident. Bumpers returned to Charleston with his new wife, a former Charleston classmate, Betty Lou Flanagen. He became the only attorney in Charleston and practiced law there for eighteen years, losing only three jury trials, and also took over the operation of his father's store. In 1966 he sold the hardware store and began operating a 350-acre Angus cattle ranch.[21]

While running the hardware store and practicing law, Bumpers became an important part of his community. He led the choir and taught Sunday school in the Methodist church. He served as city attorney as well as president of both the school board and the chamber of commerce. Bumpers' first entry into politics outside his hometown proved unsuccessful. In 1962 Bumpers ran for the office his father had once held in the state house of representatives. Although he won 90 percent of the vote in Charleston, his opponent carried the other districts and won the election. Bumpers considered running for governor in 1968 but decided to wait and prepare for the future. Bumpers crisscrossed the state speaking to youth groups, civic clubs, and local bar associations.[22]

Although Bumpers had already begun preparing himself for a gubernatorial campaign, Faubus's attempted political comeback finally convinced him to run. Bumpers entered the race saying that he could not look his children and grandchildren in the eye if he sat idly by while Faubus came back to power. Many voters recognized a voice of concern that echoed their own fears. Arkansas voters, Bumpers would remember years after the election, "knew they didn't want to go back to the Faubus era and so it was a question of which of these other seven guys they were going to vote for." Virtually anonymous outside his hometown of Charleston, Bumpers sought to capitalize on his political obscurity. He conceded the difficulty of overcoming so many old pros in the race, but also saw advantages to his situation. "I think the people are honestly looking for a new face," said the political novice. Bumpers downplayed campaign issues as difficult to define, focusing instead on several broad themes. The state faced "a crisis of confidence." The people had lost trust and respect for their leaders. Arkansans yearned for a fresh new leader who "really cares." Bumpers sought to portray himself as a leader voters could trust, a word seldom associated with his main opponent. The young challenger traveled the state incessantly that summer talking with people. Bumpers told them all that he wanted to change the political climate of Arkansas.[23]

The zeal of the young candidate as well as the sophistication of his campaign were described in a memo to Faubus from one of his supporters in northeast Arkansas: "Bumpers was on our local television as well as Memphis stations almost constantly during the last week. He sent a computerized letter to every woman in our county seeking support. He attached a door knob card to every door in Jonesboro. He advertised heavily in our daily paper and had tapes on all three radio stations and he personally campaigned in Jonesboro, not one but on four different occasions."[24]

His energetic stumping of the state produced results. Dale Bumpers had charisma; his personality served as his greatest asset, and "exposure to the voter was all it took," wrote Bill Lewis in the *Arkansas Gazette*. Bumpers did not make personal attacks on his opponents, but emphasized the stark contrast between himself and the politicians of the past. "I think the day of the screaming speech is over," Bumpers told voters familiar with the Faubus style of campaigning. "I'll tell you what sells better than anything else, and that's candor and sincerity."[25]

Bumpers sought to convey this emotional sense of trust through the relatively new political medium of television. "It was the first time television was used appropriately," said Deloss Walker, Bumpers' political advertising consultant in 1970. Walker defined "appropriately" as "communicating emotion." And television could be utilized to convey that sentiment dearest to politicians: trust. "Voters don't know how to solve issues," explained Walker years later. "They want to elect someone whose motivations they trust." Bumpers communicated this sincerity better than any of the other candidates. Ernie Dumas, reporter for the *Arkansas Gazette* and one of the most astute political observers in the state, recalled later that his mother had alerted him to the candidate's talent. Mrs. Dumas told her son early in the campaign that she was going to vote for "that Bumpers fellow" she had seen on television. Bumpers invested a chunk of his $50,000 start-up money, donated by his brother and sister-in-law, to make a two-week television blitz. "Back in those days," Bumpers would recall twenty-six years later, "you could get a thirty-second spot for 150 bucks and so we ran television spots which were nothing but introductions saying, you know, I'm a great guy and here's what I believe in . . . that saved my spending ten minutes with everybody I shook hands with telling who I was and where I came from and so on. Even after that very limited television time, you walk into a town and people began to recognize you." Archie Schaffer, Bumpers' nephew and campaign manager, believed the turning point in the campaign came on television about three weeks before the preferential primary election. The Little Rock NBC affiliate televised a forum for the eight Democratic candidates that featured a five-minute statement by each. Bumpers spoke first and gave a forthright talk that the other candidates could not match. When the *McGehee Times* endorsed Bumpers during the runoff, they wrote that the candidate came across on television "like a polished professional and leaves you feeling that he is absolutely right about everything he says." Arkansans began to see something special in this candidate, and they began to listen to what he said.[26]

Deloss Walker told Bumpers that it would take $100,000 to get into the runoff; after that, he advised, money would not be a problem. Consequently, most of what was left of the $95,000 in Bumpers' campaign chest, raised in part by the sale of the candidate's cattle, went for a television blitz in the final two weeks of the contest. Articulate and appealing on screen, Bumpers left viewers with an impression of sincerity. No desk came between the candidate and the viewers; Bumpers sat on a stool, used no script, looked into the camera, and spoke in an earnest and effective manner. One sixty-year-old man, after seeing Bumpers for the first time on television, remarked: "He just looks like he's a cut above the kind we usually have running for governor."[27]

Orval Faubus, who also depended heavily on that medium, realized that he could reach a great many more voters through television than by traveling around the state. But the former governor did not understand the essence of television nor could he adapt his stump-speech oratory to this new campaign tool. Faubus's use of television was "a waste of money," according to Dale Bumpers. "As a matter of fact it probably hurt him because his television was not good. He projected a sort of old guard, old politics image." Faubus taped black and white programs sitting at a desk alternately reading, preaching, or shouting from a script. Bumpers, by contrast, employed short color messages, talking quietly as if sitting in the viewer's living room discussing the problems of the state and suggesting commonsense solutions. "When a voter lets you into his home by watching your television broadcast, you don't scream at him when you get there," explained Bumpers, contrasting his own style with that of Faubus without ever mentioning the former governor. On the night before the election Bumpers held a live question-and-answer session that furthered the candidate's effort to portray himself as someone whose openness, candor, and judgment voters could trust.[28]

Dale Bumpers did not vilify Faubus, or denigrate the other candidates, or malign busing, or even say much about the issues. He ran a positive campaign emphasizing that he was not running against anybody, but was running *for* governor. Bumpers' refusal to engage in slander about other candidates not only deviated from the political norm, but actually cost the inexperienced challenger some powerful support.

Almost every moderate to liberal Democrat opposed Faubus's return to political power and feared that the former governor would somehow pull off another victory. After all, Faubus had never lost an election in Arkansas. The opposition therefore sought to marshal its forces against Faubus. Influential elements within the Democratic power structure, including the Pulaski County (Little Rock) Democratic Party head, assessed their party's contenders. This group of powerful Democrats decided that, with the proper guidance, Dale Bumpers just might win. Moderate, attractive, and unencumbered by ties to the old political machine, Bumpers seemed the perfect beneficiary for their support. These politically savvy individuals reminded Bumpers that he stood little chance of success, indeed had almost no statewide organization. Then they offered Bumpers a deal: in exchange for their powerful political backing, which would almost certainly guarantee at least a spot in the runoff, he would malign the record of the former governor. The Faubus record of corruption and political favors provided a great deal of ammunition for such attacks. When Bumpers replied that this was neither his style nor the type of campaign he wanted to run, he received an admonition and ultimatum. Their support rested on these requirements; he should think it over and let them know the next day.[29]

Bumpers left the meeting and called Ted Boswell for advice. In the last governor's race, Boswell had, much like Bumpers, risen out of obscurity and come on strong, only to barely miss the runoff. Boswell had run against what remained of the Democratic political machine of the Faubus days in power. When Bumpers explained the situation and asked Boswell what he would do, Boswell told him no one would have had to ask him to attack Faubus; he would have been attacking him from the start. But Boswell said that Bumpers would probably lose the election anyway and afterwards would have to live with himself. If Bumpers did not feel comfortable attacking Faubus, Boswell reasoned, then Bumpers should follow the positive path he had been traveling. When Bumpers informed his erstwhile supporters that he would not agree to their terms, their response strongly suggested that Bumpers possessed little intelligence. "Some people have advised me to really take the gloves off and get rough," Bumpers said publicly, "but I decided not to."[30]

Shortly thereafter he delivered a speech remarkable not only in its dissimilarity to the politics of the past, but extraordinary in its assessment of the moral malaise present in society and its appeal to the better angels of Arkansans' nature. Bumpers called on voters to look inward to find the root of their problems. Selfishness and a "complete disregard for others," according to Bumpers, had become the "predominant driving force" in society. "For the common good of mankind, we must rekindle the attitude of concern for our fellow man," Bumpers said. Radicals and conservatives hated each other. "The whites and blacks seem to be directing more ill-will toward one another than ever before." The energy squandered in hating could be put to "countless worthwhile uses," Bumpers asserted. "With the right spirit and leadership, we can get our state together." This candidate sought something very different from the electorate. Rather than exploiting emotional issues or pandering to polls, Bumpers called on voters to look within. The basis for this appeal was both risky and brilliant. If people would accept moral suasion as a basis for solving the dilemmas of the uncertain present, then perhaps the candidate who suggested it, who seemed sincere and trustworthy, could lead them into the future.[31]

On the Friday before the primary vote, the *Arkansas Gazette* highlighted four Democratic candidates whom they considered responsible and "capable of restoring principle and respect to the Democratic Party in Arkansas." Dale Bumpers made the short list; Orval Faubus did not. Bumpers was "probably the most articulate and polished candidate in the race," wrote the paper. The Democratic Party could "either turn backward into a discredited past or move forward with principled new leadership toward brighter horizons."[32]

One political analyst commented on the eve of the election that the most remarkable aspect of the campaign had been Bumpers' meteoric climb out of political obscurity. Indeed, the obstacles overcome by the young challenger constituted nothing less than a political miracle. Fifty-five days before the election Bumpers could expect only 1 percent of the vote. A month later he hung well below 10 percent. The next week only 5 percent of Democrats polled thought Bumpers would make it into a runoff, while only 1 percent of those Democrats believed he could win the party's nomination.[33]

But Bumpers took off in the last week. The last poll before the preferential primary, conducted by Area Market Research Associates, indicated that Attorney General Joe Purcell would capture a spot in the runoff with Faubus, who led in everyone's polls. The poll predicted that Purcell would garner 23 percent with Bumpers in third with a little over 18 percent. On election day, Tuesday, August 25, Faubus held to his front-runner status, leading all other candidates with 36 percent of the vote. During election night Bumpers and Purcell moved back and forth between the second and third positions. The outcome remained in doubt until Saturday, when Purcell conceded. Bumpers, with 20 percent of the vote, would face Faubus two weeks later in a two-man race to determine who would capture the Democratic nomination.[34]

When reporters asked the runoff candidate if he intended to begin attacking Faubus, Bumpers responded by saying that he was running for governor, emphasizing the word for. Bumpers expressed confidence that he would win the runoff, asserting that Faubus received "substantially less" than enough votes to assure a victory in the runoff. "We expect to get virtually all of the votes cast for all of the other candidates but Faubus," Bumpers said. The tactic made sense. "Bumpers has plenty of ammunition if he chooses to use it," wrote the *Twin City Tribune* at West Helena during the runoff. "We doubt that he will—he's conducted a clean campaign thus far and probably sees no reason to change his style."[35]

No one had to ask Orval Faubus his strategy. He opened the runoff by attacking his opponent and revealed that he had selected busing as the major issue in the runoff campaign. "I understand that Mr. Bumpers doesn't think it is an issue," Faubus said. When a reporter pointed out that Bumpers said that busing could not be an issue because all the candidates opposed it, Faubus responded that Bumpers was trying to "soft pedal." Did Faubus mean that he was more against busing than Bumpers was? "I certainly do," he answered. When pressed Faubus conceded that the governor could do nothing about busing, but asserted that the governor must speak up for the victims of forced busing. As Faubus put it in a televised address on August 30: "The governor is the representative of the people. He speaks for the people many times. Who would be the better person to stand up and tell Washington that the people of Arkansas are opposed to this busing?" If Bumpers won the governor's chair, Faubus declared, "every bureaucrat in Washington and every federal judge is going to say, 'Why this busing is all right that we're pushing on the people because down there they have elected a man that says busing isn't an issue.'" The reaction by many to Faubus's attempt to make this the issue was reflected by an editorial cartoon in the *Arkansas Gazette*. It showed a banner that read: Faubus for Gov. Again and Again and Again and Again, *ad infinitum*. Under the banner the former governor spoke: "Busing is the only issue in this campaign although there's nothing a governor could do about it"[36]

Few in Arkansas could forget that Faubus had acted as the point man for resistance to federal pressure to integrate thirteen years earlier. Therefore, busing seemed the perfect issue for the former governor. While the changing climate of politics in the state militated against appeals to racism, the busing issue struck a chord of resentment among even the growing number of moderates in the electorate. Students from the Little Rock area would ride buses as part of a court-approved desegregation plan beginning September 8, the same day voters would choose the Democratic nominee. A letter to Faubus from a woman in Little Rock during that primary season reflected the attitude of many voters. "I would definitely like to see our schools remain segregated but that is impossible and we might as well accept it. The 'busing' for no other purpose except to mix races is another matter entirely." This reluctant acceptance of integration led Faubus to realize that the electorate had changed. While staking out the busing issue as his own, he also claimed that his stand against busing had nothing to do with race. Busing constituted a burden for parents and children of both races and an unnecessary expense for taxpayers, declared Faubus. He even sought to distance himself from his own school closing in Little Rock during the 1958–59 school year. "I didn't close the schools," Faubus claimed. "The people voted to close them and I merely acted to carry out the law." Faubus failed to mention that he had sponsored the bill that gave the governor the power to close integrated schools and pushed it through the legislature. Faubus realized that the current electorate would not stand for school closings even if those schools faced integration.[37]

Many saw through Faubus's charade and criticized his exploitation of the busing issue. The *Times* of North Little Rock ran an editorial cartoon of a man labeled "demagogue" whipping a school bus labeled "busing issue" as if riding a horse toward a sign pointing to "political goals." The caption under the cartoon read "Riding the Hot One." Bumpers refused to ride the hot one. He avoided the debate over who opposed busing more. Years later he conceded that Faubus had employed the busing issue in order to frighten people. "That was one of the knottiest issues I faced because it was a very volatile issue. People were just paranoid about it." Bumpers rejected what he called "sensationalism" in 1970. "The people are in the mood for common sense." When asked what he considered Faubus's greatest weakness, Bumpers pointed out that his opponent had been governor for twelve years. "He has nothing new to offer. His election would be a step backward."[38]

Bill Wells did not think so. The fifth-place candidate in the recent Democratic primary quickly endorsed Faubus because of what he called the "liberal tendencies" of Dale Bumpers. Even though Wells and Faubus had battled over possession of the busing issue during the primary campaign, they still shared the same ideological bed. When the Citizen Council of Arkansas circulated an eight-question "Report of the Candidates" to all those running in the primaries, Faubus, Wells, and Walter Carruth, running on the George Wallace–inspired American Independent third party, had all responded favorably. These three candidates had checked boxes indicating that they favored states' rights and opposed federal control of public schools and busing. Bumpers and Governor Rockefeller refused to even reply to the questionnaire.[39]

With Wells's support for Faubus, the right side of the political spectrum had solidified around Faubus. The left and the large center, however, moved toward Bumpers. Joe Purcell, the third-place Democratic candidate, endorsed Bumpers, saying that Bumpers more closely shared his own views. When the state AFL-CIO's Committee on Political Education threw their support behind Bumpers, Faubus said he had confidential information that labor leaders from the North had dictated the endorsement. Such antiquated antics, though, no longer stirred the electorate. A man from Stuttgart, Arkansas, writing to the *Arkansas Gazette*, compared Dale Bumpers to "a fresh breeze on a hot summer night." The Stuttgart writer did not dislike Orval Faubus and even admitted to voting for him in the past. "I could enjoy his showmanship if the times were not so fraught with danger."[40]

Faubus called Bumpers a "country clubber" with no experience in government who had deserted the Democratic Party in previous elections and reached the runoff as part of a plot directed by Rockefeller and the editor of the *Arkansas Gazette*. Faubus accused Bumpers of being linked to the "colossal Rockefeller machine which has fastened its hold upon the state." Faubus said that his runoff opponent had been stalled in fourth place until the Rockefeller people "moved for Bumpers." Faubus claimed they aimed to defeat him in the primary so Rockefeller would win the governor's chair again. The charges did not ring true. One elderly black man rejected these claims as he ate hot dogs at a Bumpers political rally. "I know Rockefeller didn't put you in the race," the man told Bumpers, "'cause he feeds better'n this." Faubus charged that Bumpers and Rockefeller appealed to the same type of voters. "Therefore," Faubus said, "if the choice is between two flaming liberal look-alikes, that vote will go to the flaming liberal with 500 million dollars." When Faubus claimed that a lot of Democrats for Rockefeller supported his runoff opponent, Bumpers agreed and responded that he had invited them back into the party. Bumpers noted that it took 220,000 crossover votes to elect Rockefeller to his first term. "These people left the party because of Faubus," Bumpers pointed out. "I want them to come back . . . I say the only way we can win in November is for them to come back, and they are not going to come back if Faubus is our nominee."[41]

Perhaps sensing the veracity of Bumpers' statement, Faubus's political tactics became increasingly desperate and bizarre. Faubus even launched an attack when a news service quoted a member of Dale Bumpers' Sunday school class. The man said that Bumpers always made their class interesting and gave as an example speculations as to whether God parted the Red Sea when Moses led the Israelites out of Egypt or whether an earthquake might have caused it. Bumpers had read this out of a book to stimulate discussion, but Faubus saw grave danger in this questioning of biblical authority. "This kind of teaching by the bogus liberals," charged Faubus, "will destroy faith in the Bible." Faubus even took out newspaper advertisements asking: "What about the Bible, Mr. Bumpers? If the Bible isn't all true, can any of it be true?" Bumpers turned the incident around to portray Faubus as a political anachronism lacking the confidence to face the future. In a televised appearance Bumpers asserted that the strength of his religious faith allowed him to consider rationally new concepts without being shaken. "It is not men of faith," Bumpers insisted, "but men of secret doubts who are afraid of new ideas." The incident emphasized the different characters of the two candidates. Faubus seemed stuck in the past, while Bumpers embraced new ideas. Faubus had given Bumpers an opportunity to affirm his religious faith for the many fundamentalists in Arkansas and had made himself look foolish by attacking a man for the way he taught his Sunday school class.[42]

In early September Faubus leveled new charges at his opponent. In a thirty-minute telecast carried on ten stations in the region, Faubus accused Bumpers of believing that the Supreme Court under Chief Justice Earl Warren was "a great court." The Warren Court had earned special disdain in the South because of its many liberal rulings, including the *Brown* decision that outlawed segregation in public schools. The charge was vintage Orval Faubus: focus on a point of voter discontent, link that complaint with your opponent, then exploit, challenge, accuse, and finally seem to prove the charge by innuendo. This must be Bumpers' view, the former governor reasoned in a typical Faubusian leap of logic, because the *Arkansas Gazette* would not have supported Bumpers if he did not hold that opinion. Bumpers calmly responded by pointing out that many other newspapers not known for liberal leanings had also endorsed him. These included the *Blytheville Courier News*, the *Springdale News*, the *Marked Tree Tribune*, and the *Paragould Daily Press*, the last of which had not supported any political candidate in twelve years.[43]

The *Arkansas Gazette* threw its support to Bumpers as did virtually every small-town newspaper in the state. The *McGehee Times*, for example, depicted the candidates in stark contrast. Orval Faubus was "a face, a politician and a man of the past . . . his administration was pocked with scandal, riots and, in the end, a splintering of the Democratic Party from the dissatisfaction. Now he's asking the people of the state to give it all back to him." The paper characterized Bumpers as "a dynamic, energetic young lawyer from a small town who has literally exploded on the Democratic scene." The *Springdale News* called Bumpers "a man of dignity, integrity and ability." The *Helena–West Helena World* maintained that "the state needs some new political blood and that is what Bumpers will give us." The Warren *Eagle Democrat* asserted that Bumpers offered "every asset of the clean young unknown who catches the imagination of the electorate." *The Times* of North Little Rock believed Bumpers would "breathe new life into Arkansas's sagging Democratic Party," while the nomination of Faubus "would guarantee a fall campaign based on innuendo and emotion . . . and place the Democratic Party back under the sway of the wheeler-dealers."[44]

As journalistic support around the state grew in favor of his opponent, Faubus said that these newspapers wanted to set up in the general election "the same sort of gently contested race you would find for king and queen of a charity ball at some country club—Bumpers versus Rockefeller, battling it out, tux-to-tux, cocktail-to-cocktail, boyish-grin to boyish-grin. No hard feelings, it's nothing serious."[45]

The attempts by Faubus to link Bumpers to Rockefeller, to portray himself as a man of the people battling against great odds and wealth and power, had worked for him in the past. He had been raised in the traditions of populism and had used these appeals successfully in his many political campaigns. But times had changed, and Faubus could no longer portray himself as tilting against entrenched power. The brand of populism that Faubus had employed had been replaced. This new populism favored outsiders who could convey trust and respectability over screaming demagogues who railed against a few basic issues held dear by rural farmers. No one understood the appeal of character more than the self-styled country lawyer from the small town of Charleston, Arkansas. Bumpers discounted conservative or liberal labels for himself or his future administration. "What the state of Arkansas needs and deserves now as never before is a man of common sense, good judgment and a man who will be dignified and conduct the affairs of the state in a decent manner." Perhaps sensing that he had staked out a position too far on the right of the political spectrum, Faubus tried to remind people that he had cut his political teeth as an economic populist. Heretofore accusing Bumpers of being a "flaming liberal," Faubus now claimed credit for implementing liberal programs during his administrations instead of just talking about them. Calling himself "the true liberal" in the race, the former governor said he had brought "social progress instead of just going out and talking about it in platitudes and generalities as Mr. Bumpers is doing and as Mr. Rockefeller has been doing." Faubus also told the *Commercial Appeal* in Memphis that he considered himself a liberal. When the reporter asked why he championed so many conservative views, Faubus responded that the first duty of a politician was to get elected so that he could get things done. "I wish none of us had to say the things we have to say," Faubus lamented.[46]

Apparently most of Arkansas's voters agreed. They did not like the things the former governor said during the campaign either. As ballots came in during election night Bumpers took an early lead and watched it increase to 58.7 percent of the vote. Faubus called his own showing "remarkable," considering the odds against him. He blamed his defeat on Senator Fulbright, the AFL-CIO, the Arkansas press, "and every other 'liberal' and 'pinko' force."[47]

Rather than sinister forces out to get Faubus, the Democratic runoff demonstrated the political realities of 1970. The campaign presented a stark contrast between the two figures contending for leadership of their party and state. The newly chosen Democratic nominee voiced motivations that may have explained his admirable campaign. "My father taught me that politics is a noble profession," Bumpers said, "and I wanted to prove it." The candidate, who had nothing to lose, gambled that a campaign of "visible honesty" might succeed. Bumpers got his message across by constant stumping of the state and by employing television in a more effective manner than any other candidate in Arkansas could manage.[48]

When Faubus bellowed about busing, Bumpers spoke soothingly; all the candidates opposed busing, but the Court had not yet made a definitive ruling so that was not really an issue. When Faubus admitted that a governor could not do anything about busing other than raise his voice, Bumpers seemed to benefit from the electorate's desire for quiet moderation. "By 1970, people were tired of racial politics," Bumpers recounted years later. "Most people then realized that integration was a fact of life. They were going to have to learn to live with it and they hated the chaos and confusion and outright violence that had been going on and they wanted a more serene setting and they wanted somebody who would lead them into the 1970s who would take a different tack."[49]

When Faubus attacked his opponent's religious beliefs, Bumpers' Sunday school teacher character stood in stark contrast to the former governor whose administrations held the taint of corruption and whose recent divorce and remarriage bothered many of the moral-minded voters of Arkansas. Once the issue of trust became central to the campaign, all the invective Faubus hurled at his opponent did not seem to matter. The unflappable Bumpers turned every assault to his advantage. Dealing with problems in a quiet, calm, rational manner, Bumpers further demonstrated the dissimilarities between himself and the former governor.

Several erstwhile supporters lamented Faubus's personal life. One woman from Hot Springs wrote to Faubus identifying herself as "a humble female public servant" and suggested that the former governor lost this race because he left his wife for his young secretary. "From principle I could not vote for you this time." The note had attached a picture of Faubus's new wife cut out with pinking shears. Another unsigned letter claimed: "Arkansas lost the best governor she ever had because of a young ambitious girl who looked like an Indian squaw." Other Faubus supporters contributed different assessments of the campaign. A Baptist preacher from Stuttgart, Arkansas, wrote Faubus that of all the candidates in the first primary he had feared Bumpers would be the most difficult for the former governor to defeat in a runoff. "He was 'new' and all the enemies of sixteen years jumped on his bandwagon," wrote the preacher. "He had no record and never really said what he would do about anything. Couple this with a nice set of dentures and you have a winner." Faubus's own later assessment characterized the election as inevitable. No one could have defeated Bumpers in 1970, Faubus reasoned, because "a man and the mood of the voters suddenly and inexplicably got in tune."[50]

State Republican chairman Odell Pollard said that the Democratic primary reflected the electorate's appreciation of the two-party system that the GOP had brought to the state. The public now knew of "the evils of machine politics." In other words, the large vote for Bumpers essentially indicated a rejection of Faubus. "I distinctly think it is an anti-Faubus vote," said Governor Rockefeller. "Remember, you've got a predominance of Democrats in the state of Arkansas and I think they were so refreshed to have a fine, honest, attractive young man who might come in and give the Democratic Party that which it had been denied for 16 years." The governor's assessment of the primary also accurately portrayed his own precarious position. Thousands of moderate and liberal Democratic voters who had rejected the legacy of Faubus machine politics by supporting Rockefeller returned to their political home. John Harkey, a former insurance commissioner under Governor Rockefeller, returned to the Democratic fold to support Bumpers. "Yard signs are sprouting all over this town in front of homes of people who always voted for Rockefeller," Harkey said. "[N]ow we've got someone to vote for rather than having to vote against someone." State Democratic chairman Charles Matthews saw "tremendous appeal" in Bumpers' campaign, "a new face, new leadership, the themes of unifying the state and the Democratic Party."[51]

The rejection of Faubus signaled a new day for the state and the South. Arkansans felt proud of themselves, and observers near and far vindicated their self-esteem. "If in Arkansas Orval Faubus has been beaten overwhelmingly, then there must be some message," wrote the *Arkansas Gazette*. "The message may be that segregation is fading as the overpowering issue in Southern politics." Many agreed and commented further on the importance of the Faubus defeat. The *Paragould Daily Press* applauded Arkansas voters because they had "told the world that they are ready to look to the tomorrow—rather than the yesterdays . . . They chose the high road . . . They chose a man as Democratic standard-bearer not identified with racial hatred and strife or demagoguery." National commentators also heralded the political demise of Faubus. "Old demagogues like old prizefighters keep coming back for more," the *New York Times* observed. When the former governor retired in 1966, "most Americans were more than content to see and hear the last of him, but there was no way of telling for certain whether his fellow Arkansans shared that view. On Tuesday evening he found out that they do."[52]

With Orval Faubus dispatched, the general election could proceed without the specter of demagogic demons of the past. Bumpers would face a very different sort of man than his rival in the Democratic primary.

Winthrop Rockefeller could only claim Arkansas as his adopted home, having moved there in 1953. Not surprisingly, the wealthy, liberal, cosmopolitan Rockefeller seemed oddly out of place in the Ozark state. He sprang from one of the richest families in America and benefited from the education, cultural background, and refinements that come with great wealth. Although not a typical Arkansan, Winthrop was not a typical Rockefeller either. At six feet four inches and 240 pounds, Winthrop did not even look like the rest of his family, and he certainly did not act like a Rockefeller. He had dropped out of Yale and worked as a roughneck in the Texas oil fields. Then, almost a year before the Japanese attack on Pearl Harbor, Winthrop enlisted in the United States Army as a private. He later attended officer candidate school and quickly rose to the rank of major. Rockefeller saw a great deal of combat in the Pacific. He fought in the battles of Guam and the Philippines and suffered wounds in the invasion of Okinawa during a kamikaze attack. By the end of the war he held the rank of lieutenant colonel and had received the Bronze Star with Oak Leaf Cluster as well as a Purple Heart. After the war Rockefeller returned home to New York where he worked a desk job and pursued the pleasures of bachelorhood. In 1948 he married a model carrying his child, but divorced her a few months later. Feeling the need for a change, he called an army buddy in Little Rock, who suggested he move to Arkansas. Rockefeller accepted the offer and bought 50,000 acres atop Petit Jean Mountain seventy miles northwest of Little Rock. He called it Winrock Farms and began farming and ranching. The operation included 6,000 head of Santa Gertrudis cattle and 17,000 acres devoted to rice, soybeans, and grain. He built roads, silos, barns, an airfield, and a mansion.[53]

Although Winthrop may have been a maverick, he could not escape his family tradition of public service, and Arkansas became the beneficiary of Rockefeller's philanthropy. Education, medicine, the arts all received millions in contributions. Rockefeller also initiated an economic rebirth of the state as head of the Arkansas Industrial Development Corporation.[54]

A lifelong Republican, Rockefeller by 1959 had seen enough of the Faubus political machine and decided that the state desperately needed a two-party political system. In a 1960 address, broadcast on both radio and television, he argued that a two-party system would create a "healthier condition in Arkansas politics." Rockefeller established a Committee for Two Parties and funded the Arkansas Election Research Council to monitor electoral corruption. A year later, Rockefeller became the Arkansas Republican national committeeman presiding over a small, reticent party driven by patronage. No party organization existed. The GOP did not even have a list of potential supporters. Whatever voter information that might benefit the party resided in county courthouses controlled by Democrats. Rockefeller began collecting names in a haphazard manner. These early efforts would eventually lead Rockefeller to become the first politician in America to maintain and pay for his own private computer and experts used strictly for political analysis. Rockefeller also ran public opinion polls. In late 1960 and early 1961 voters rated four well-known Arkansans including Faubus and Rockefeller. The results suggested that Rockefeller was "a potentially strong candidate for governor."[55]

In 1964 Rockefeller decided to challenge Faubus for the governor's chair and began his campaign pointing to the corruption within the Faubus administration. Faubus emphasized his own seasoning in office compared to an "untried, inexperienced former New York playboy." Faubus had a field day contrasting Rockefeller's lifestyle to that of most Arkansans. Faubus criticized the outsider's admission that he got his hair cut in New York, that he served liquor to guests, and that he had divorced his first wife. The Rockefeller fortune served as the perfect foil to play on the prejudices of an abundant underclass in the state. "This election will show if a poor boy can still beat a millionaire. . . . Why, his grandaddy was that oil magnate who raised the price of kerosene sold to the po' folks . . . if we owe the Rockefellers anything, we've been paying it a long time."[56]

Faubus often reminded voters that he, unlike his rich northern opponent, shared a common heritage of hardship with Arkansans. One day on the campaign trail, passing a wagon drawn by mules, Faubus remarked that he had driven such a wagon in his youth. His publicity man ordered the car to stop. Faubus got out and drove the wagon. The accompanying press entourage dutifully lapped up this homespun photo opportunity. When the pictures made the newspapers Rockefeller commented that Faubus would keep Arkansas in the mule-drawn wagon era while he wanted to move the state into the jet age. But the stunt portrayed Faubus as a man of the people, while Rockefeller remained a city slicker who could not imagine the difficulties of poverty.[57]

Rockefeller failed in 1964, although the 43 percent of the vote he received topped any Republican candidate since Reconstruction. Several factors contributed to the loss. The challenger's own post-election polling showed that Faubus's personal attacks had found a receptive audience. The Republican challenger had also failed to unite his own party. The presidential campaign of 1964 had increased divisions because Rockefeller supported the candidacy of his brother, Nelson, over the eventual nominee, Barry Goldwater. Winthrop conceded to the *New York Times* that his brother's campaign hurt his own bid for governor of Arkansas because "Nelson is branded throughout much of the South as a liberal."[58]

In the South the word "liberal" almost always held racial connotations. And Rockefeller worked hard to overcome his liberal image as he laid out his beliefs cautiously. Integration should be solved on a local basis, he suggested, "with encouragement." While advocating better educational opportunities for blacks, he opposed the pending 1964 Civil Rights Act, fearing the bill granted "certain police powers to the administrative, Executive branch of the government." Faubus accused Rockefeller of being an "ardent civil rights advocate" and suggested Rockefeller's moderate stance was an attempt "to change his spots on the racial issue." Rockefeller's caution went for naught in 1964, but his moderate approach to racial issues continued. After the election, John Ward, a Rockefeller aide, outlined an approach that reflected the changing temper of the times among southern voters. Rockefeller "should never become completely identified with either extreme. He should maintain an attitude that takes into account the feelings of both sides of the issue, offering guidelines for both leading to a solution both can accept." This advice fit well with Rockefeller's own views and feelings about race and served the candidate well in the next campaign.[59]

Although Rockefeller could not slay the race king in 1964, he did begin to form a coalition that would destroy the efficacy of racial politics in the state. Along with the eight traditionally Republican counties in the northwestern part of the state, Rockefeller carried the four counties that contained Arkansas's largest cities. More important for building a winning coalition in the future, Rockefeller had made inroads into the black vote. The poll tax had kept the number of registered black voters low in 1964, and the 84 percent of the black vote Faubus received in that election indicated that the Democratic political machine controlled those votes. On the same day that he made his concession speech, Rockefeller announced he would run again in 1966. In the next two years Rockefeller traveled the state attacking the political abuses of the "Faubus Machine." The news that Faubus was building a palatial new home added credence to the Republican charges of corruption.[60]

In 1966 Faubus decided not to seek reelection. The Democratic primary eliminated the candidates that early polls suggested held the best chances of success. Jim Johnson, a staunch segregationist, captured the

Democratic nomination. The nominee had founded the Arkansas White Citizens Council, and his outspoken criticism of school integration in 1957 had prompted Faubus to resist the court-ordered integration plan in Little Rock. On the campaign trail in 1966, Johnson refused to shake hands with black voters.[61]

But these tactics would no longer serve Arkansas politicians. The increased black vote could constitute a significant portion of a winning coalition. The poll tax ended in 1964, and even though the 1965 Voting Rights Act did not require federal monitoring of elections in Arkansas, it encouraged thousands of independent-minded blacks to register. Jim Johnson was the last candidate that newly liberated black voters would choose in a governor's contest, particularly in a year in which no national campaign competed for party loyalties. Approximately 95 percent of the seventy-five thousand black votes cast went for Rockefeller and provided his margin of victory. The Republican candidate could make outright appeals to black voters without fearing a white backlash in this more moderate electorate; the strong segregationists stood solidly behind Johnson anyway. And the growing white moderates in the state had moved out of the shadow of ardent segregation. According to an August poll a plurality of voters believed that racial integration had benefited the state and that Rockefeller would handle the racial situation better than his Democratic opponent. In late September only 11 percent of voters polled wanted to see the next governor fight integration guidelines with "all forces at his command," while 66 percent wanted him to "keep things as orderly as possible." Arkansans wanted racial peace; they believed this would improve their national image, and 59 percent believed Rockefeller would make their state look better in the eyes of the nation.[62]

On election day in 1966 Rockefeller garnered 54.4 percent of the vote. In addition to capturing the black vote and the traditional Republican vote, Rockefeller won the support of industrialists seeking an improved business climate for the state as well as hundreds of thousands of disaffected Democrats. Most agreed the election had not reflected a desire for a two-party system. Republicans captured only three of the 135 seats in the state legislature. Even the newly elected governor saw the election as an anomaly. "In '66 the people were not necessarily voting for me," Rockefeller admitted. "Certainly they weren't voting for a Republican. They were voting against a system they had wearied of." John Ward, a Rockefeller aide, agreed; he believed that people voted for his boss because "they didn't think he would steal from them, and they liked his positive attitude, he was someone they could be proud of and they could feel good about his going off and representing the state."[63]

As governor, Rockefeller seemed intent on reforming and modernizing the state. He presided over rewriting the century-old state constitution. He pushed through the state's first minimum wage law, expanded state aid to public education, and increased teacher and university faculty salaries. He supported a Freedom of Information law requiring governmental bodies to allow public access to meetings, as well as a code of ethics for government executives. The Rockefeller administration cracked down on illegal gambling and legalized liquor by the drink. He was a champion of major prison reforms and incentives for luring new industries to the state, and he appointed blacks to important government jobs.[64]

Despite these reform efforts, Rockefeller faced some real problems in his bid for reelection. Rather than his accomplishments in office, the public focused on his personal flaws. One element of indignation concerned the governor's enjoyment of strong drink, which he never tried to hide. Many voters resented the fact that Rockefeller seemed to spend too much time out of his office, and out of the state. And when he was in the state he could never make it anywhere on time. To many, Rockefeller also seemed ineffectual. Even one of the governor's chief aides called Rockefeller a "terrible" administrator. And when the governor called a special session of the legislature that achieved nothing, people began to believe that a Democrat could accomplish more. In early September 1968, Eugene Newsom, the governor's pollster, reported that at that moment a Democratic challenger could win 60 percent to Rockefeller's 40 percent.[65]

But the Democrats blundered when they nominated Marion Crank, a remnant from the Faubus political machine. Sterling Cockrill, a longtime Democratic force in the state house of representatives, said that the party leadership was handed to Crank "by the status-quo Democrats, the county politicians, the Court House group, the whatever machine there was left." If any doubt about Crank's connection with the corrupt political past existed, it disappeared when information surfaced about what Republicans called the "Family Plan." While Crank had served in the legislature, his entire family, including his eight-year-old daughter, drew a state payroll check. The Democratic nominee for lieutenant governor, Bill Wells, a former legislator, had the same problem. The increasingly large group of moderate Democrats who had deserted their party's ranks in 1966 would not return to support an Old Guard politician and stayed within the Republican fold. Arkansas's two major newspapers, the *Democrat* and the *Gazette*, endorsed Rockefeller over Crank. Rockefeller's pollster forecast a 51 to 49 percent victory for the incumbent. The projection proved nearly perfect. Rockefeller received 322,782 votes to Crank's 292,813.[66]

Rockefeller's coalition had held firm. Rockefeller carried eleven of the twelve counties with black majorities, including three that had voted for Democratic presidential candidate Hubert Humphrey. Once again Rockefeller won the Ozark and northern counties where GOP strength dominated. Metropolitan counties gave the incumbent 59 percent of their vote, and counties with at least one city of 10,000 contributed 55 percent. Rockefeller did well among affluent voters, receiving 59 percent from the highest category of per-capita income. And yet Arkansans did not embrace the GOP. Republican strength in the legislature increased from two to only five. All Republican candidates for statewide races lost with the exception of the GOP's candidate for lieutenant governor, who barely beat out the Wallace Democrat. Independent George Wallace carried the state in the presidential balloting with a plurality of 38 percent ahead of the Republican candidate, Richard Nixon. And a liberal Democrat, J. William Fulbright, won reelection to the senate. Rockefeller's second victory did not reflect a rise of Republicanism in the state, but demonstrated that a moderate on civil rights who emphasized good government and economic progress could sustain a majority even in a state holding an 83 percent Democratic majority.[67]

During Rockefeller's second term his difficulties in accomplishing his desired reform measures increased. The obstinate Democratic legislature turned downright hostile, and Rockefeller did little to make it easier for the legislators. He refused to engage in the kind of quid pro quo that previous Arkansas governors had practiced. Rockefeller disdained politics as usual and described the legislators as "shortsighted, petty men" unwilling to face up to the state's real problems.[68]

Arkansas's real problem, in Rockefeller's mind, stemmed from a lack of revenue, so he began his second term in a determined effort to raise taxes. Upgraded services and new programs that would keep the state "in step with the rest of the nation" would require millions per year, Rockefeller told voters on television. If the legislature would pass his fiscal program it would contribute ninety million the first year in new revenues and $105 million the next, with 50 percent going to education. His proposals to raise sales taxes, personal and corporate income taxes, and cigarette, tobacco, and alcoholic beverage taxes would have amounted to an increase of about 90 percent in general taxes. Rockefeller called on citizens to sacrifice. He launched into a public relations campaign using the slogan "Arkansas Is Worth Paying For." Although taxes never command a great deal of voter sympathy, Rockefeller's proposals garnered outright hostility. Most Arkansas voters found it difficult to accept the notion of sacrifice on their part when one of the richest men in America had made the suggestion. Critics of the tax increases began to turn the slogan around: "Is Rockefeller Worth Paying For?"[69]

Although the campaign to increase revenues did eventually sway the majority of voters to the inevitability of some tax increases, the huge increases that Rockefeller proposed found little support with the public or in the legislature. Lawmakers rejected the governor's tax proposals outright, passing their own modest revenue measures that produced less than a quarter of those proposed by Rockefeller. Even those voters who applauded the governor's reform efforts could not ignore the fact that this Republican governor could no longer accomplish much, if anything, when faced with a stubborn Democratic legislature.[70]

Rockefeller had promised back in his first campaign that he would only seek two terms, but the governor despaired of accomplishing his goals within his self-imposed deadline. In October 1969, some of his aides prepared a memo debating the pros and cons of another campaign. Recognizing the governor's political liabilities, such as drinking and marital problems, difficulties with the legislature, and their candidate's tarnished reform image, it gauged the chances of success in 1970 with "at best a cautious optimism." Nevertheless, the memorandum held that "the best interests of Arkansas and the Republican Party would be served" if Rockefeller sought a third term. An opposing group within the administration observed that support had dropped lower than "it had ever been in previous campaigns," and that the governor's chances of winning a third term seemed remote.[71]

Rockefeller chose to act on the more positive assessment. In April he wrote to the state's Republicans to warn them that he might break his two-term pledge. "It is painful to admit an error, and reverse oneself, but my commitment to the Republican Party and to my own convictions are more important than my one statement. . . . Yes, we have made great progress, but we have not yet dismantled the Old Guard!" It was the specter of the Old Guard that motivated the incumbent to run again. "To quit now," said Rockefeller in his formal announcement, "would impose on me a feeling of guilt all of the rest of my days." A large part of that guilt sprang from the fear that Orval Faubus, the leading Democratic contender, just might win. Rockefeller could not bear the thought of seeing his fledgling reforms trampled under Faubus's feet. "Well that's it," said Rockefeller when he learned that Faubus had entered the race. "I can't hand it back to him."[72]

All of Rockefeller's research and polling had targeted Faubus. Ample evidence of corruption, an old guard political machine run by cronyism, and regressive policies provided potent ammunition to use against him. But a candidate very different from Orval Faubus emerged with the Democratic nomination. Dale Bumpers had none of Faubus's liabilities. Rockefeller would have to try to tie Bumpers to the Democratic political machine and emphasize the need to prevent corruption by retaining a two-party system in the state. In addition, the incumbent governor would campaign on his administration's record. Rockefeller could point to his four years in office and boast of the creation of a new job every thirty-eight minutes, a new or expanded industry opening every one and a half days, three pay raises for teachers, and the state's first minimum wage law. Despite these achievements, the task of securing a third term against Bumpers seemed nearly impossible. A poll conducted after the Democratic runoff vote indicated that the challenger led the incumbent 70 percent to 20 percent with 10 percent undecided.[73]

An intensely shy man who had never enjoyed campaigning, Rockefeller found it difficult to motivate himself against such overwhelming odds. Shortly after Bumpers secured the Democratic nomination, the governor publicly doubted if he could "muster the spontaneous enthusiasm" of his opponent. In 1966 and 1968 Democrats had deserted their party because they opposed "bigotry and machine politics," said Rockefeller. Now he conceded that he might lose that support to Bumpers. "I think many Democrats are happy that they do have a Democrat whom they can rally around—an honest new personality." The major issue in the race, according to the governor, would be which candidate could do the most for the state. He had the advantage of a record to stand on. "I think it will be very interesting for Mr. Bumpers to come forward with a program to outdo the ongoing program of the present administration," Rockefeller said.[74]

Two weeks later in a poll conducted between the first and third of October, Bumpers led 61 percent to Rockefeller's 24 percent with 2 percent favoring Walter Carruth, the candidate running on George Wallace's American Independent Party. In this same poll dozens of voters commented about the campaign. A sampling of their responses speaks volumes about the race. When asked for their candidate preference some

Rockefeller supporters alluded to his strong points. "He 'sho' has helped us colored folks," said one respondent. "He likes to help the underprivileged," remarked another. A few voters saw the one glaring weakness of the Democratic nominee. "Bumpers hasn't got a program that I can see. He is just a fresh chicken." Those voters who preferred Bumpers seemed to define their support by the things they did not like about Rockefeller: "Mr. Rockefeller can't accomplish too much with a Democratic legislature. Two terms are all he asked for. Bumpers will give the state a good image. He is his own man," answered one of those polled. "Just don't want Rockefeller in office again," said another. "Change horses once in awhile —makes a better ride." Some voters liked the challenger enough to switch parties. "Bumpers—He doesn't drink and is very good on TV. I'm a Republican, but when it comes to the Governor's race I'm voting for Bumpers. I think he's a good Christian man, an educated man, and a sincere man." The pollster summarized the range of comments on the two candidates. "Bumpers is the new, fresh face. He has said nothing of consequence. He probably will get better cooperation out of the legislature. But Rockefeller's sincerity comes through. He says what he means and is not afraid to take a stand."[75]

Seemingly more interested in sparing their client from the harsh realities of the campaign than in furnishing him with accurate predictions, Rockefeller's pollsters grasped at every straw of hope. After the early October poll positioned Bumpers 37 percentage points ahead of the governor, they predicted: "The guess on Bumpers' win is down to just about an even plurality." Two weeks later another poll indicated that Bumpers still held a commanding lead of 63 percent of the electorate, but that Rockefeller had increased his support by 7 percentage points. The summary of the poll referred to a recent British election that had gone against projections. "I don't think this race is over by any means," wrote one of the pollsters. "Bumpers has played his cards well—although I don't really think he has much of a hand to play with."[76]

Two weeks before the election Bumpers' support had dipped to 51 percent while Rockefeller's had climbed to 35 percent. Bumpers began to campaign in earnest with public appearances and addresses on radio and television. He also began to state his position on the issues. Rockefeller had criticized the challenger for his silence. Now Bumpers began to state his position on the issues in a calm and reasonable manner that once again instilled confidence in the voters without inciting controversy. Rockefeller, desperately trailing, went on the offensive with an advertising blitz and appeared around the state transported by jet helicopters. This obvious display of campaign spending carried consequences. Polls indicated that Bumpers' lead was growing while the governor's support had peaked.[77]

The polls showed just how difficult achieving a third term would be for the incumbent, and events conspired to stack the odds even more heavily in favor of the challenger. National leaders of Rockefeller's own party did irreparable damage to the governor's campaign. In September a reporter for *Women's Wear Daily* quoted Attorney General John Mitchell as saying that Rockefeller could defeat Bumpers by buying enough votes from "the far left or the hard right or the black vote." Although Mitchell denied the remark, the comment struck a raw nerve among many voters. The *Fordyce News-Advocate* believed that Mitchell's statement "pretty well put the finger on the situation in Arkansas." Although Rockefeller had a squeaky clean reputation without a hint of scandal, people could not help but suspect wrongdoing, or at least take offense at the large amounts spent on Rockefeller's campaign.[78]

Some spoke directly to the resentments many Arkansans held toward Rockefeller's great wealth. "We're not going to let our state be bought by any jitterbugging dilettante New York liberal with a bag full of money," said Bob Riley, the Democratic nominee for lieutenant governor. Senator J. William Fulbright also spoke out about Rockefeller's campaign spending. "The use of his tremendous private fortune to subvert the democratic process is what offends me," Fulbright said. "If we are going to restrict candidates for governor to millionaires, how many candidates are we going to have?" The Democratic challenger, conducting a low-key, low-cost campaign, complained about his opponent's extravagant spending. "The expenditures of my opponent in this campaign—the callous disregard for money and the amount of it that's being spent, so much of it wasteful," said Bumpers, "lends credence to the idea in people's minds that money is spent lavishly in state government." The charges of excessive campaign spending rang true. When expenditures of the two gubernatorial candidates became public, the figures indicated that Rockefeller had outspent Bumpers by more than four to one.[79]

While Mitchell's statement still buzzed in voters' ears, Spiro Agnew came to town to show the Nixon administration's support for the state's Republican gubernatorial candidate. Divisions developed among the governor's staff over the wisdom of inviting the vice president, and although Rockefeller decided in favor of the invitation he conceded that Agnew would probably cost him some votes. The problems for Rockefeller began as soon as the vice president arrived. Agnew began by attacking Senator Fulbright. This did not sit well with many of Rockefeller's supporters who had also voted for the senator. The comments also offended many who saw no reason for the vice president to attack Arkansas's senior senator who was not even running in the election. Agnew compounded the damage by making a gratuitous and insulting attack on Rockefeller's opponent, calling Bumpers a "grin and grunt" candidate. This did not ring true. "Anyone who has seen Dale Bumpers in action," wrote the *Arkansas Gazette*, "knows that he is one of the truly articulate on the Arkansas political scene." The visit had cost the governor votes, the paper believed, because "Agnew knows nothing about Bumpers except what Rockefeller's speechwriters have told him."[80]

Perhaps most damaging, the Agnew visit associated the very vocal antidesegregation rhetoric of the vice president with the Republican governor who had proven that racial politics no longer guaranteed success in the state. Black voters, Rockefeller's most solid group of supporters, as well as the white moderate Democrats who had supported the governor in the past, had no stomach for the politics of racial divisiveness championed by Spiro Agnew. The *Arkansas Gazette* called the governor "bold (not to mention ambidextrous) to bring Spiro T. Agnew, the lion of Mississippi segregationists, for a GOP rally even as the Rockefeller organization banks once again on getting 90% of Negro votes." The paper also reminded blacks that "as they lined up with the party of Winthrop Rockefeller, that they were lining up with the party of John Mitchell and Spiro Agnew as well."[81]

Indeed party politics in Arkansas offered peculiar and incongruent enticements for black voters. While the party of Richard Nixon developed a strategy designed to appease southern whites unhappy with federal desegregation mandates, the Arkansas Republican party, under the leadership of Winthrop Rockefeller, included blacks in party politics as well as state government. Rockefeller had transformed the specter of racial politics by openly appealing for black votes. These appeals demonstrated the political sagacity of building an inclusive coalition. Rockefeller's past support included not only Arkansas Republicans and black voters but the large body of moderate whites weary of fiery racist rhetoric and corrupt Democratic machine politics.

The Rockefeller family tradition had long been to provide financial assistance to black colleges, and Winthrop had been active in the National

Urban League, but Rockefeller did not come to Arkansas for the purpose of changing race relations. Although Rockefeller believed that everyone deserved equal opportunities, he neither patronized blacks nor gave special privileges to those who served in his administration. Rockefeller represented a turning point in Arkansas race relations. The governor filled state jobs with qualified blacks and had special assistants to keep close tabs on the hiring of minorities. After the assassination of Martin Luther King, Jr., Governor Rockefeller became the only governor in the nation to call for and lead a memorial prayer service for the slain civil rights leader on the steps of the state capitol. When *U.S. News and World Report* reported that racial disturbances racked Arkansas in the wake of the assassination, Rockefeller telegraphed the editor, calling the report "misleading and unjustified." The governor expressed pride in the conduct of Arkansans during this tense situation. "In this spirit we are moving forward and hopefully will set a pattern for the nation, but such reporting . . . makes our job unjustifiably more difficult and may even be a disservice to those of us who are sincere."[82]

Although racial incidents did occur in Arkansas, Rockefeller exhibited his sincerity in trying to ameliorate racial tensions. In 1969 when racial disturbances racked Forrest City, Arkansas, the governor worked diligently to avert a crisis. When black activists there planned a "poor people's march," Rockefeller met with blacks and whites to ease racial tensions. The governor opposed the march, but did not believe he should prevent a legal march. Instead he persuaded black leaders to postpone the march, allowing tempers to cool. In the next year Rockefeller tried in vain to prevent confrontation in Earle, Arkansas. Still, many people appreciated the exertions of the governor in response to racial problems. "We in Earle were spared from what might have been a far worse situation," wrote one woman from that troubled town to the *Arkansas Gazette*. "Above all, we needed and had the attention of a governor who remained in close touch all night, and in those days following, ready and anxious to help in bringing . . . peace in the most beneficial manner for both races." The Earle woman went on to place the actions of the governor in a wider context. "Arkansas has had less racial difficulty than any other state in the South," the woman reminded readers, "with more advancement in the field of human relations than any other southern state." The movement in this direction, she continued, "had to have strong leadership, and it received a dynamic push from one Win Rockefeller."[83]

In April 1970 Rockefeller sought to ease the tension over school desegregation. Arkansas at the time was operating forty-nine dual-system school districts in violation of the Civil Rights Act of 1964. The governor asked the Justice Department for a delay in order to give the districts involved time to comply voluntarily. But unlike southern governors of the past who sought to delay desegregation by any means available, Rockefeller seemed sincere in his desire to work toward an amicable solution. Two months later Rockefeller telegraphed President Nixon when the administration backed off an earlier decision to force a desegregation deadline for the fall school term. Rockefeller implored the president not to "break faith with the black community" by slowing the pace of school desegregation. The relaxation of the deadline, the governor warned, would compromise "the position of those who have courageously gone ahead with objectivity and a sense of justice—if not always with enthusiasm—in the implementation of Federal desegregation guidelines."[84]

Yet Rockefeller wavered in his firm rejection of racial politics and succumbed to the politically popular position of opposing busing. Rockefeller did not believe that as governor he should interfere in local school districts with busing problems. He had supported the Southern Governor's Conference statement in 1969 calling for a "quality, nondiscriminatory education for every child" and urging "restraint and good judgement in the use of any busing to . . . achieve racial integration." In January 1970, Rockefeller said that busing should not be disregarded "in implementing the court orders, and the law working toward sound integration." Some praised the governor for his stand. The *Arkansas Gazette* applauded it and called the southern cry against busing "hypocritical" considering that "whole generations of whites and blacks alike were bused all over kingdom come to keep the schools totally segregated." But the *Gazette* did not speak for the majority of Arkansans, and Rockefeller knew it. In February Rockefeller backpedaled on the busing issue. "I have not recommended busing—and am not recommending it now." In a futile attempt to garner support from conservative elements, Rockefeller compromised his coalition. "If the governor's strategy was to antagonize those who have admired his courage and candor," observed the *Pine Bluff Commercial* after the Rockefeller statement on busing, "then he succeeded this weekend." In that same month, previewing his role as chairman of the 1970 Southern Governor's Conference, Rockefeller called on the president to issue a "forthright statement we can understand" on busing schoolchildren to achieve integration. When Harry Dent, Nixon's southern strategy advisor, contacted Rockefeller, the governor agreed "to avoid this subject from a critical standpoint." Rockefeller also admitted to Dent that big delegations of blacks and whites taking opposite positions on busing caused him "to waffle his position by saying he wanted the President to clarify his stand." Dent added in his memo that "his position really is that he favors all kinds of busing."

Dale Bumpers, the Democratic nominee for governor, had no such qualms about letting his real position be known. Once again he handled the politically explosive issue adroitly as he had during his primary contest against Faubus. The challenger maintained his opposition to busing, yet told voters that if the Supreme Court mandated busing to achieve racial balance in classrooms, the state would have to comply. "If they [the Court] declare busing mandatory, then, of course, that is the direction we will move," Bumpers said.[85]

Rockefeller had wavered from a brand of politics that he pioneered in the state, maintaining a moral position regardless of where the racial chips might fall. Ironically, Rockefeller's approach had by 1970 benefited his political opponents. His inclusive coalition made it possible for a Democratic moderate to reclaim state leadership, as Dale Bumpers admitted after his election. Many others noticed the transformation as well. "The day Arkansas changed," observed Leroy Donald of the *Arkansas Gazette*, "was the day after Martin Luther King, Jr.'s assassination when Rockefeller stood on the capitol steps singing, 'We Shall Overcome.'" Black and white Arkansans shared this opinion. "While Governor Rockefeller helped free the black man in Arkansas from the oppression of Jim Crow," said Sonny Walker, the African American Rockefeller had nominated as director of the Office of Economic Opportunity, "he also helped free the white man of our state from the prison of his prejudice."

Some in the state, however, saw the black vote as a liability reflecting the ambivalence of many Arkansans. While the desire to move beyond the bad old days of racism pervaded the body politic, some resented a concentration of power derived from a minority voting as a bloc. The *Helena–West Helena World* urged voters to support Bumpers because "Rockefeller has a strong backing and a big block of voters who will be all out for him," referring to the overwhelming black support for the governor. "These people, will exert every effort to pool all their strength, while so many of the Tax Payers, the people who support the state government financially, will not take the trouble."[86]

After Rockefeller's victories in 1966 and 1968, the state Democratic Party reorganized and reassessed political expediencies. The party had moved away from the corrupt political machine of the Faubus years and abandoned the old political ploy of espousing segregation and white supremacy at election time. After Rockefeller's winning example of appealing to the growing body of white liberal and moderate voters, open appeals for black votes no longer threatened Democratic candidates. Dale Bumpers could not be linked to the bad old days of racist, corrupt Democratic machine politics. Refusing to concede the black vote to his opponent, the Democratic nominee now sought to reclaim those votes residing in Republican ranks. After all, the national Democratic Party spoke much more directly to the needs and wishes of black voters in 1970 than did southern-strategy Nixon Republicans. In October, Bumpers told a group of skeptical blacks that he wanted them involved in the Democratic Party and the state government. "I'm opposed to discrimination in every form," Bumpers maintained. He reminded the black group that he had campaigned all summer without appealing to emotions, an obvious reference to his calm response to Faubus's fiery rhetoric in the Democratic primary. A faculty member from a predominantly black college in the state asked Bumpers if his racial appeal might hurt him with other voters. "It might," Bumpers replied, but he added that he made the appeals because it was morally right.[87]

At almost every campaign stop voters asked Bumpers questions about race. A rabbi asked the candidate how he felt about Rockefeller's appointment of a black leader to the Board of Trustees of Arkansas State University. Bumpers responded: "I would not hesitate to appoint black men to such positions if I knew them and had confidence in them." A student at the University of Arkansas asked him what he would do to make integration fact "rather than fantasy." Bumpers said he did not believe integration was a fantasy. He said that all Arkansas school districts had gone to a unitary school system and that he was sure that the federal government would enforce the law. When asked by another student why the only blacks seeking public office in Arkansas ran as Republicans, Bumpers pointed to his efforts to recruit blacks to return to his party. And he asserted that participation in the Democratic Party would best serve the interest of black people. Bumpers' attempts to lure black voters demonstrated a transformation of politics in the South. The challenger's lead in the polls suggested that he did not need to openly court the black vote, which would largely support Rockefeller anyway. But the effort reflected the recognition of the changes in the South.[88]

Winthrop Rockefeller knew he could count on most of the black vote, but he had serious doubts about those disaffected Democrats who had deserted their party during the last two campaigns. Rockefeller ran commercials suggesting that the "same old crowd" would control the Bumpers administration. To support this allegation, Rockefeller pointed to the fact that Bumpers had not spoken to the issues but expected to take office by "looking pretty on TV and trying to win with a smile, a shoeshine and one speech." Bumpers resented the commercials, saying that if the old crowd was waiting in the wings they would never get out of there as long as he was governor. These attacks fell on deaf ears for the most part; Bumpers had no connection with the Democratic old guard and no record to attack. Rockefeller did sway some support by pointing to Bumpers' reluctance to discuss the issues or to engage the governor in a televised debate. "Whatever one thinks of Governor Rockefeller's program, it is clear that he has one," wrote the *Pine Bluff Commercial*, "while Mr. Bumpers as late as this week was still getting away with generalities like being in favor of both quality education for all and a conservative spending policy. He hasn't been very specific about how the state could achieve both." The *De Queen Bee* lamented the fact that twice the governor had challenged the Democratic nominee to debate the issues. "And twice now . . . Bumpers has kept a tight lip before making any public pronouncement about said debate." The *Stone County Leader* at Mountain View, Arkansas, summarized the two candidates' positions as Rockefeller "dwelling on the inexperience and shallow platform of Bumpers, while Bumpers is picturing himself as being up against a Goliath-type financial machine." The paper believed that Bumpers should "dwell on the issues and problems, for although money still plays a big role in electing politicians, people are interested in his opinions and plans and most votes will be cast on those merits."[89]

Even this chink in Bumpers' armor proved impenetrable. Rockefeller's editorial endorsements from Arkansas newspapers declined dramatically in 1970; his political appeal could not match that of his young challenger. Indeed, Rockefeller seemed in an untenable position. The *Arkansas Gazette*, having supported Rockefeller's gubernatorial attempts in the past, now applauded his reform proposals while at the same time backing Bumpers, who they believed would have more success guiding Rockefeller's reform measures through the Democratic legislature. This contention fit right in with Bumpers' general election campaign theme. Even if the two candidates agreed on every problem and every solution, Bumpers insisted, the overriding issue in the campaign remained: "Whose judgement do you best trust to deal with those problems, who do you think will work the hardest and who do you think will be able to resolve the legislative stalemate and get our state moving?" When a student leader of a Young Republican organization at the University of Arkansas asked Bumpers a question concerning prison reforms proposed by Rockefeller but stalled in the legislature, the candidate responded: "If you want those things, vote for me."[90]

The final predictions in the governor's race had Bumpers leading with over 50 percent of the vote. But on election day, pollsters, Rockefeller, Republicans, and even Bumpers himself expressed astonishment at how strongly the challenger finished. Bumpers' vote margin of 62 percent exceeded that of any gubernatorial candidate in Arkansas history. Rockefeller had only 32 percent of the vote, with Walter Carruth of the American Independent Party receiving 6 percent. While Rockefeller received his usual group of stalwart Republicans and dominated the black vote with 88 percent, the incumbent governor carried only two of seventy-five counties. Bumpers dominated northwest Arkansas, where Rockefeller had always done well, and still carried the moderate and conservative Democratic areas of southern Arkansas.[91]

Jim Ranchino, a political scientist from Ouachita Baptist University active in Arkansas political polling, thought that Rockefeller had fallen out of contention in the last week because of a backlash over excessive campaign spending. Representative John Paul Hammerschmidt, the state's only successful major Republican candidate in the general election, agreed. Newspapers around the state seemed to bear out this suspicion. The *Arkansas Gazette* ran an editorial entitled "The Arrogance of Spending," denouncing the "fantastic level of spending" in the Rockefeller campaign, even employing "not one but two helicopters." Rockefeller had "saturated newspapers, radio stations, billboards and recently, placed a conglomeration of mail to the voters that would break any postmaster's back," the *Marked Tree Tribune* remarked. These lavish practices may have been acceptable in large states, said the paper, "but in Arkansas, the campaign staged by Mr. Rockefeller got to the point where it only negated his real accomplishments." The *Dumas Clarion* agreed that campaign expenditures had become so lavish that the state should implement some controls. Even though "the Republicans may well have spent six-fold as much as the Democrats," the paper asserted, Dale Bumpers proved that "an attractive, personable candidate can win a nomination even if he is underfinanced." The *Times*, in North Little Rock, marveled at the fact that

Bumpers had won without the Democratic old guard and states' rights factions. The Democrats who had deserted the party and independents "found Mr. Bumpers attractive not only because he was a new face in the Democratic Party unallied with any of the old factions or leaders but also because he eschewed narrow partisanship and made no promises other than to work on the state's problems as best he could." The *Newport Daily Independent* agreed. "Although we supported Governor Rockefeller, there is no question that the Democrats this time came up with an able leader, one not identified with formerly powerful factions that the Rockefeller forces could link him with."[92]

One group of the electorate more than any other contributed to Bumpers' success: white moderates returned to the Democratic party in 1970. The great middle class of voters, that group responsible for Rockefeller's past electoral successes, observed Jim Ranchino, "had moved from a rather conservative, intolerant posture in 1960, toward a greater degree of tolerance and moderation in 1970." Ironically, Rockefeller, who had done more than any other politician in Arkansas to bring about this moderation, suffered defeat due to what he had wrought. The Republicans experienced an electoral disaster statewide. They ran candidates for thirty-six seats in the house and ten in the senate. None of the challengers made it, and the party held onto only two seats in the house. According to Philip D. Carter of the *Washington Post*, Bumpers' election "proved that given a choice between a Democrat and a Republican saying the same things, Arkansas—like the rest of the South—will still usually choose a Democrat. And so the New South in Arkansas was born." Indeed, gubernatorial elections across the South in November 1970 seemed to prove that the Republican southern strategy of catering to racial fears would no longer play to the majority of voters below the Mason-Dixon line.[93]

"The future I envision must be shared by all Arkansans—old and young, black and white, rich and poor," declared Dale Bumpers in his inaugural address. "This administration will be one of concern, compassion, and reality . . . We must not waste the awakening of our people." Perhaps a New South had indeed arrived.[94]

4

Florida

In his classic work of 1949, *Southern Politics in State and Nation*, V. O. Key considered Florida "scarcely a part of the South. It votes Democratic, it is geographically attached to Georgia and Alabama, it occasionally gives a faintly tropical rebel yell, but otherwise it is a world of its own." By 1970 the state did not look much different; compared to other states below the Mason-Dixon line, Florida seemed not at all southern. Unlike the rest of the region, Florida had seen widespread urbanization, gains in wealth, and tremendous growth in population. The first southern state to have the majority of its inhabitants reside in cities, almost seven of ten Floridians lived in metropolitan areas by 1970. In the next few years, the Sunshine State replaced Virginia as the southern state with the highest per capita income. Every decade of the twentieth century saw the percentage increase of Florida's inhabitants grow at a rate at least double that of the rest of the nation. During the decade of the 1950s the state experienced 78.8 percent growth, and 37 percent in the 1960s. In the twenty years prior to 1970 nearly three million people moved into the state, swelling the population to nearly seven million people so that barely a third of its residents in that year could claim to be native Floridians.[1]

Considering the incongruent nature of Florida's growth, one might expect that the state would have abandoned its southern traditions. Because of a disproportionate representation scheme, however, the politics of the state had maintained a remarkable resemblance to politics in the rest of the region. The locus of political power lay in the Panhandle, that strip of land at the top of Florida attached to Georgia and Alabama that remained, according to Jack Bass and Walter DeVries, "strongly Democratic and racially conservative, with a populist tradition" in a state that lacked a "sense of place, kinship, tradition, and ties to the land." The Panhandle had been the area least affected by immigration, with the highest concentration of African Americans in a state with fewer blacks in proportion to the population than any other southern state except Texas. The northernmost part of the state, in other words, exhibited the most southern characteristics, and that area dominated the politics of the state. According to the 1960 census, 12.3 percent of the voters elected a majority of the state's senators and 14.7 percent elected the lower house. The five most populous counties, containing over half of the population, had only 14 percent of the state's senators representing them. Although 68.6 percent of Floridians lived in metropolitan areas, the state had no city as large as 550,000. The many cities that spread around the state dissuaded representatives of those widely spread urban counties from voting together. Representatives from the Panhandle and other rural counties wielded power through a cabal known as the "Porkchop Gang" that doled out state money for their own areas and interests, one of which was to maintain the racial status quo.[2]

Following the 1954 *Brown* decision that struck down segregated public schools, Florida lawmakers, like those of several other southern states, moved to draft laws that would prevent implementation of the Supreme Court order. In 1955, the legislature passed a bill that would, as a "last resort," close public schools forced to integrate. Governor Leroy Collins vetoed the measure, which was narrowly sustained. With the leadership of Collins and the support of a small group of legislators, several measures such as the "last resort" bill never reached fruition. As a result, racial turmoil had not occurred in Florida with the same frequency or intensity that other Deep South states experienced in the aftermath of *Brown*. While other southern governors shouted for massive resistance, Collins spoke quietly in favor of measures to ease racial accommodation in the state. In his 1957 reelection inaugural address, Collins presented integration as inevitable and suggested that Floridians obey the law of the land. Collins pointed out that blacks did not enjoy equal opportunity and accordingly were "morally and legally entitled to progress more rapidly."[3]

In 1970, however, a different Florida governor would seek to enhance his political career by creating a furor over busing and challenging federal authority concerning desegregation more directly than Orval Faubus or Ross Barnett or George Wallace ever had.

The 1970 gubernatorial campaign did not bode well for Florida Democrats. They faced a Republican incumbent governor who seemed to represent a vibrant and growing party that would replace the corrupt, decrepit, and discredited Democratic political machine of the past. The domination of the legislature by the Democratic Porkchop Gang had ended in 1967, when the U.S. District Court in Miami ordered the state to reapportion in accordance with the "one man, one vote" requirement of *Baker v. Carr.* The GOP had captured the governor's chair in 1966 and a U.S. Senate seat in 1968, and when the incumbent Democratic senator announced that he would not seek reelection in 1970, the prospects of a GOP sweep of the state's three top elective offices seemed very real indeed. Compounding the Democrats' problems, Attorney General Earl Faircloth and former governor Farris Bryant seemed likely to gain the Democratic gubernatorial and senatorial nominations, and they represented the discredited old order that had controlled Florida politics for decades. Claude Kirk, the incumbent Republican governor, could also take comfort in a poll of legislators, elected officials, and lobbyists, conducted in January by the Sarasota *Herald Tribune*, that indicated that the majority of these savvy political insiders believed Kirk would easily win reelection.[4]

Claude Kirk had entered Florida politics in 1960 as the state chairman of "Democrats for Nixon," but shortly thereafter switched parties. Two years after an unsuccessful run for the Senate in 1964, Kirk became the first Republican governor in Florida since Reconstruction. He seemed to offer a refreshing change from Democratic machine politics in which small-county representatives (the Porkchop Gang) had dominated state affairs. Under the gang's control, the legislature had neglected urban problems, divided up state-funded local work projects, and merely approved the Democratic governor's measures. Kirk described himself as a "tree-shaking son-of-a-bitch." In fact, he did seek to use his office as a bully pulpit; he would focus attention on some difficulty or politically popular issue and attack with little regard for compromise or real effort to solve the problem. His confrontational tactics seemed to gain support, at least for a while, from an electorate tired of politics as usual. Kirk set the tone of confrontation during his inaugural address when he unexpectedly called for a special session of the legislature to draft a new constitution to replace the existing eighty-five-year-old document. The complex work of revising the constitution had been under way for some time, and the governor's speech denigrated the efforts of the legislators. Kirk's words seemed calculated to win public support at the expense of lawmakers and served notice that compromise would be replaced by conflict.[5]

The new governor continued his belligerence with the legislature when he opposed a salary increase for that body. A bipartisan group supported higher salaries to attract better-qualified representatives, and Governor Kirk had promised his support. When the pay raise reached his desk, however, he refused to sign it. Kirk delivered his veto message before a joint session of the legislature in which he criticized the legislators for ignoring public feelings and voting themselves an "overwhelming" pay raise. "As Governor, I can have no alternative but to respond to the people when the people's cause is right and just." Kirk not only opposed the salary increase that he had promised to support, he publicly accused lawmakers of incompetence, irresponsibility, and even corruption. He did so the same year that a governmental audit revealed that the governor himself had used state money improperly for a honeymoon to Europe, flowers, cards, food, and travel associated with his bid to gain the 1968 vice presidential nomination. Legislators of both parties wasted little time in overriding Kirk's veto.[6]

Kirk's vice presidential ambitions isolated the governor from his own party, opened him up to criticism from Democrats, and led to financial problems that plagued his administration. Just months after Kirk took office, he hired a publicist for the state, William Safire, a speechwriter for President Nixon, who received a $90,000 contract. Opponents of Kirk quickly realized that the state's publicist spent more time promoting Kirk than Florida, and they pointed to a secret memo from Safire to Kirk that said in part: "Is George Wallace planning an appearance in Florida soon? You ought to go and 'welcome' him as part of your 'confrontation' politics." Safire advised Kirk to challenge Wallace and supplied the words for the meeting. "'You talk about crime in the streets, George. What about crime in Alabama?'" Kirk did not confront Wallace, but he did stump several Alabama courthouses telling listeners, "I know ole George and I like him, but he just can't win across the country."[7]

Kirk, on the other hand, believed that he had a realistic chance to capture the vice presidential nomination. Richard Nixon had attended Kirk's inauguration in 1967 and told Kirk's former father-in-law that he intended to run for president with a young southern Republican in 1968. During the New Hampshire primary in March of that year, William Loeb, the conservative editor of the *Manchester Union-Leader*, urged a vice presidential write-in campaign on behalf of Governor Kirk. Loeb reasoned that selecting Kirk would convince southern Democrats that the Republican Party had its "foot in the door of the South" and intended to walk in. It would also show George Wallace that "there is a difference between states' rights and racism." Nixon, however, selected another running mate. Never one to bow out gracefully, Kirk then threw his support to the candidacy of Nelson Rockefeller, which angered many Florida Republicans who strongly supported Nixon.[8]

In addition to his very public squabbles, Kirk also engaged in private battles with fellow Republicans. Kirk had an enormous ego and wanted to control the GOP. Even before Kirk won the governor's chair he had initiated a feud with the most powerful Republican in the state, Congressman William Cramer. In 1954 Cramer had become the first Republican representative since Reconstruction elected in Florida and, until Kirk came along, had also served as the guiding force of the state party. In 1970, Cramer, with the urging of President Nixon, entered the race for the vacant seat in the U.S. Senate. The prospects of recapturing the governor's chair and placing a Republican in the open Senate seat in the same race made some sort of accommodation between Kirk and Cramer seem compelling, but the intense animosity between the two men coupled with Kirk's confrontational political style solidified opposing forces within the GOP and led to internecine warfare in the Republican primaries. Both men sought to run candidates against the other. Cramer found the perfect opponent for Kirk in drugstore millionaire Jack Eckerd. With little hope of gaining contributions in a race against an incumbent, Eckerd could spend large amounts of his own money. He also had the advantage of statewide name recognition and a powerful campaign team that included William Murfin, the former state party chairman, and Roger Ailes, a television adviser to President Nixon. Adding to Kirk's woes, a former ally and state senator, Skip Bafalis, also challenged the governor in the GOP primary battle. The resulting competition within his own party seemed to pose particular danger to the governor. Conventional thinking at the time, expressed in several newspapers and supported by a number of polls, suggested that Kirk could defeat any of the Democratic challengers, but that he faced real problems capturing his own party's nomination.[9]

While Cramer viewed Jack Eckerd's candidacy as detrimental to his adversary, Kirk saw an opportunity for revenge when the Senate rejected Judge Harrold Carswell as President Nixon's nominee for the Supreme Court. With the encouragement of Kirk, Carswell challenged Cramer in the senate race. Kirk saw several positive benefits in a Carswell campaign. He believed that sympathy for the judge's rejection could be parlayed into votes. Carswell's candidacy would also embarrass many Florida Democrats who had offered profuse endorsements of Carswell when he had been a Supreme Court nominee. Most important, if Carswell won the nomination, it would solidify Kirk's hold on the party and strengthen Kirk's chances for reelection.[10]

Many believed that the judge's leap into the senate race landed him well ahead of lesser-known figures. "There ain't no way Carswell can be beat," said one GOP state senator. Carswell, who had dominated national head-lines for weeks, possessed instant name recognition. And Carswell's rejec-tion as the second southerner Nixon sought to place on the Supreme Court propelled him to a position approaching political martyrdom. Many also appreciated the irony of Carswell's seeking to enter the very body that had rejected him. "The poetic justice of this is beautiful," re-marked a Republican legislator from Clearwater.[11]

On April 20, 1970, with Kirk and Republican Senator Edward Gurney standing next to him, Judge G. Harrold Carswell announced that he was relinquishing his seat on the Fifth Circuit Court of Appeals and entering the race for the Senate "to join President Nixon in his goals of restructur-ing our country and its government along constitutional, conservative lines." Kirk also sought to pin the presidential seal of approval on Carswell. "What a flagbearer for the strict constructionists," Kirk said of Carswell. "You have a leader here, a man singled out by the President to be one of nine on the Supreme Court." Senator Gurney called Carswell "a dream candidate" and claimed that Harry Dent, Nixon's advisor on southern political matters, and Rogers Morton, GOP national chairman, agreed that Carswell's candidacy was a "once-in-a-lifetime" opportunity. Gurney further asserted that Dent considered the Carswell candidacy "an ideal solution" and that Morton had urged Cramer to pull out of the race.[12]

Florida's House Speaker Fred Schultz said that he hoped Carswell was "not being used as an innocent pawn in a back-room power deal based on publicity he received." Former governor Farris Bryant, who intended to enter the Senate race himself and who polls suggested could beat either Lt. Gov. Ray Osborne or Cramer, commented that sympathy for Carswell should not win him the election. "I don't feel that a seat in the U.S. Senate . . . should be awarded to anyone to salve his wounded pride," Bryant said. "I don't think you can base a candidacy for the U.S. Senate on a rejection by that body."[13]

William Cramer represented an important piece in this political board game. Although Kirk knew that he could not pressure Cramer to with-draw, he hoped the entry of Carswell would take the shine off Cramer's candidacy and perhaps even dispatch Cramer from power. Cramer had no intention of pulling out for the sake of party unity; instead he sought to obstruct and frustrate the efforts of Kirk and Gurney. Cramer released a statement from his office in Washington: "President Nixon personally urged me to run for the U.S. Senate. This has not changed. He also urged Judge Carswell to remain on the bench, where strict constructionists of the Constitution are needed. I am heeding President Nixon's call and hope Judge Carswell would do likewise."[14]

Even before Carswell entered the race, the administration had sought to distance itself from the internecine battles of the Florida GOP. "The President's name has been kicked around in the Florida primary battle," Harry Dent told Bob Haldeman in a memo in March. "I have asked Ron Ziegler to get a question asked and answered saying that the President is not taking any part in the Florida primary." But the next month Dent unwittingly became the man in the middle of the feud. Kirk and Gurney misled Dent, whose endorsement of Carswell's candidacy carried with it the implication of the president's favor. The two Florida Republicans told Dent that Cramer had agreed to drop out of the race so that Carswell could capture the Republican nomination unopposed. In fact, Cramer had never been approached about withdrawing and told Dent after the story became public that he was in the race to stay. A few days after Carswell entered the campaign, national Republican leaders disavowed any part in the political machinations of Kirk and Gurney. Rogers Morton angrily denounced Kirk and Gurney for "shocking" behind-the-scenes tactics. Morton denied Gurney's claim that he had urged Representative Cramer to drop out of the race. "I'm not about to discourage any candidate to run on the Republican ticket. I'm in favor of open primaries." Morton criticized Kirk and Gurney for picking Carswell behind the back of Cramer, who had announced his candidacy seven months earlier, and then asking Cramer to withdraw. "It's unconscionable for this to have happened," Morton said. "If a few candidates are selected in some smoke-filled room, what's the use of having a primary?" Morton asked. The White House would remain neutral. One party spokesman said: "Kirk and company have put Nixon in one hell of an embarrassing position at best and infuriated him at worst."[15]

State GOP leaders also denounced the Carswell candidacy ploy. Gubernatorial candidate Skip Bafalis said the GOP state committee should replace Chairman Duke Crittenden if he was part of the "power play." Bafalis called Kirk and Gurney "kingmakers," trying to gain a "hammer lock" on the party by using Osborne and Carswell as "pawns." Crittenden denied any involvement, saying that he was chairman of all the Republicans. Alyse O'Neill, a state GOP committeewoman and wife of a Nixon appointee, in an open letter to the press urged Carswell to remain on the bench. "I refuse to substitute the temporary whims, transitory caprices and shifting political ambitions of Claude Kirk for the permanent well being of the Republican party," O'Neill wrote. Carswell responded that the decision to run for the Senate was his own, that he had not consulted with the president before he entered the race, and that he was not running "in tandem" with any other Florida politicians. He would be his own man, he said, "beholden to nobody but the people."[16]

For all the hoopla and great expectations involved, the Carswell candidacy did little more than fracture the Florida GOP. At a time when Kirk, running for reelection himself, needed to lead a united Republican effort, he divided his own party. Whatever benefit Kirk hoped to gain backfired, as GOP regulars throughout the state expressed resentment over Kirk's chicanery. "It's one thing to maneuver for power within the party," said one Republican of Kirk's ploy; "it is quite another to go off and divide the party. And I'm telling you the party is really divided." Carswell proved a poor candidate. He had not run for elective office since 1948, when he had sought a Georgia congressional seat and declared his support for white supremacy, and that campaign had helped derail his Supreme Court nomination. Cramer would go on to defeat Carswell easily for the Republican nomination, only to lose to Lawton Chiles, a young, little-known Democrat who would walk the entire state to emphasize contact with the average citizen.[17]

The machinations of Kirk in the Senate race demonstrated the continuing turmoil the incumbent created within his own party at a time when he needed to marshal all the support he could muster. But Kirk knew that it would take more than Republican support to win reelection. Kirk believed that he could tap into the resentment over busing and achieve a power base that would cut across party lines. The disruption of public education became a prime campaign issue in 1970. Many school boards and parents reacted with indignation at federally mandated desegregation plans that would move students and teachers that year. In Sarasota County the school board voted 5 to 0 to defy a federal district court order to submit a new desegregation plan with a more balanced black-white ratio. Calls from irate parents inundated legislators, according to Representative Lynwood Arnold, chairman of Jacksonville's Duval County legislative delegation. "It seems to be the only subject people are interested in . . . most of them seem to realize there isn't much the Legislature can do. But they still want to talk about it. And a lot of the calls are from Negro parents who are just as upset," Arnold said. State senator Mallory Horne reported a similar biracial indignation in Tallahassee's Leon County. The rancor had nothing to do with race, he explained; complaints were coming in from "colored as well as white communities." In his fourteen years as an elected official, the senator claimed, he had never witnessed "more resentment, more fear and more bewilderment" from parents who expressed frustration with their children being "tossed about like a feather in a reckless wind." Their frustration led the senator to entertain the notion of defiance. Horne considered direct resistance, but believed that the only hope for posterity lay in the "capacity to use the avenues of constitutional protest open to us under the law." One woman, whose husband worked for the U.S. Health, Education and Welfare Department (HEW), had no such qualms. "If my children are forced out of their present classroom in February, then I will not send them back. Period!" she threatened in a letter to the *Tallahassee Democrat*. "[A]s far as I am concerned the government can go to hell."[18]

The uproar over busing did not escape the attention of Governor Kirk. Prior to 1970 Claude Kirk's position on civil rights differed markedly from that of most southern governors. "I'm not one of those red-necked Governors like Lester Maddox," Kirk told the *Saturday Evening Post* in 1967, "I'm the only good guy in the South." When Alabama Governor Lurleen Wallace invited him to attend a conference in Montgomery to discuss stopping school integration, Kirk replied: "We here in Florida who are pursuing a war on crime cannot join in attempts to subvert or delay the law of the land as interpreted by the Supreme Court." Also in 1967, Kirk defused a potentially volatile meeting led by black militant H. "Rap" Brown. Kirk won the crowd over by urging a peaceful gathering even as he warmly welcomed Brown. As governor, he had also launched an "Operation Concern" to deal with problems of the ghetto. The governor's apparent lack of personal prejudice and past record of civil rights support could have served the state well in easing the final stages of school integration. In 1970, however, Kirk decided that the political advantages of defiance could not be ignored in an election year. "I don't think Governor Kirk was a racist," Reubin Askew remarked many years later, "I think he just exploited the issue as many politicians did. In fact, it was almost the normal thing to exploit the issue . . . He was exploiting it because he thought it would really put him in a good position." The black constituency of the state accounted for only 10 percent of the electorate and voted solidly Democratic, and Kirk believed that electoral success rested in appealing to those Democrats who most objected to desegregation pressures. Kirk seemed to have heard Barry Goldwater's 1964 advice to southern Republicans to "go hunting where the ducks are."[19]

Kirk believed that challenging court-ordered desegregation would yield flocks of voters. The Fifth Circuit Court had ruled that the public schools within their jurisdiction, including Florida's, must be desegregated by February 1, 1970. In mid-January Kirk petitioned the Supreme Court to delay that school desegregation deadline until the governor could plead the case himself. (He contended in this and later confrontations with the courts that only the Supreme Court had sufficient stature to deal with him.) Claiming he had brought "racial harmony" to Florida, Kirk maintained that desegregation could be accomplished in an orderly fashion in September but that the February deadline would lead to "havoc," particularly in wrecking the state's budget. The Supreme Court wasted little time in rejecting Kirk's petition; it ruled the same day that public schools attended by about 300,000 students in five southern states, including Florida, desegregate by the ordered deadline. "The courts apparently don't care about the education of children," Kirk claimed, only about the "social mechanics."[20]

Governor Kirk's last-minute appeal to the Supreme Court may have struck a resonant chord with some, but his actions did not impress everyone. An editorial in the *Tallahassee Democrat* contended that intervention by the state came much too late. Many school board members from the capital county of Leon, after agonizing for weeks over the threatened desegregation plan, resented the governor's political grandstanding. "Big deal," said one school board member of Kirk's actions. Another, criticizing both the governor and Commissioner of Education Floyd Christian, claimed that: "Neither Kirk nor Christian has ever gone to the press and said, look folks, the schools are in a bad situation. We have been left dangling without any advice or help on an overall plan."[21]

Others criticized the governor's actions for different reasons. Two of the state's top black leaders tore into Kirk for asking for the delay. Reverend C. K. Steele of the Southern Christian Leadership Conference characterized the governor's actions as a "ridiculous" stand against defenseless black children. Steele also called Kirk a political opportunist who thought he could get some political mileage out of the controversy. The Reverend Joel Atkins, president of the Florida National Association for the Advancement of Colored People (NAACP), in a flurry of mixed metaphors, accused Kirk of "shouldering up to the segregationists. He's changing colors like a lizard . . . playing political football with the rights of black people." Atkins admitted that busing students was a great expense for the state, but reminded Floridians that the segregated system that had operated in the state for years had also been expensive. "Governor Kirk is trying to pull a farce over on the court when he says that this instant desegregation will break Florida," concluded Atkins. "Here we are nearly sixteen years after the Supreme Court's original ruling on desegregation . . . and it seems to me mighty absurd that he should be asking for more time to do it."[22]

Those directly involved with the implementation of desegregation expressed opinions ranging from resigned acceptance to adamant disapproval. "The fact is that we must either accept it or see our schools collapse," said the education commissioner. The legislature considered calling a special session in order to allocate funds to cover the immediate reassignment of students and teachers to meet the deadline. The Leon County School Board unanimously passed a strongly worded resolution protesting the court-ordered deadline and sent it as an urgent message to Congress. The resolution called the court's action "arbitrary, unreasonable and unrealistic," contending that the mandate would "have disastrous consequences to the public school system . . . in uprooting students, faculty and equipment."[23]

Students and teachers also had mixed opinions about the moves. Many expressed concern about integration's effect on student councils, clubs, sports, and friends. "I think it stinks," said one ninth grader. "My girlfriend will have to stay here and I'll be moved." Another student chimed in that sports were "going to be goofed up." One girl worried about moving students into the varying quality of curriculums at different schools. "They're doing it so Negroes can learn as much as we are," responded one eighth-grade girl. Another eighth-grade girl from an all-black school wanted white students to come to her school. "If we can go to all-white schools then they can come here," she reasoned. But a boy from the same school did not like it. "If white boys come here, they're going to want to participate in sports. It's going to mess things up." The principal of the same black school seemed more optimistic. "I think we can do it," he said; "the attitude here seems to be that whatever the School Board comes up with, we'll do our best to make it work." Another teacher from Tallahassee contended that the school system could handle almost any situation. "I wish that we had accepted complete integration years ago, and had not waited to be forced to do so. If we were integrating under our own steam we wouldn't feel so bad about it."[24]

The immediate desegregation controversy seemed bound to occupy the center of the political arena in an election year. Hank Drane, political editor of Jacksonville's *Florida Times Union*, believed that interference with neighborhood schools was coupled with the "fact that people don't like to be shoved around is why the desegregation decision may shape the course of politics in 1970 more than any other issue." Drane wrote, "Any politician who doubts it is a major issue is far out of touch with reality."[25]

Claude Kirk had a firm grip on political realities. He believed that the desegregation issue offered him a real opportunity; even after his appeal to the Supreme Court failed, he continued to press the issue. After all, Kirk excelled at confrontation, and here was a chance to take on the federal government. On January 19, Kirk threatened to suspend county school officials who followed the orders of the Supreme Court and implemented desegregation plans during the 1969–70 school year. While maintaining that he was not defying the Court or "standing in the schoolhouse door," Kirk again asked the Court to reconsider its February 1 desegregation deadline order. Unlike the other four southern states included in the Supreme Court decision, Kirk argued, Florida had led the South in integration and racial progress. He urged the Court to give the state extra time to continue its orderly desegregation. "We are not defiant in Florida," Kirk said. "We are accomplishing integration, desegregation. The reason I am here today is to show that I am sincere." The state cabinet imitated the governor's sincerity by passing a resolution that prohibited busing to achieve racial balance in schools ordered to desegregate. The general counsel for the state board of education maintained that there was no requirement in the Supreme Court order that pupils must be bused to achieve racial balance in the schools. The governor agreed wholeheartedly. "We can have complete resistance to forced busing and still be in compliance with the law of the land," Kirk reasoned.[26]

The education commissioner, however, disagreed. "I am strongly and unalterably opposed," declared Floyd Christian, "to any action that would place Florida and Florida's school personnel in violation of legal federal court orders." Christian accused Kirk of holding out "false hope" while "looking for votes." He was not the only one who objected to Kirk's actions. Marvin Davies, the state NAACP field secretary, wanted to put the governor in jail. David Cook, the associate editor of the *Tallahassee Demo-*

crat, characterized the governor's actions as "a needless exercise in futility." Cook believed that Kirk might reap a political bonanza from the situation but that he had set himself up for a conflict with the court that he was sure to lose. "The court will prevail, no matter how wrong it is," Cook wrote. "It would be a shame, however, if [Kirk] has raised any false hopes of avoiding complete desegregation. That can't be stopped—even by the master confronter of them all."[27]

Governor Kirk dug in his heels. He again threatened to suspend county officials who implemented court-ordered desegregation plans. The Leon County school board attorney, Graham Carothers, pointed to the difficult position in which Kirk's order put a school board. If the governor went through with his threat, he would "place the board in the position of having to choose between the risk of being in contempt of court . . . or being subject to removal by the governor," Carothers said. State senator Frederick Karl of Daytona Beach also worried about the school board's predicament. Karl, chairman of the committee that acted on all gubernatorial suspensions, said that school officials would be placed in an "untenable position" should the Kirk order be implemented.[28]

Kirk maintained that the effect of his threatened suspension of school board members would put him "in between the Supreme Court and the boards." A few days later the governor said that he would be willing to go to jail to prevent "forced busing" in Florida schools. Kirk made the bizarre assertion that such a jailing would be "for a philosophical cause, just as our prisoners in Vietnam are in jail for a philosophical cause." The governor's legal aide, Gerald Mager, blasted the Leon County school board for "abdicating its responsibilities to the children" by "throwing in the towel" on the February integration order. Mager said he was "shocked and surprised" that the board had not gone back to the Court to appeal the present order. The Leon County school board attorney answered Mager's attack: "I am frankly appalled at the irrational statement attributed to the governor's legal aide." The attorney labeled the free legal advice as "obviously politically inspired" and "repugnant to an orderly solution of legal problems."[29]

One week before the February 1 deadline, Kirk filed another suit requesting that the Supreme Court establish a national standard for a unitary school system and direct HEW secretary Robert Finch to apply these uniform guidelines in funding for education. "We are going to be in compliance by September 1," said Kirk. "We don't want to see our tax dollars shipped off to other states which are not in compliance." Kirk also blamed education commissioner Floyd Christian for his inactivity, labeling him "about as useful as hip pockets on a hog." Kirk reasoned that Christian "implied support of forced busing by doing nothing." Christian responded to Kirk's statement by contending that the governor had decided to cash in politically on the emotions generated by the recent Supreme Court decision.[30]

Others believed the governor's anti-busing stand coupled with his promises to go to jail rather than succumb to pressure from the courts had made him unbeatable in his bid for reelection. "It's got him elected," declared one Democrat. Another political observer wrote in the *Florida Times Union* that people out in the hinterlands believed that at least the governor tried to do something. "That is what they will be reminded of and remember in the fall when most of the court ordered mixing plans take effect and the election campaigns are under way."[31]

Kirk had little chance of going to jail, but the mere threat of martyrdom would strengthen his chances in November. Two counties had already gained delays from district courts, and only two other counties were directly under court order to desegregate in February. The chances, therefore, seemed favorable that some sort of delay would occur that would allow the governor to claim his tactics had succeeded.[32]

But Kirk's efforts to sway the court and gain more time for the desegregation plan failed. In a unanimous decision, the Court denied Kirk's plea for a rehearing. "The governor saw this as an opportunity to capitalize on an emotional situation for his own political advantage," said Floyd Christian, "and it has backfired." Indeed, Kirk's failure came as no surprise. An editorial in the *Tallahassee Democrat* admitted that the Supreme Court had done some strange things in the past, "but considering appeals for rehearing by people who weren't party to the litigation would be a little too much for it."[33]

Kirk's exercise in futility continued when he issued the executive order he had been threatening in Volusia and Manatee counties. The order barred student transfers and busing to accomplish school desegregation. "The issue in Volusia, the issue in Manatee, the issue everywhere we've been involved has been busing," said Kirk's legal advisor. Some critics countered that the issue involved the governor's reelection. "He has preferred to publicly fight with teachers, with the commissioner of education, and now with school boards and superintendents, in order to perpetuate himself in office," said Wally Johnson, executive secretary of the Florida Education Association. Ray Dunne, Volusia County school superintendent, ordered by a federal district judge to transfer 2,800 students and 145 teachers to accomplish school desegregation, faced contempt charges if he did not comply and dismissal from the governor if he did. Accordingly Dunne complained that "I'm caught between the proverbial rock and hard place." Attorney General Faircloth informed school officials that federal orders outranked Kirk's executive orders and advised them to obey the Court. "Those direct orders may not be agreeable to us," wrote Faircloth, "but they are of superior rank in our system of jurisprudence— under our government of laws."[34]

Kirk faltered on his threat to fire the school board members, and criticism poured in from all sides. Democratic representative Jerome Pratt castigated the governor for playing politics with the school issue. Even Kirk's pastor admonished the governor. The busing issue that the governor played upon was "a phony issue," the rector of St. John's Episcopal Church told his congregation. And the Florida field director of the NAACP labeled Kirk's stand against busing as that of a bigot and blamed the violence that accompanied the desegregation process in several schools on the state's "stinking leadership."[35]

Kirk experienced the hazards of playing politics with the volatile busing issue, but he had not yet learned his lesson. In April, the culmination of Kirk's stand against busing came in Manatee County. After the Volusia County warm-up, some feared that Kirk would do something drastic. U.S. district judge Benjamin Krentzman had ordered an integration plan in Manatee that would have reorganized its busing patterns so as to eliminate token integration and provide the same 80/20 white-black ratio in its schools as found in the county's school-age population. On April 2, education commissioner Floyd Christian wrote to Kirk: "I believe when we have exhausted all our legal remedies and although we are not happy with the Court decision, we are left no other choices but to obey the law. . . . I trust that in the exercise of your executive power, you will not take any precipitous action in attempting to remove the School Board members and Superintendent for their compliance with the Federal Court Order." Christian had good reason for concern. Over the next week not only Florida, but the entire nation watched the governor challenge the federal judiciary. The *New York Times* carried the story on page one for seven days, while the national television news reported it among their top stories for most of the week.[36]

On April 6, after the Supreme Court had denied a delay, Kirk suspended the Manatee County school board and placed the school system "under the trusteeship and custodial supervision of the governor of the State of Florida." Calling the school officials "valiant, courageous and eminently qualified," Kirk maintained that the takeover would relieve them from implementing an "educationally unsound and illegal" order. In his new role as superintendent, Kirk told a meeting of principals that he would stand between them and the courts "tomorrow and tomorrow and tomorrow." Manatee County school board superintendent Jack Davidson challenged the suspension, saying that the sudden shift in plans would produce mass confusion in the schools. "It's about time everyone took their hands off our school system, Judge Krentzman, Governor Kirk and everyone, and let us get on with the business of educating our children."[37]

The next day Judge Krentzman ordered Kirk to step down immediately as head of the school board and to appear in court to show cause why he should not be held in contempt. Calling the order "a horrible illegal act of forced busing," Kirk claimed that he had acted not in defiance of the court, but on behalf of the schoolchildren of Manatee County. "The only man who in any way is in defiance of the system of justice is Judge Ben Krentzman," Kirk said. "Do not confuse a lawful contest of sovereign authority with defiance of the courts," the governor told legislators.[38]

Many in Manatee County applauded Kirk's actions. Crowds gathered at the school administration building. Some of them carried signs proclaiming "Manatee County Loves Governor Kirk," "I Am Proud of my Governor," and "God Bless Governor Kirk." Comments from area residents also demonstrated support. "It is very refreshing to find someone as high in government," one radio caller said of Kirk, "who has enough guts to take a stand and hold to it." Manatee County Commission chairman L. H. "Bud" Fortson declared: "People all over the country should start standing up to the courts." One of the suspended school board members resigned and published a letter supporting the governor and criticizing the federal courts; another member came to the administration building to join in the demonstration of local support. The mayor of Bradenton, Manatee's county seat, also backed the governor's actions.[39]

The Florida press did not join in the praise offered by many of the Manatee County residents. Even Manatee's local paper, the *Bradenton Herald*, criticized the governor's actions. The *St. Petersburg Times* called Kirk's actions "totally reprehensible." And the *Tallahassee Democrat* editorialized that tyranny usually begins with good intentions but that we must "hew to the Constitution and law. Anything else leads to anarchy, which eventually requires dictatorship."[40]

Attorney General Faircloth declared that Kirk's actions had "opened a legal barrel of snakes." Reubin Askew, a state senator from Pensacola contemplating entering the upcoming gubernatorial race, called the suspension order "sheer demagoguery." Democrats controlled the Florida legislature and would have impeached the governor, but feared that if they pursued removal it would make Kirk a hero and get him reelected.[41]

Kirk's confrontation placed President Nixon in a precarious position. In developing its southern strategy, the Nixon administration had sought to put the onus of desegregation on the judiciary. Nixon had publicly opposed busing, but Kirk's defiance could force him to send in federal marshals to enforce busing. On the other hand, if he ignored Kirk's actions, Nixon could face severe criticism for hypocrisy. Representative Abner Mikva of Illinois reminded the House that during the 1968 presidential campaign Richard Nixon had delivered impassioned speeches on how his administration would provide vigorous law enforcement. "Where is the President now when a governor of his own political party openly and shamelessly flouts the orders of a federal court?" Mikva asked. The *St. Petersburg Times* pointed to the same contradiction in an editorial saying that Kirk's actions had "exposed the danger which the Nixon Administration's 'southern strategy' poses for the law of the land. The President's silence before such open defiance by a governor hardly discourages rebellion by others."[42]

Meanwhile, the Manatee County school situation remained unresolved. Judge Krentzman ordered local officials to reclaim control of the school board and ignore any mandates the governor might issue to the contrary. The governor promptly ousted the school board again and directed aides and sheriff's deputies to seize the school board offices. Judge Krentzman ordered federal marshals to arrest them. The governor promised that his men would fire on the marshals if they attempted to take control of the schools. When the marshals arrived they found the Manatee County sheriff, several deputies, and about a dozen state troopers in riot gear forming a barricade outside the superintendent's office, where the governor's aides had locked themselves in and refused to come out. The sheriff, speaking at the governor's behest, told the marshals that his men would use force to prevent them from taking anyone from the building. The marshals served arrest warrants but took no prisoners, saying they considered the aides, the sheriff, and his deputies under arrest even though they were not actually in custody. U.S. attorney John Briggs promised to take control of the Manatee County schools even if force were required. Late that afternoon Governor Kirk, surrounded by about seventy policemen, arrived at the school administration building, telling newsmen: "Anybody who lays a glove on a sovereign is committing an illegal act. There is nobody who can bodily force the head of a sovereign state into court."[43]

Several high-level administration officials tried to reason with the governor. Attorney General John Mitchell as well as the assistant attorney general for civil rights repeatedly implored Kirk to stop his defiance. But Kirk remained unmoved. "We will resist force with force, effort with effort." Kirk even challenged Judge Krentzman's authority to order the head of a sovereign state to appear personally. "Whoever wants to arrest the governor must rassle the governor," warned Kirk.[44]

On Friday Kirk warned of a "grave danger of loss of life." Claiming that he did not intend to release control of the school system until the Supreme Court ruled on the legality of forced busing and that he would use force if necessary, he allowed federal marshals past the scores of guards to serve subpoenas on nine of his aides. "If this is the way to get to the Supreme Court, I'll give them every member of my staff." Meanwhile, during a hearing before Judge Krentzman, Kirk's senior assistant, Lloyd Hagaman, broke into tears and sobs as he reaffirmed his intention to heed the governor rather than the court. "I don't want to disobey the court order, but I have to stand by my governor."[45]

It would be tough to stand by Governor Kirk. The next day Judge Krentzman, finding Kirk guilty of contempt, ordered the governor to stop disobeying his school desegregation orders or pay a fine of $10,000 a day. Krentzman rejected Kirk's contention that there had been a violation of the principle of separation of powers. The judge ruled that the conflict was between the judiciary of the federal government and the executive branch of a state government, and the precedents were clear that the "state government must yield." The judge also pointed out that the contempt order placed Kirk in the company of earlier southern governors who had defied the courts concerning desegregation—all of whom eventually yielded to federal authority.[46]

On Sunday evening Kirk threw in the towel and promised to return control of the schools to the Manatee County school board and to direct its officials to put the court-ordered integration plan into effect. He tried to cast his surrender as a tactical victory. "Florida and the Department of Justice," said Kirk, "agree the solutions to our problems must lie in the duly constituted courts." Kirk added that he had received a promise from the Department of Justice that it would join with him in an appeal. "Disobeying a District Court and paying a $10,000-a-day fine is not going to solve anything," he said. "If I thought that or going to jail would do so, I would be in that jail."[47]

Although Kirk did not say who in the Justice Department had given him promises concerning the Manatee case, some in the department clearly had not been party to any such assurances. Solicitor General Erwin Griswold charged in a memorandum filed with the Supreme Court that "any confrontation between the governor and the United States would be entirely of his own making." Griswold opposed Governor Kirk's effort to remove the Manatee County school case immediately to the Supreme Court without going through the normal appellate steps. "It is inadmissible that any officer—high or low—should assume the stance that he will not obey the order of any court but this Court," Griswold concluded.[48]

Florida newspapers weighed in with their opinions concerning the governor's actions. The *Miami Herald* called for Kirk's impeachment. The *Tampa Tribune* excoriated the governor for his defiance. "A court order must be respected whether it be directed against a Governor or a Black Panther. Otherwise, government falters and no man's rights are secure." The *Orlando Sentinel* assessed Kirk's actions more favorably. Kirk, it said, asked only for equality in integration practices for the South. The *Tallahassee Democrat* contended that the nation needed a ruling on the forced busing issue, but questioned Kirk's methods "for the excesses of state constitutional authority it seems he has indulged . . . the approach of a bull in a china shop." The *St. Petersburg Times* said the governor had "brought embarrassment and danger" to the state. And the *Florida Times Union* thundered that the governor and the federal government should settle their differences in a courtroom rather than in a schoolroom.[49]

Citizens near and far also reacted to Kirk's defiance. In a Republican poll taken in areas of the state expected to provide 75 percent of the Republican vote in the upcoming primary, reaction was evenly split between those who approved of the governor's recent actions and those who either disapproved or had mixed reactions. And most of the letters Kirk got from Floridians expressed disapproval of his actions. One woman from Key West wrote that even though she was a Republican and opposed forced busing she was ashamed of the governor and believed him to be an egomaniac, "a red-neck racist, and a grandstanding show-off." A Tallahassee woman wrote that it was inexcusable for a governor to defy a federal court order, and a man from Eustis believed that Kirk should not only be put in jail but impeached. And the writer of a letter to the *Tallahassee Democrat* questioned the governor's sanity. "Has our Governor gone mad? In twice defying a federal court order, and allowing his agents to make threats of armed violence against marshals, Kirk has taken a giant step towards destroying the rule of law in this country."[50]

Kirk remained unrepentant. In explaining why he yielded to the contempt citation, Kirk maintained that he knew from the beginning that he "could only go so far" in attempting to block the court-ordered desegregation plan in Manatee County. He knew he could "go up to the point of force, but not beyond." Kirk called the students and parents of Manatee the "front line soldiers." If they "stick with it," he asserted, "and if we do our job in the courts, forced busing will fade away and die."[51]

On Tuesday, April 14, the day after Kirk abandoned his position as school board superintendent, Manatee County's desegregation plan went into effect. Buses rolled on double shifts to accommodate the additional student load. Eleven white women marched outside the school board building carrying signs that read "Who runs Florida—Kirk or Krentzman," and "Don't Bus, Join Us." About a dozen black parents also gathered at a bus stop to demonstrate their objections to the busing plan. But the school opening went smoothly, with absenteeism only slightly higher than normal. Reinstated superintendent Jack Davidson, speaking from his office as workers removed a battery of telephones Kirk had installed the week before, characterized the transition as "really going very smoothly. . . . The people still don't like forced busing. I don't like it either, but the great majority of our people agree that the place to settle the question is in the courts, not the streets."[52]

The superintendent's assessment aptly characterized the feelings of most Floridians. Governor Kirk's defiance seemed steeped in political opportunism and reaffirmed those critics who assessed his administration as one of confrontation without recourse to remedy. Kirk believed he could ride the irresistible force of public resentment of busing, but he met the immovable object of federally court-ordered desegregation. Kirk played out the old politics of race in April, before the campaign really began. This tactic allowed the other candidates to stand back and see if defiance could translate into votes. They could criticize Kirk's continuing confrontational tactics without taking a firm stance on busing. Kirk's actions proved the futility of defiance. Not only did he fail to prevent court-ordered busing, he did not gain significant support from voters who overwhelmingly disapproved of busing.

The political efficacy of the busing issue had died at Manatee, but Kirk attempted to revive it and place it at the center of his bid for reelection. Florida schoolchildren were being bused around "like pawns in an insane numbers game played by a handful of irrational federal judges," Kirk charged. To reinforce his point, Kirk sought and received the backing of Vice President Spiro Agnew. In a campaign swing through Florida, Agnew labeled Kirk an "action-oriented . . . stand-up governor." The vice president praised Kirk's defiance in the Manatee school desegregation incident, saying that Kirk "did a good job and served a very useful purpose in bringing the situation to the attention of the people and prodding court action." Kirk agreed. In a televised discussion of the issues, Kirk blamed a "permissive liberal philosophy" for implementation of compulsory busing of schoolchildren to achieve racial balance. Every week Kirk reminded voters that he had not given up in his defiance of court-ordered desegregation. When the Internal Revenue Service announced that they would do away with the tax-exempt status for private schools, Kirk said he would be the number one defender of those schools, many of which had been established to avoid racial integration. And Kirk sought to link tax exemption of private schools with his favorite topic: busing. Kirk claimed victory in his Manatee County public school desegregation fight and said he would not let private schools be picked off by federal agencies. "We have stopped busing in its tracks, and we are winning in Manatee whether you read about it or not." Kirk said he would call a seminar for the heads of private schools throughout the state to devise a course of action. Kirk also promised that Florida would join any school district in suits fighting what Kirk called "forced busing." Kirk's leading Republican opponent, Jack Eckerd, accused the governor of plotting "the most desperate, most reckless, most dangerous confrontation of his show biz career." Everyone was against forced busing, Eckerd contended. "Do we solve it or do we exploit it?"[53]

No matter how hard Kirk tried to focus the campaign on an issue of his own choosing, the other GOP candidates aimed their criticism at Kirk himself. Eckerd said he would use Kirk's record, his promises compared to his performance, to bring down the governor. Kirk was a liar and a desperate man who was "stooping to lies and vicious character assassinations in an attempt to save his own political hide," Eckerd charged. Skip Bafalis believed that Florida had become the laughing stock of the country under Kirk and charged that renominating the incumbent would guarantee a victory for the Democrats in November because the governor had "unified the Democrats on a single issue: Kirk himself." His adversaries not only made public statements criticizing the governor, they also financed a political biography meant to embarrass him. Published in the midst of the primary campaign, the 124-page paperback hatchet job entitled *Claude Kirk, Man and Myth* contended that Kirk was a "bush-league Huey Long" whose lifestyle was always "one jump ahead of his income." Concerning Kirk's political intrigues in Manatee County and in the Carswell Senate candidacy, the book stated: "In one instance he had played politics with human life, playing the school bully and then chickened out. In the second, he had used a man's reputation in an attempt to pull his own political chestnuts out of the fire."[54]

Whether he liked it or not, Kirk, rather than his opponents or the issue of busing, had become the focal point of the campaign. Two weeks before the first primary most voters appeared apathetic and undecided about gubernatorial candidates with the major exception of Kirk. One voter said the governor was "too much of a showman. I voted for him last time but never again." Another said he liked Kirk's "frankness and boldness." Even bumper stickers reflected the electorate's opinions of the governor. One stated "Kirk for Governor," while another proclaimed "Happiness is a New Governor." One group calling itself the "Conservative Citizens Committee" mounted a crusade to defeat the governor because he was too liberal. Major Holbrook Scott, a longtime GOP activist and chair of "Veterans for Kirk" in 1966, headed the group. Scott called Kirk "the most extravagant, wasteful spendthrift of any governor in the history of Florida." And Scott believed the incumbent had "been completely disloyal to the Republican party and the independent Democrats who elected him." The group's avowed purpose was to advise the voters about which candidates were truly conservative and which were liberal, but Scott readily conceded that what he was really interested in was "defeating Claude Kirk." Thomas Whol, a banker, builder, and Kirk appointee to a county planning board, announced he would head the Eckerd campaign in his county. "I'm disappointed in Governor Kirk," Whol said. "It's nice to have a flamboyant governor, but there comes a time for responsible leadership."[55]

While Kirk suffered at the hands of his own party, Democrats began to gear up for their challenge of the Republican incumbent. While several well-established political leaders sought to secure their party's nomination, one obscure Democrat challenged Kirk directly and ignored the Democratic front-runners. Reubin O'Donovan Askew believed there was an urgent need for responsible leadership in Florida. Many Democrats had voted for Kirk in 1966 in hopes of finding new leadership, but instead got government by impulse and antics, Askew told people. "I think the people are ready for a new leadership, keyed to results rather than who gets the credit." Admitting that he did not have all the answers to the problems facing the state, Askew promised to work hard and apply all of his "training, experience and ability to develop a meaningful partnership with the people in an earnest attempt to find solutions." Askew had already earned a reputation as a hard-working legislator who shunned political expediency in favor of doing what he believed right. Even though Askew's remarks did not differ markedly from those of other politicians running for office, he delivered them with an air of believability. His ability to project sincerity, particularly over television, would serve him well in the 1970 campaign.[56]

Askew was born in 1928 in Muscogee, Oklahoma, the last of six children. His father, an itinerant carpenter with a sixth-grade education, left the family when Reubin was born. When he was eight, his mother moved with the children to Pensacola, Florida, where she had been raised, and took a job as a hotel maid. Reubin's first job was going door-to-door taking orders for pies and cakes his mother baked at night. "My mother had an enormous influence on me," Askew would say years later. "Mother taught us to hold our heads high and work." And Reubin's mother said of her youngest son that "he was the most determined boy I've ever seen, anything he did, he had to do perfectly, even if it was just cleaning the yard." Askew attended Florida State University, where he received a degree in public administration, and the University of Florida, where he earned a law degree. He served as a paratrooper in World War II and as an air force officer during the Korean conflict. Elected to the Florida legislature in 1958 and again in 1960, he moved over to the senate in 1962 for the first of four terms, eventually rising to become president pro tem of that body. He won numerous legislative awards, was named one of the outstanding young men by the state Jaycees, and worked extensively on behalf of underprivileged and retarded children.[57]

Askew had also demonstrated that he belonged to a new breed of southern politician that shunned racial bigotry. Askew attributed this trait to his mother, who he said had worked with a lot of black women as a housekeeper in a Pensacola hotel. "She related to their plight and as a result I guess that was translated to me so that I came along and I really felt strongly that the whole system was so morally wrong . . . to deny someone the freedom of their own God-given talents to develop was more than I could really take." In 1950, while Askew served as student-body president at Florida State, the university prevented an integrated student government delegation from holding a meeting on that segregated campus. Askew supported a resolution that called upon the legislature to integrate all state graduate schools. Eight years later, during his first campaign for the legislature, controversy over racial integration dominated the political contests of the day. Askew refused to say that he supported segregation. "Some of my closest advisors said that you've got to say it," Askew remembered. The young candidate refused. "I'm not going to say it. If that's what it takes to get elected, I'm just not going to do it," he told his advisors. During that same campaign a man called him a "niggerlover." Askew responded: "The difference between you and me is that I'm trying to overcome my prejudices and you're not." Even though his position seemed out of step with that of his constituents, he won election and re-election. "Ol' Rube [Askew's nickname] got some funny notions 'bout the colored, but you can't help respecting a man for saying what he thinks," remarked an old man from Pensacola. First elected to the legislature only four years after the *Brown* decision, Askew resisted efforts to close public schools rather than succumb to integration. "I guess because I was from Pensacola people just naturally expected I'd be part of the conservative bloc, but I took the position from the beginning that I'd never do anything to shut down schools," Askew said. "Without public education I never would have had any opportunities."[58]

In 1970 Askew decided to run for governor against very long odds. After losing their hold on power, Florida Democrats seemed unusually united behind the clear front-runner, Attorney General Earl Faircloth. In late April a poll in the Tampa–St. Petersburg area suggested Faircloth would win easily. Askew, however, did not campaign as if Faircloth would capture the Democratic nomination. On the first of August, Askew contended that the Democratic primary was wide open and that he would pose the greatest threat to the incumbent in the general election. "Democrats who want a change are going to vote for the man who has the best chance to beat Kirk," said Askew. Not everyone agreed with Askew's assessment. Even Askew's hometown newspaper, the *Pensacola News-Journal*, endorsed another Democrat. In an editorial the paper said that senate president John Mathews was better qualified and more likely to capture the nomination than Askew. Most voters in North Florida, according to one paper there, believed that Faircloth or Mathews would be in the

Democratic runoff. But the paper noted that even though Reubin Askew was not well known, several voters commented that they were leaning toward him.[59]

Although few voters outside the Pensacola area knew of Askew, several political observers soon began to appreciate the potential of this young, attractive candidate. In a report on the Florida gubernatorial race dated 18 June 1970, Harry Dent wrote that Kirk would likely win the Republican nomination and defeat any prospective Democratic challenger, but that state representative Reubin Askew concerned him. Askew, Dent wrote, "seems to be the front-running conservative Democrat as Attorney General Faircloth has faltered." Oddly enough, the incumbent realized this before almost anyone else. In early June, when Askew resigned from the state senate to enter the gubernatorial race, Kirk told him: "I hope the Democrats don't have sense enough to nominate you, you're the only one who can beat me." Indeed Kirk had hoped to run against almost any other Democratic candidate.[60]

Askew presented a sharp contrast to the incumbent governor. A self-described "non-smoking teetotaler and a Presbyterian elder," Askew's personality could not be described as flamboyant nor his rhetoric dramatic, but his honesty and sincerity came through. Often on the campaign trail Askew would relate that all of his life people had been saying that he was too serious, "but don't you think it's time for some seriousness in the governor's office?" he would ask the crowd. "That was the one line that always got applause," Askew would remember years later. Askew's campaign differed from the norm. He sought to run a campaign steeped in optimism. He based his television commercials on "issues, nothing negative, I talked about issues." Many seemed to appreciate this approach. "I'm just glad to see a candidate have the guts to say what he thinks," said one public official. And Askew said what he thought directly to the people by means of television. His media advisor, who initially had maintained that a candidate should never be featured in a political advertisement, reversed himself after he saw Askew in front of the camera. "So every one of my commercials," Askew remembered, "were me talking to the people and I think that had a tremendous impact." Askew contended that he had broken all the political rules and offered a new approach to government. "It's a new day, for the poorest and the wealthiest, for the black and the white. We've got to start talking about the things on which we agree, not our disagreements."[61]

Askew emphasized the need for new leadership and financial responsibility. Unless Florida had "strong executive leadership and a new tone in the governor's office," Askew declared, "our problems of conservation, taxation and education will continue to grow with no solution in sight. If we could talk away our problems," he quipped, "we wouldn't have any left because we've had one of the best talkers in the country in the governor's office these last four years. Kirk's input into government has been air and the product has been hot air." When Kirk made a no-new-taxes pledge Askew said the promise was "just as phony today as it was in his campaign four years ago." Askew hammered away at what he labeled the primary issue of the campaign—the need for genuine tax reform in Florida to reduce the load on low- and middle-income families. His "fair share" tax plank would repeal the 4 percent sales tax on utility, telephone, and garbage bills because "these items are as essential as groceries and medicines," Askew said. He repeated his opposition to taxes on personal income, groceries, and medicine. When Democratic candidates agreed on the inevitability of new taxes, Askew attacked them all. John Mathews, who proposed a grocery tax, became "Food Tax Jack." To accept Mathews' plan was "just another way of saying that we're going to load more taxes on the middle and low income people and leave the special interests alone," said Askew. "When someone calls for a tax on groceries which feed our families, it is unfair and unthinkable." Askew railed against another candidate that favored a personal income tax and charged that the leading Democratic candidate's proposed increase in the capital stock tax would endanger small business. Instead of listening to consumers, Askew said, these politicians "are listening to and obeying the special interests which put money into their fat campaign treasuries—and escape their fair share of the cost of government." This issue would serve Askew well. In recommending Askew for the Democratic nomination, the *St. Petersburg Times* contended that "when many others were catering to prejudices, Askew was talking about tax reform. He has kept himself free of the entangling commitments that entwine Kirk."[62]

The growth of support for Askew had been steady and impressive. Six months prior to the primary only 4 percent of the state's electorate could recognize his name. At the end of June Askew's own polling assigned Faircloth 44 percent of the vote, followed by Mathews with 11 percent; Chuck Hall had 8 percent, Askew was last with 7 percent, and 30 percent were still undecided. One month later Faircloth's support had dropped 6 percentage points; Mathews, Hall, and Askew had all risen 4 percentage points, with 24 percent undecided. By the end of August, Faircloth commanded 35 percent, Mathews 13 percent, and Hall and Askew both 14 percent, with 24 percent undecided. These numbers held steady through the next week just prior to the primary vote, and Askew received endorsements from approximately half the state's newspapers. The momentum of support for Askew seemed to be increasing and, even more significant, at least one poll suggested that most voters believed Askew represented the only Democratic candidate that would beat Faircloth in a runoff.[63]

In the first Republican primary, held September 8, Kirk led the field with 172,888 votes, but Skip Bafalis's 48,378 votes denied Kirk a majority and forced him into a runoff with Eckerd, who polled 137,731 votes. Kirk's 48 percent fell far short of his predicted 60 percent victory. The incumbent had suffered serious damage from these two challengers, indicating a lack of strength within his own party.[64]

In the Democratic primary Earl Faircloth led the polling, while Reubin Askew ascended to a second-place runoff spot in the closing days of the campaign. Political observers had from the beginning of the campaign season predicted that Faircloth would become the Democratic choice for governor, but Askew's late surge into the runoff convinced many, including the Kirk camp, that Askew would capture the nomination. Faircloth's support had faded during the busing controversy. Some voters believed that Faircloth had shirked his duty as attorney general when Governor Kirk challenged busing plans in the courts. While many did not support all of Kirk's tactics, they saw Faircloth's acquiescence to Kirk's resistance as a sign of weakness in a gubernatorial candidate. Kirk also believed he had undermined Faircloth's political appeal and wanted to face him in the general election. In fact, Kirk wanted anybody but Askew. Some Republicans saw Askew's rising star as the eclipse of their own. "The Democrats have no finer man in Tallahassee than Reubin Askew," said a top-ranking Kirk aide. "It's not Jack Eckerd we have to worry about."[65]

In 1966 Kirk had been the forlorn Republican running against entrenched Democratic control, but in 1970 he had to answer for his actions while wielding power over the last four years. Kirk became the center of attention and the target of attack for the entire field of candidates from both parties. Jack Eckerd said that if Kirk were renominated he would drag down GOP candidates all over the state and erase gains the party had taken a hundred years to achieve. The primary, Eckerd's campaign manager noted, "proved that even a majority of Kirk's own party doesn't want him." William Cramer, who won the Republican nomination for the Senate, worked against Kirk because he believed that the governor had stabbed him in the back by pushing Judge Carswell to run against him. And state Democratic chairman Anne Cramer worried that the GOP infighting might spoil their chance to run against Kirk. "We've been waiting four years for a crack at him, and we know we can beat him."[66]

Several newspapers agreed that the elimination of Kirk would benefit the state. Two Tampa Bay–area newspapers endorsed Eckerd and Askew for their party's nominations. "Four more years of Kirk would be bad business for Florida," according to the *Tampa Times*. The *St. Petersburg Evening Independent* wrote that Askew was "known to his colleagues for his integrity, a welcome virtue for a governor of Florida." The *Miami Herald*, citing the incumbent governor as the major issue in state politics, also backed Eckerd and Askew. Nominating these two would "restore sound, honest, dignified government to Florida after four nightmarish years of buffoonery and turmoil," the paper contended.[67]

But those who hoped to see Kirk eliminated from Florida politics would have to wait. Jack Eckerd, Kirk's Republican challenger who had forced a runoff primary, proved unequal to the task of driving the incumbent from office. On September 29, Kirk won 56.8 percent in the Republican runoff. Kirk would face the Democratic nominee in the general election.[68]

On the Democratic side, in a move that surprised many, Secretary of State Tom Adams, who had turned down offers from two other Democratic contenders, accepted an offer to be Askew's running mate. Adams brought with him perhaps more ability and experience than any other Democrat in the state, not to mention a well-established political organization. Besides governmental experience, the Askew-Adams team could point to grassroots financing. Askew had been running on a shoestring budget, and Adams had gone broke in politics. Askew praised Adams as the only political figure who admitted a campaign deficit. Adams said he accepted the offer to run for the number two position because Askew refused "to take a dime unless the person who gives it wants it reported. This just ain't so with other candidates in the election."[69]

Although Faircloth led the first primary, his lackluster campaign could not contend with the refreshing candidacy of Askew nor the organization of Adams. Askew captured the Democratic nomination with a 119,000-vote margin of victory. Askew's 400,000-vote total exceeded by 50,000 votes the total Republican vote cast for Kirk and Eckerd in their runoff. Kirk had invigorated the Democratic Party by providing competition from the GOP for the first time since Reconstruction. It seemed the

Democrats had shaken off the image of the discredited old order with new faces and new ideas.[70]

Askew reflected this freshness by calling for a "new tone" in the governor's office that was "both responsible and responsive and conducive to finding solutions to the problems facing Florida." Calling his runoff win a "victory for the people," Askew said his fair-share tax reform campaign would be financed solely by the people. The Democratic nominee expected special interests to extend offers of assistance now that he had the nomination, but he promised he would not take any funds with any strings attached. "We are going to continue in raising our money in the same way we've done in the past and that is on an individual basis."[71]

Askew proved appealing to a wide array of voters. In the 1968 presidential campaign George Wallace and Eugene McCarthy had represented the extreme ends of the political spectrum. The Florida campaign chairmen for each of these two 1968 presidential candidates threw their support to Askew in the 1970 general election. The former Wallace campaign director saw Askew as simply the best man for the job, while the McCarthy chairman compared Askew's appeal to the old populist political coalition. "I'd hate to put a tag on Mr. Askew as far as conservative or liberal," said the Wallace supporter. "He's more of a middle of the roader." The McCarthy man agreed and pointed to qualities in the candidate that seemed to reach across ideology: "he's a very sincere guy that is not owned by the traditional special interests in Florida. He's a pretty free man, really." These sentiments foreshadowed trouble for the incumbent, who won in 1966 with the help of thousands of Democrats who came to believe, with Kirk's help, that their party's candidate, Robert King High, was too liberal. Kirk had emphasized High's open endorsement of integration and the public accommodation section of the 1964 civil rights bill, and his tenure as mayor of Miami when race riots racked that city. Kirk had also exploited the widespread frustration of many Floridians with President Lyndon Johnson's "Great Society" by linking High with national Democrats whom many associated with the excesses of liberalism that plagued the 1960s. But in 1970 Kirk would have a much more difficult task in trying to label Askew as an extreme liberal. While High hailed from Miami, a city that many considered a liberal Sodom and Gomorrah, Askew grew up in the most conservative part of the state. And it was impossible for Kirk to link Askew with the political problems of the recent past when a Republican president and Kirk himself had been presiding over the nation and state.[72]

These difficulties did not stop Kirk from attempting to reimplement his earlier strategy. Kirk claimed that the *New York Times* had labeled Askew a liberal. "And you can't hardly beat the *New York Times* for picking out liberals—flaming liberals," said Kirk. "I want all the permissive liberals to vote for Askew. I want all the discerning Democrats and wise Republicans to vote for me." Kirk also attacked Askew's ability to be governor. "Goody Two-Shoes . . . a nice, sweet-looking fellow," Kirk said, but being governor was "a tough job and just being a momma's boy won't get the job done." But Askew had earned a reputation for taking on tough jobs. In the senate, Askew had often drawn the tedious non-headline assignments because of his record of accomplishment. He had served as chairman of both the Appropriations and Constitutional Amendments committees and was credited with doing most of the work on the complicated revision of the trial court system.[73]

Kirk seemed unable to sit back and rest on the laurels of his administration, even though he had accomplished a great deal. He had opened up Florida politics to public scrutiny, led the fight for governmental reform and constitutional revision, sought educational improvements, taken measures to protect the environment, and formed the first state law enforcement agency. But Kirk's brand of confrontational politics dictated that he attack his opponent. In the past slinging the mud of racial liberalism had served southern politicians well. By 1970, however, diverting attention away from the issues with political invective proved ineffective. Coupled with the diminution of the race issue was the fact that Kirk's adversary in 1970 remained impervious to the incumbent's attacks of excessive liberalism, corruption, or incompetence. Askew's earnestness and wholesome image seemed, to many voters, more suited to governance than the confrontation and dissension created by the incumbent. That Askew had entered the race as an unknown in most of the state enhanced his fresh-face appeal among an electorate disgusted with politics as usual. Kirk sought to counter this appeal. "Askew is not a new face at all," Kirk charged. "He's been around for twelve years. The reason the people knew nothing about him is that he never did anything."[74]

If Kirk did not understand the dynamics of this particular campaign, Askew's campaign manager, Elmer Rounds, did. Before the candidates even began running, Rounds traveled to sixty counties in the state. "I discovered the public was in a foul mood. They were angry at government and politics," Rounds said. "I could see Reubin would have a good chance because he was unknown. It was the same advantage Kirk enjoyed in 1966."[75]

Askew deftly sidestepped Kirk's criticisms by reminding voters of the incumbent's antics while in office. "I think the people are tired of government by crisis," Askew said. "We can't have government by personality. We must have government by law, by diligence and by commitment." Askew turned Kirk's accusations that he was a liberal into a joke. "Kirk's definition of an ultraliberal is anybody who runs against him," said the Democratic nominee. Askew pointed out that Kirk had supported the 1968 presidential bid of Nelson Rockefeller, whom many saw as representative of the extreme liberal faction of the GOP. And Askew produced a 1967 *New York Times* story in which Kirk called George Wallace a "flaming liberal." Askew rejected being positioned on the political spectrum. He said that labels were not important. "I have never been fearful to take a stand on any issue. Look instead at the men you are putting into office. The governor's record is one of inefficiency." After the election even GOP Senator Edward Gurney conceded that Republican efforts to label Democratic candidates as liberal had not succeeded. "There was no clear-cut liberal-conservative battle," Gurney said. "The candidates tried to make it that way but it didn't work out."[76]

The Kirk campaign even sought to link Askew's tax reforms to liberalism. Kirk's campaign manager, Robert Lee, charged that Askew had "surrounded himself with the most wild-eyed liberal elements in Florida." Lee claimed that Askew and a Miami state senator were "co-architects of the new pork chop liberalism" that was "just a new disguise for the old liberal Democrat tax-and-spend philosophy." Lee charged that Askew's "alleged tax reform package" would increase taxes and spending. Governor Kirk also accused Askew of favoring big spending. While in the legislature the Democratic nominee "never failed to vote for more spending," Kirk claimed. "Big spending doesn't solve anything. When he talks about tax reform, I don't know whether to laugh or cry." The governor saw dangers in Askew's proposed corporate income tax. "I enjoy this game that we're involved in—free enterprise and democracy," said Kirk. "My adversary is trying to kick around the corporations. Ain't nobody going to kick around the corporations."[77]

Askew supporters had warned him from the beginning that his campaign should not advocate a corporate income tax. "You didn't have much chance before, now you've got none," the United Press International bureau chief in Tallahassee told Askew after he announced that he would make his fair-share tax program the centerpiece of his campaign. "Any kind of tax proposal, my friends assured me, was political suicide," the candidate admitted. Many political observers had predicted that after his primary victory Askew would downplay his corporate income tax since it would open him up to Republican charges of being anti-business, but the Democratic nominee continued to emphasize, and even clarify, his plans for tax reform. Askew devoted more space to his fair-share tax program than to any other issue in his "13 pledges" campaign statement. Kirk renamed his opponent "Reubin Taxyou," contending that Askew's reforms would cost each household in the state at least $150 per year. "The working man is realizing, finally, that this is not a tax on corporations; it is a tax on him. If 'Taxyou' is elected," Kirk told a breakfast audience, "all of these eggs and grits and gravy and biscuits will carry a tax." Askew struck back at Kirk's criticism of his tax program by labeling the incumbent as "Tax-Fraud Claude." Askew reminded a gathering in Miami that in 1966 Kirk had been totally opposed to any advance or increase in the sales or gasoline tax. "But two years later he proposed the largest single increase in taxes in history—a 5 percent sales tax." Askew also reminded his audience that Kirk still advocated a one-cent increase in gasoline taxes after the legislature had rejected it in a special session. Askew denied that his proposed corporate tax was anti-business, as Kirk had charged, and contended that it would merely require corporations to pay a fair share of the tax load. "Florida ranks forty-sixth in the nation in the amount of taxes corporations pay, but we've got one of the highest consumer taxes in the nation."[78]

As the election neared, Florida newspapers made endorsements. Jacksonville's *Florida Times Union* supported Kirk, whom the paper characterized as "controversial, colorful and sometimes downright cantankerous." The paper contended that the incumbent had been good for the state. "He didn't cave in under every pressure that was brought to bear on state government. That's not his way. . . . He won some and he lost some. He backed away from none. . . . He got the people more involved." Almost every other Florida newspaper, however, did not like what the governor got the people involved in. Calling the Kirk administration "four years of divisive and destructive buffoonery," the *St. Petersburg Times* endorsed Askew for governor. "Governor Kirk's tenure has been a lark for the governor but an albatross for the state," said the editorial. "The Askew record on the other hand portrays quiet, responsible, progressive leadership."

The *Tampa Tribune* said that Florida was "too important a state and too proud a state to have to endure four more years of a governor who turned this high office into a traveling circus." The paper praised Askew for conducting himself honorably and for his stand on the corporate income tax. The *Miami Herald* also supported Askew. "It is time in Florida . . . for a new generation of leadership," said the paper. Askew is "a breath of fresh air in Florida politics . . . he has captured the imagination of a state which plainly desires new leadership." According to Kirk it only made sense that the state's newspapers supported his opponent. Askew was a tool of Florida's "foreign-controlled, permissive-liberal press," Kirk charged.[79]

Voters weighed in with their own opinions. At a defense plant one employee believed that Kirk had "stood up against many obstacles. He didn't accomplish much but he tried." A black employee said that Kirk was "an extremist on the right." State senator Verle Pope of St. Augustine considered Askew a man of great ability and courage. "We are starting with a product we know is good," Pope said. "He can lead the state out of the wilderness we have been in for the past four years."[80]

In the final days of the campaign Kirk used pollution as a metaphor for all the ills he claimed Askew represented. While campaigning in Askew's home county of Escambia, Kirk pointed to an executive order that he had issued to clean up Escambia Bay. Kirk claimed that if he remained in the governor's office there would be no more fish kills. If his opponent won the election, however, the contamination would return because Askew was a "patsy of the polluters." Kirk then launched into a wide-ranging litany of charges against Askew. "He wants to pollute your homes with forced housing. He wants to pollute education with forced busing. He wants to pollute your minds with pornography. He favors those who pollute your bays." Askew had the luxury of being defended by the press. "Although he doesn't like the nickname 'Mr. Clean,'" wrote the *Gainesville Sun*, "Mr. Askew earned it by his legislative conduct." The Democratic nominee himself responded to Kirk's charges by subtly reminding voters that Kirk had been running the state for the previous four years. "From the way he is talking," Askew observed, "everything wrong in Florida is my fault." One older man at a campaign rally agreed, telling the Democratic challenger that he was going to win because he refused to indulge in the same type of politics as the governor. "The state's tired of that type of politics." Rather than hurling insults back at the governor, Askew labeled Kirk's charges "the politics of a desperate man who knows he's fixing to lose."[81]

Polls seemed to bear out Askew's assessment. In a *Miami Herald* poll of 600 registered voters statewide taken in late October, Askew led with 62 percent to Kirk's 35 percent. Kirk scoffed at the poll. "I bet my last buck a third of the voters out there haven't made up their minds," Kirk said. But the incumbent also admitted that winning reelection would not be easy. "It's an uphill fight," Kirk said. "But I have confidence. It's been uphill every day I have been in Tallahassee." And the governor's campaign efforts gave no indication that he was engaged in a losing effort. He pursued a relentless campaign schedule, while maintaining his enthusiasm and optimism. Typically his campaign DC-3 took off close to dawn with bleary-eyed campaign workers and journalists stumbling aboard to find the candidate for reelection fresh, immaculately dressed, and upbeat. Kirk would crisscross the state attacking his opponent as a liberal in sixteen- to twenty-hour days, while conducting the affairs of the state with occasional stops at the capital.[82]

All of Kirk's campaigning, however, failed to sway nearly enough voters to give him four more years in office. On election day voters sent a resounding message to their confrontational governor. Askew won 57 percent of the vote, a landslide margin of 291,083 votes.[83]

When the primary season began, most political observers considered the incumbent unbeatable, but after four years of confrontation the electorate opted for a less colorful candidate and a more cooperative government. Askew had stressed his desire to work with the popularly elected cabinet, which his predecessor had sought to abolish, and the legislature, which the governor had battled with during the nine special sessions he called during his tenure. Kirk's confrontational tactics had solidified opposition against him. One of the few successful GOP candidates in the election called Kirk a "unifying force for the Democrats." Many blamed Kirk for not only uniting the Democrats, but for dividing the GOP during a four-year battle to establish personal control of the party. "He's tried to set up his own party," one Republican leader complained.[84]

Kirk's defiance of court-ordered desegregation that required busing also contributed to his political demise. After the election Kirk conceded that the racial emphasis of his campaign probably cost him the election. The governor sought to place himself between the federal government and the school systems attempting to implement court orders. Kirk's challenge harkened back to the old southern notion of interposition; the states had created the Constitution by compact, so when the federal government overstepped its authority, the states had the right and the duty to interpose themselves between the offending action and its execution. Southern governors had attempted to justify their resistance to federal mandates in the past with interposition and failed. Although polls showed that nearly 90 percent of Florida's voters disapproved of busing, very few had any illusions that they could successfully resist federal court orders. That Kirk's motivations seemed transparently political further reduced the popularity of his stand. Furthermore the tumultuous decade of the 1960s had illustrated the social upheaval that resulted from defiance of the law and strained the willingness of most southerners to mimic the protestors and rioters they had so roundly castigated. Indeed much of the criticism of Kirk's actions pointed to militants of the recent past who broke the law in testing aspects of society they considered unjust. Kirk had fallen out of step with the mood of the electorate. His philosophy of governance did not reflect the feelings of the voters.[85]

Reubin Askew, on the other hand, mirrored the concerns of Floridians. "I wasn't for busing; no one was for busing at that time," Askew would say years later. He was not against integration, but believed busing merely complicated the determination of a reasonable racial balance. Askew had not been forced to take a strong stand for or against busing, as Kirk's showdown at Manatee occurred before Askew became a serious candidate. "I knew that if I tried to take it on hard the only thing it would do was help him so I never really pursued it as an issue," Askew would later recall. "African Americans knew from my record in the legislature that I would be fair with them . . . I did not want to inflame the issue because if you get elected you've created your own problem. I wanted to settle the thing as best I could, so while he mentioned it I simply didn't pursue it with him because he was vulnerable on too many other issues."[86]

While avoiding disruptive racial issues, Askew's reliance on populist issues served him well in 1970. Askew ran on a shoestring budget, provided full disclosure of his contributions, and refused special-interest money. Running a campaign financed solely by the people added credibility to his main campaign theme of taxing the corporations in the state in order to reduce personal income taxes. When Kirk tried to portray Askew as a tax-and-spend liberal Democrat, the charges did not ring true. Askew had established a conservative fiscal record during his years in the legislature, even voting against the legislative pay raise that Governor Kirk had made such a fuss over early in his administration. And the governor's own unpopular proposals to raise gas and sales taxes did not lend credence to his charges against Askew. Kirk also had public problems with his personal and campaign finances. The contrast between the two candidates' personalities also contributed to the electoral success of Askew. Kirk showed up at his own inaugural with an attractive woman he would only refer to as Madame X; the governor had a reputation as a hard drinker, his language could be coarse, and his appetite for confrontation was legendary. Askew, on the other hand, described himself as a nonsmoking teetotaler and Presbyterian elder who had married his high school sweetheart, and, most important, he had a convincing air of honesty and sincerity that he communicated to the public.

That candor played particularly well over television. Askew could appear on-screen and speak to voters in a frank and earnest manner. Television, therefore, allowed an attractive candidate to emerge from obscurity in a manner that no amount of stumping the state could achieve. "When I came along, not because of me, but because of the time, television came of age," Askew asserted years later. Coupled with these positive reactions to an appealing candidate, the overwhelming, near unanimous editorial support reinforced the affirmative feelings Askew conveyed over the airwaves. "Television and editorial endorsements played a very important role in my case because my name recognition was only about 4 percent a year before the election. So that I happened to hit it right with television and it worked out pretty well for me."[87]

The frankness and positive approach to solving problems that Askew demonstrated in the media seemed indicative of a new attitude for a New South. In his inaugural address he spoke of the need to do more than "give pious lip service to the justifiably urgent needs of our black citizens." After the election he expressed hope that a New South might lead the country into a new era of racial accommodation. "The rest of the nation has tried to teach us justice in the South by mandate and court order," Reubin Askew would later tell his constituents. "Now perhaps it is up to us to try to teach them in a much more effective way—by example."[88]

South Carolina

In his 1949 study of southern politics, V. O. Key contended that the preoccupation with race in South Carolina supplanted political conflict. "In part, issues are deliberately repressed, for, at least in the long run, concern with genuine issues would bring an end to the consensus by which the Negro is kept out of politics. One crowd or another would be tempted to seek his vote." By 1970 the consensus concerning black involvement in politics had ended. As Key had predicted, only one crowd sought the black vote while the other sought to mobilize the fears of the majority of white voters concerning federal pressures to achieve racial balances in schools and the perception that blacks could exercise undue influence by voting as a "bloc."[1]

Five years after the publication of Key's book, the Supreme Court ruled that segregated schools must end. South Carolina, like other southern states, challenged the *Brown* decision, but when desegregation came, South Carolina acquiesced, if not enthusiastically at least with a modicum of decorum. Not without irony, integration began at Clemson University, built on the cotton plantation of John C. Calhoun, the antebellum South's leading spokesman for slavery and states' rights.

In 1963 as his tenure in office drew to an end, outgoing governor Ernest "Fritz" Hollings signaled a determination to deal with the problems that integration posed for his state in a positive manner. "If and when every legal remedy has been exhausted," Hollings told the legislature, they "must make clear South Carolina's choice, a government of laws rather than a government of men. As determined as we are, we of today must realize the lesson of 100 years ago, and move on for the good of South Carolina and our United States. It must be done with law and order." The incoming governor, Donald Russell, continued these efforts at easing the transition by opening up the inaugural barbecue to black citizens for the first time.[2]

In 1968 South Carolina sent its first integrated delegation to the National Democratic Convention. It was the only Deep South delegation that went unchallenged. In 1970, as part of the three-hundredth birthday of South Carolina, *Porgy and Bess* was performed in Charleston, the first performance of native son Dubose Heyward's musical play about black life in the city in which it was set. A decade earlier city officials had barred even the movie version. Also in 1970, when four southern governors pledged to defy federal desegregation plans that included student busing plans in their home states, Governor Robert McNair promised South Carolina would obey the law. The 58,000-pupil Greenville County school system faced a midyear desegregation order that involved extensive busing. The governor received over 15,000 telegrams. "Everybody wants the governor to do something," an aide said, "but nobody has any suggestions for what he could do that would be legal." McNair told his constituents in a statewide telecast: "We've run out of courts, and we've run out of time, and we must adjust to new circumstances." The governor said he would oppose any attempt to close schools or abolish compulsory school attendance laws. "We've seen what defiance will lead to," McNair said. "I don't think the people of this state would want to defy the order of the court after we've run the course legally. We don't want federal troops in South Carolina. We've built a reputation for obedience to the law."[3]

The example set by the chief executive helped community leaders accomplish complete integration with "grace and dignity," as one national wire service characterized it. Even though McNair saw his popularity decline as a result of the conciliatory speech, most South Carolinians had moved into the ranks of moderation. "The people down here know they've lost the battle," observed one Democrat. "They'd like to continue fighting, but they realize they can't win. So they don't want trouble stirred up." This seemed to sum up the attitude of white moderation in the state. Resistance had proven disruptive, and most whites seemed willing to live with integration in exchange for tranquility.[4]

By 1970, South Carolina seemed poised to accept integration, even in that most jealously defended bastion of southern segregation: schools. "White folks feel they're becoming more moderate," explained M. Hayes Mizell, a white civil rights activist who scored an upset victory in a 1970 Columbia school board election. "They are doing things they didn't do a few years ago, like sitting down with Negroes at lunch counters, participating at meetings where Negroes are present, their kids are going to school with at least some Negroes. With all this peace, and tranquility, they think everything is OK, that they're more liberal." More than 50,000 white children in 1970 were attending formerly all-black schools in the state. Although the movement to establish new private schools to circumvent integration reached its peak in 1970, public school enrollment declined by only 2 percent that year. The University of South Carolina included 400 black undergraduates in the fall of 1970.[5]

In anticipation of the upcoming election of 1970, two South Carolina college students sought, by employing census figures, to find the county most representative of the state and survey one hundred random voters. The search indicated that Laurens County, with a population of 47,609, was *the* average county in the state. Laurens County lies in the northwestern quadrant of the state midway between Greenville and Columbia. The county contained a 70/30 percent racial split and a 60/40 percent urban to rural ratio. Politically the county had followed the state pattern in its choice for presidential candidates in the past three national elections, supporting Kennedy, Goldwater, and Nixon. Of the one hundred voters employed for the survey eighty were white and twenty black. The political affiliation of the white respondents included thirty-eight Independents, fourteen Republicans, and twenty-eight Democrats. All the blacks participating in the survey, with the exception of one Independent and one Republican, indicated a preference for the Democratic Party. Of the total number of respondents eighty-three considered themselves members of the "Silent Majority" that Richard Nixon had appealed to. Eighty-eight read a newspaper and eighty-four watched television news. Forty-nine said that the news media influenced their political thinking more than family, friends, or fellow employees. Fifty-eight viewed public officials as "basically honest and effective," while sixty-seven believed the situation in the state was hopeful. The one hundred random respondents in this most average county in South Carolina designated two problems that most concerned them on the national and state level. Of national issues, thirty-one worried about crime, twenty-nine Vietnam, and twenty-seven race relations. Of state issues sixty-eight expressed concern over education, twenty-six taxes, and twenty-one crime. The authors of the study noted that the overwhelming response to education was because of race mixing and student busing associated with a recent desegregation court order of "intense concern to respondents" in neighboring Greenville County. The study concluded by pointing to the possibility of Republican gains in South Carolina because of two popular Republicans—South Carolina's U.S. Congressman Albert Watson and President Richard Nixon.[6]

A Republican had not sat in the governor's chair in South Carolina since Reconstruction, but 1970 seemed to hold great promise for the Grand Old Party. While token school integration had proceeded smoothly under freedom-of-choice plans, new and drastic changes threatened the state. Several South Carolina school districts faced pressures to desegregate that included termination of federal funding, and the 58,000-student Greenville County school district struggled in January 1970 with the midyear court order that included extensive busing. Some Republicans sought to exploit what they considered drastic and intrusive federal orders. These Republicans, led by Watson and Senator Strom Thurmond, believed that the McNair administration's moderate approach exhibited weakness that had encouraged more stringent federal desegregation measures. Closely associated with the McNair policies, Lieutenant Governor John West appeared certain to capture the Democratic nomination. But polls discovered that many white voters agreed with the following comments about West: "Weak, doesn't do anything; goes along with McNair; can't stand up for his own beliefs; bland." Some Republicans saw West as a vulnerable candidate. They maintained that West lacked the personal charisma of the popular Watson. They also believed West could be linked unfavorably with the present governor and attacked as more liberal than the electorate.[7]

Albert Watson had begun his political career as a Democrat serving in the South Carolina House before moving on to the U.S. Congress in 1962. In 1960, Watson headed up Democrats for Nixon and in 1964 supported Senator Barry Goldwater, the Republican nominee for president. As a result of his support for Goldwater, Democrats in the House of Representatives stripped him of his seniority. Watson then resigned his seat and entered a special election as a Republican. Watson recaptured the office with 70 percent of the vote and retained the seat in 1970. This win led many Republicans to see Watson as the strongest potential Republican candidate in the state and they urged him to run. Republican Senator Strom Thurmond, who had also left the Democratic Party after supporting Goldwater in 1964, saw Watson as a kindred spirit. At a November 1969 Republican gathering 900 party contributors heard Thurmond introduce Watson as the "future Governor of South Carolina."[8]

Many hoped that Watson could combine the strong Republican support spearheaded by Senator Thurmond with an appeal to those voters who had voted for Wallace in 1968. Richard Nixon had carried the state in 1968 with 39 percent of the vote, largely through the efforts of Senator

Thurmond, while Wallace had received 32 percent. Distress over desegregation measures that included busing seemed to permeate the state, and Watson looked like the perfect candidate to take advantage of the issue. Watson had no qualms about exploiting white fears concerning desegregation or even black voting rights. In the special congressional election of 1965 to fill the seat Watson had resigned, his campaign flyers proclaimed in bold lettering that the South was under attack and that Democrat bosses planned to rule with the Negro vote. "Remember," one flyer warned, "A man who is elected by the Negro bloc vote will have to answer to the NAACP every time he casts a vote in congress. Is that the kind of congressman you want in this congressional district?" Watson would campaign for governor wearing a white tie that he privately admitted represented his segregationist supporters. Watson accused Governor McNair of "surrender" for advising compliance with court-ordered desegregation and described himself as "an ardent fighter for the rights of the majority against the vocal, violent minority."[9]

But Watson did not speak for all Republicans. Arthur Ravenel, Jr., a racial moderate from Charleston, also sought his party's nomination in 1970 and thought a different approach could win the governor's chair. Senator Thurmond's endorsement of Watson left Ravenel "very disappointed." In December 1969 Ravenel, responding to the touting of Watson as the Republican nominee for the upcoming governor's race, said that the South Carolina GOP was "racist oriented," on the "unrealistic or ridiculous right," and should follow him to a position closer to the center of the political spectrum.[10]

Ravenel believed that the Republican Party had to reach out to black voters in order to have any hope of success in statewide races. "How can we win elections by appealing to only 65 percent of the voters?" Ravenel asked. "I believe you've got to openly appeal to the black voters. . . . I'm going to do it openly, not sneaking around in alleys." Ravenel had been advocating this approach of racial accommodation for some time. In 1968, serving as the GOP district chairman in Charleston, he had promised that as long as he held that position, "this will not be a racist party." The *Greenville News* took notice. Under an article entitled "GOP Should Take Ravenel's Cue," the paper pointed to Ravenel's open-door approach as the only way to "break the Democratic party's virtual monopoly on the growing Negro vote."[11]

Ravenel could point to two southern Republicans, Lynwood Holton in Virginia and Winthrop Rockefeller in Arkansas, who had gained the governor's chair because of black support. "And all Black people want," wrote Ravenel to one Republican activist in the state, "is the same thing White people want. And what's wrong with that?" It all seemed so simple to Ravenel that the direction of his own party in 1970 confounded and upset him. Ravenel believed that "polarization forces" were pushing Watson into the gubernatorial race. Ravenel contended that this "bunch" included "reactionaries" whose cause was hopeless. "Not being able to get any Black or moderate support, they're going to have to push harder for the seg and racist vote."[12]

Those close to Ravenel shared his alarm at the possibility of a Watson nomination. James Duffy, who became Ravenel's campaign manager in 1970, after hearing Watson suggest that parents keep their children from attending court-ordered desegregated schools in spite of the state compulsory education law, asked an associate incredulously: "A governor who will not uphold the law?" And in reaction to Watson's tactics of urging resistance, Duffy echoed his candidate's attitude regarding the latest round of court-ordered desegregation in South Carolina. "It is an issue that might have some political appeal," wrote Duffy to a supporter, "but has no room for legitimate problem solving because it has all been tried since 1954."[13]

The Ravenel camp was not alone. A moderate group of Republicans had emerged who objected to the racial message Watson would send to the state and nation. Like Ravenel and Duffy, James Henderson, the GOP candidate for lieutenant governor, advocated a very different approach from that of his party's top candidate. "If I have anything to do with it, we're going to pay attention to all the races," Henderson promised. "No party can hold public office without recognizing that one-third of South Carolina's population is black."[14]

Some young people in South Carolina, who had no doubt been affected by the civil rights movement, saw Watson as a political menace. In the February 20 issue of Clemson University's student newspaper, the *Tiger*, an editorial proclaimed that Watson's election would be a political disaster. "His slick rhetoric and reactionary non-thought," wrote the paper, would confuse the uninformed voter, "and the key to his campaign is a raucous, negative attack on the forces of progress in our state government." Although the state had not suffered the disgrace of electing a George Wallace or a Lester Maddox, the editorial contended, Watson had "the charisma, oratorical expertise and Thurmondesque to capture the votes of masses of South Carolinians. Watson . . . preys off the fears and frustrations of people caught up in America's social revolution."[15]

Even Republicans who could barely vote saw the need for black support. In January 1970, the Clemson Young Republicans organized a forum on the "future of the Negro in the South Carolina Republican Party" and invited several prominent political figures including blacks and GOP members. "As a concerned Republican," the president of the group wrote to Ravenel's campaign manager, "you are no doubt aware of the acute need for our party to gain a part of the Negro vote in this state."[16]

An issue of even more immediate concern to Ravenel than reaching out to black voters was how the party should choose their candidate. Ravenel and his supporters believed that he could win the nomination if allowed to compete in an open primary. A small but determined cadre advocated the primary rather than the customary convention in which the candidate would be chosen by the party leadership. One member of the state Republican Convention wrote an open letter to his fellow delegates. "To open the future for our party we must open our ranks by going to the primary method of nomination," wrote Dr. William Hunter of Clemson. Hunter believed that their party's poor percentage of officeholders resulted from selecting candidates by the convention method and pointed to a recent poll indicating that 84 percent of Republicans in the state desired a primary. But the powers that controlled the state GOP, led by Senator Thurmond, party chairman Ray Harris, and Republican national committeeman Drake Edens, believed that Watson had a good chance to capture the executive office and did not want to diminish Republican strength in primary battles. In correspondence the party faithful often referred to what they called the eleventh commandment: "Thou shalt not criticize thy fellow Republican."[17]

One South Carolinian in the Nixon administration was keeping close tabs on the political situation in his home state. Harry Dent, counsel to President Nixon for southern political affairs, was a former state GOP chairman and an aide to Senator Thurmond who maintained an active correspondence with Republican leaders in the state. In January Ravenel offered Dent his assessment of the state's upcoming elections. "Polarization forces," according to Ravenel, were pushing Watson into the race. "The Democrats are licking their chops at the prospect of eating him up in the fall. He can get absolutely no Black vote and very little support from the White moderates whose numbers are rapidly increasing." And if

Watson ran for governor, Ravenel feared, the Republicans had no one who could hold the congressional seat that Watson would vacate. Ravenel argued that the party, not to mention his own chances for the nomination, would be better served by selecting the Republican candidate in a primary rather than a "controlled convention." Ravenel knew that if Thurmond gave his approval the state GOP chairman would set the mechanics for a primary in motion. Ravenel thought that he could win the Republican nomination in a "free and open primary" and that his chances would be "excellent of winning in the fall" because he believed he could secure "with honor and without any deals as much as 40% of the Black vote and most of the moderates."[18]

The GOP moderates, however, would not gain the sympathy of South Carolina's senior senator in this election. In 1970 Strom Thurmond abandoned his tradition of remaining neutral in state elections and threw the full force of his considerable influence behind Albert Watson. James Duffy had participated in Republican politics long enough to see which way the wind was blowing. He wrote to Ravenel with the news that Thurmond had released one of his assistants to run the Watson campaign. "So we [k]now how that works. The Thurmond people and our official Party leaders are about the land getting the convention firmed up." Thurmond's support seemed obvious to most political observers. John West later observed that "Thurmond ran harder for Albert than Albert did." Thurmond's papers prove the accuracy of this assessment, revealing that he solicited scores of his own supporters to get behind Watson. In dozens of phone calls and letters he asked for contributions to "Citizens for Watson," and thank-you notes from the senator acknowledged thousands of dollars worth of contributions. Thurmond appealed to multimillionaire H. L. Hunt in Texas for financial assistance to his protégé, and he asked the actor John Wayne, a Republican activist, to sign a letter that would be sent to potential Watson contributors.[19]

In February Lieutenant Governor John West, as expected, entered the gubernatorial race. Facing no serious Democratic opposition, West began his campaign running against Watson without having to worry about a primary opponent. West's personality and campaigning style contrasted sharply with Watson's. While Watson employed fiery rhetoric, West spoke in moderated tones. In interviews Watson gave short answers designed to grab headlines; West gave detailed, candid, at times rambling replies. Ike McLeese, a prominent member of West's campaign strategy committee, assessed his candidate's strengths and weaknesses in a confidential campaign memo. McLeese judged his candidate "eminently qualified." West, however, could not be called "Hollywood pretty," nor was he "an aggressive flesh pumper. . . . John leaves the average person with the impression of being a good man, who would understand if you perhaps voted for the other candidate." Watson, their "slick, articulate" opponent, McLeese believed, went to the opposite extreme by "leaving an individual with the impression that the wrath of God will descend upon him if he does not vote for Albert Watson." McLeese complained that there was little they could do about their opponent's attributes, but that the Republicans had "one major and hopefully colossal weakness," and that was the candidate himself. "To put it bluntly," McLeese wrote, "Albert Watson is a no good son-of-a-bitch." McLeese qualified this assessment by charging that the Republican candidate had defrauded the United States government while he was a congressman by renting his own office building from himself with federal money and, as a private citizen, by failing to file his federal income taxes for four consecutive years. Watson, in McLeese's mind, had "enough dirty laundry and skeletons in his closet" to keep the West campaign busy until the election.[20]

The background of the two men also differed. Watson had abandoned the Democratic Party and gravitated to those elements of the Republican party in the South that sought to resist federal pressures to desegregate. John West, on the other hand, had been among those southern politicians who led the way toward a slow adjustment to the changing racial situation. West had been elected to the state senate in 1954 shortly after the *Brown* decision and continued to serve for twelve years in that body. Years later West would remember that the legislature in those days had measured every action against the effect on schools and segregation. Nevertheless, West fought against the Ku Klux Klan and in 1961 cast one of only two votes against a measure that would require the closure of any college or university that was forced to integrate. West also stood almost alone against repeal of the compulsory school attendance law designed to assist parents opposed to integration. Elected lieutenant governor in 1966, West did something no white politician in South Carolina had ever done. In 1969 he attended and spoke at a South Carolina dinner in honor of NAACP Executive Director Roy Wilkins. West's political career had sought inclusion of all South Carolina's citizens, but 1970 would test those notions of acceptance.[21]

After the Supreme Court ruled that "freedom of choice" desegregation plans would not satisfy federal requirements, district courts began to demand immediate massive school desegregation throughout the South in the middle of the school year. These court orders would test the growing body of white moderates in the state. Although token desegregation had gone smoothly in South Carolina, many whites wanted these further changes to proceed slowly, thereby allowing time to adjust. The prospect of trouble bothered most moderates more than moral qualms about equal educational opportunities. The black student who integrated Clemson University in 1963, Harvey Gantt, accurately characterized the core of moderation in his state when he said that, "if you can't appeal to the morals of a South Carolinian, you can appeal to his manners." The midyear desegregation orders tested even their manners. To many these federally imposed plans seemed unreasonable. They argued that the integrate "at once" orders forced an unusual strain on both schools and the children that attended them. And to make matters worse, many of the plans included busing to achieve racial balances. Busing inspired overwhelming opposition combining a wide spectrum of friends and foes of integration. Those whites who did not want integration at all naturally opposed busing, but most moderate whites also saw these plans as disruptive of the neighborhood school concept and local control of education. One political survey observed that, "if anyone could come up with a way to achieve integration without busing, he would draw a great deal of support—integration not withstanding." Little wonder that some candidates believed that resistance to desegregation, particularly when implemented by means of busing, would yield political dividends.[22]

When John West announced his candidacy, he sought to avoid a campaign tug-of-war over desegregation. He called Watson's remarks "emotional rhetoric" that sought to derive "political capital out of a difficult situation, but does nothing to solve it. I shall leave that path to others. The lives and future of our children are far too important to be used as political footballs."[23]

While West threw his hat into the ring, Watson drew a line in the sand. On February 22, Albert Watson spoke in Lamar, South Carolina, where 2,500 whites gathered and circulated petitions calling for "freedom of choice" desegregation plans. The Darlington County school system, which included Lamar, had recently come under a federal court-ordered desegregation plan that increased the number of black students attending integrated schools from 400 under the freedom-of-choice plan to 7,000. "I have been called a racist, a bigot and a political buzzard," Watson told the rally, "but I intend to tell the people where I stand and tell it like it is.

. . . Every section of this state is in for it," said Watson, "unless you stand up and use every means at your disposal to defend [against] what I consider an illegal order." Amidst cheers and applause Watson said that he had been criticized for speaking to this group of "hard core rednecks." In answer to those criticisms, he told the gathering: "God bless anyone interested in their children. I applaud you. I stand with you."[24]

The day after the Lamar rally James Duffy wrote a memo to Arthur Ravenel. "Watson has had a field day with the school situation and West sounded like a weak 'me too.'" Duffy recommended that Ravenel make a statement enumerating his beliefs. The candidate should say that he supported freedom of choice and disapproved of the timing of the recent court orders because they created such a rush in allocating students to schools. But he also should say that he opposed any school boycotts and point to the success of Greenville County in meeting the court-ordered desegregation schedule and continuing the education of their children. Ravenel should promise that as governor he would oppose any federal law that was alien to the beliefs of the state, would strive to alter those laws, but would nevertheless support and uphold the law. Duffy suggested that Ravenel say, "To do otherwise would be deceitful to those that elected me." [25]

Shortly after Watson's appearance in Lamar, an ugly incident there captured the attention of the entire nation. While protesting the implementation of the court-ordered desegregation plan, an angry mob of whites attacked and overturned two buses that had carried black children to school. This spectacle of white violence aroused criticism and disdain. Governor McNair condemned the protest. In a news release Senator Strom Thurmond said that "the spectacle of a school bus filled with students being attacked by adults has sickened South Carolina and the nation." Even Albert Watson spoke out. "As do all thinking South Carolinians," said Watson, "I deplore violence and there is no justification for it whatsoever." A state senator from the Lamar area attributed the trouble to a small minority who had hurt themselves by their actions, "when you talk about maybe hurting children—black or white—decent people won't stand for it." The general public, in the words of one local official, were "appalled and a little scared" by the Lamar incident.[26]

The largest newspaper in South Carolina, Columbia's *State*, condemned the actions at Lamar in an editorial. While opposing "drastic measures ordered by federal courts," the editorial demanded that criminal charges be brought against those who incited and participated in the riot.

The paper pointed to two decades of responsibility and reason by the people of the state that set them apart from some of their fellow southerners. "The truth is," the paper said, "violent reactions not only do not delay desegregation, in many instances they hasten it.... It is demonstrably stupid to invite retribution and punitive federal legislation by breaking laws, breaking heads, or breaking down buses and buildings."[27]

On the night of March 2, 1970, all three national network news programs led off their broadcasts with coverage of the incident and closely followed events stemming from the Lamar incident over the next two days. Eric Severeid of CBS delivered an editorial warning that other southerners might follow the example of Lamar if the government did not take strong measures. The *Atlanta Constitution* blamed Nixon's desegregation vacillations for the Lamar disturbance. The government's southern director for civil rights enforcement resigned, accusing the administration of a failure of leadership. Two HEW regional heads, one in Atlanta and one in Dallas, did so as well, declaring ineffectiveness on the part of the administration in handling civil rights.[28]

While some pointed to the Nixon administration, others placed the blame much closer to home. The local NAACP president said that Watson's appearance at the "freedom of choice" rally in Lamar "poured gasoline on the fire." The editor of the weekly newspaper in the neighboring town of Hartsville wrote that Watson's appearance at the rally "lent an air of respectability" that the protestors did not have before. Governor McNair's press spokesman claimed that Watson caused the incident. "He helped create the public attitude that led to this." Senator Thurmond countered by blaming the governor, who was responsible for maintaining law and order. If the governor could not control a mob of 150 people, Thurmond contended, he should have requested federal assistance. "Those in the state who seek to parcel out blame by suggesting that Republicans caused the disturbance by speaking out strongly for freedom of choice fail to realize an important element of human psychology," said Thurmond. "People are less likely to resort to violence if they have faith that their leaders will stand up for them by using every legal resource provided within our system." Drake Edens, the GOP national committeeman for the state, also blamed the Democratic administration. "If the action of any public official brought this thing on," Edens said, referring to Lamar, "it was probably the surrender statement by Governor McNair when he said 'we've run out of courts, we've run out of time.' That left a group of frustrated and hopeless people with no place to go, no way to seek relief."[29]

Not all Republicans, however, could forget Watson's role in fanning the fires of racial frustration. One woman from nearby Darlington wrote to a party official describing her disappointment at the handling of the school situation by her fellow Republicans. The woman asserted that she knew of no one who would not have preferred to keep freedom of choice. "However, a force has grown up in our county that upsets the vast majority as much as forcing integration." Her letter went on to assess the mood of her community.

> The majority in our county are people who want their children in school while our state and county leaders try sensibly to solve this problem. I feel we would be on the road to normal now if these few men had not continuously kept stirring up crowds. In Watson's speech to this crowd in Lamar a week before the outbreak, he . . . advocated openly forcing the schools to close. Had he not further incited this already emotional filled crown [sic]—the buses may not have been overturned. . . . Please tell me how the Republican Party can support men such as this?[30]

Another woman, active in GOP political circles, assigned both the blame and the appropriate spin for the Lamar incident in a letter to James Duffy. "If there's any rope to be pulled you can bet I want in on the Albert Watson lynching. . . . If there's any way to do it, I think that the Lamar tragedy should be deposited on the back of one state Democratic administration of which Mr. John West is such an 'integral' part."[31]

Ten days after the buses were overturned, James Duffy sent a memo to Ravenel and his top advisors. "Each of us have heard from people, personally and by mail, who are appalled over the Lamar incident." Duffy stated that the situation was encouraged by Watson and that other party leaders supported him. "This puts . . . the Republican Party stamp of approval on the affair. The issue is racism. We can define it as bussing, freedom of choice, supreme court interference, etc., but the truth is simply race. That the process followed by the court was difficult and unreasonable might well be defended. However, it was the law." Duffy further expressed his disgust in a letter to a political consultant working for the campaign. "Our Party leadership has definitely gone to the racist format of a campaign and it remains to be seen how successful this strategy will be. Regardless of how effective it does not seem to be a basis for building the Party, state, or nation."[32]

Ravenel spelled out his own feelings in a letter to a GOP supporter. "Quite frankly, I am appalled at the prospect of our party running a racist campaign with Albert Watson heading our ticket. Whether such a ticket could win or not is immaterial to me, for I believe that this type appeal would be wrong for South Carolina."[33]

Arthur Ravenel failed to steer his party toward a more moderate racial course. He also failed in his bid for a statewide primary to select the party's nominee. Albert Watson gained the nomination at the state Republican convention held March 21, 1970. The Republicans, however, closed ranks, at least publicly. Dr. William Hunter, who served as finance chairman of the 1970 Committee for a Republican Primary, issued a statement conceding that the decision to nominate by convention, and the resulting nomination of Watson, "was made openly and clearly by the delegates of our party. . . . Those of us who favored the primary system and hoped for Arthur Ravenel's nomination abide by the results of the convention's action." Hunter lamented that the race issue had been raised in the campaign but that he could not conceive of Watson "in the role of a racist, or of his being unfair to any South Carolinian because of race, creed or religion." The statement of principles adopted at the convention, however, reflected the hard-line stance of the Watson forces. Under education the principles statement read: "We believe that education in South Carolina is undergoing a grave crisis. The requirements of massive integration are creating burdens which are always difficult and often impossible." The statement condemned "the vacillation and defeatism of the McNair-West Administration on the issue" and urged that the federal government maintain the tax-exempt status for private schools. The statement also recommended that elected officials "speak out firmly and in protest against unwarranted Court orders, and that every legal avenue to upset these orders . . . be explored to the fullest."[34]

After Watson garnered the Republican nomination, Harry Dent offered the candidate suggestions on strategy that were reminiscent of George Wallace's tactics. "Go hard for the country music–working man vote," Dent wrote in a memo. Watson should travel with a country music band and visit country music radio stations to do campaign spots. Dent also told Watson that the average man, who "feels a little alienated . . . will like your 'square' virtues. . . . Remember, he is 40, earns less than $7,000, didn't finish high school, likes bowling and stock car racing, and is a Baptist." Dent also advised Watson to emphasize his relationship with Nixon-Agnew and stress that he could do more for the state because of access to a friendly administration. On the other hand, Watson should tie West to Governor McNair, paint West as a national Democrat, and link him to Hubert Humphrey.[35]

Watson and the Republicans took much of Dent's advice to heart. In September the state *Republican Newsletter* wrote that the voters would have to decide if they wanted to be led by John West, "who supported liberals like Kennedy, Johnson, and Humphrey or someone like Albert Watson who has consistently supported conservatives right down the line from Nixon in '60 to Goldwater in '64 and Nixon again in '68. Watson has the conservatism of Thurmond and West has the liberalism of Hubert Horatio Humphrey." West had indeed been a strong supporter of Humphrey in the 1968 presidential campaign and refused to disavow that support. During the gubernatorial race Humphrey read an article in the *Washington Star* that detailed the Republican ploy of associating West with the former vice president. "I hope and pray that your friendship with me will not be a political liability in your state," Humphrey wrote. West thanked him for his concern and responded: "My public support for you was the right thing to do and I will never feel other than proud of it. I shall always remember your statement in 1968 . . . how one gets elected is more important than the office itself. This classic statement has been, and is, a source of inspiration to me and I am following it in the campaign."[36]

The Republicans also tried to link West with the NAACP. They criticized West for publicly praising the NAACP's Roy Wilkins. And a campaign flyer blamed the NAACP for the rejection of South Carolina judge Clement Haynsworth's appointment to the Supreme Court and for "destruction of freedom of choice in our public schools," then admonished West for using "the prestige of his high office to dignify the aims and activities of this organization." Watson employed the same campaign slogan that George Wallace used in Alabama: "Your kind of man." To erase any doubt as to the meaning of his slogan he ran newspaper advertising under the caption: "Which men are your kind of men?" The left column of the advertisement stacked pictures of liberal Democrats with little support in the state: Hubert Humphrey, Edmund Muskie, Lyndon Johnson, and Birch Bayh, a Democratic senator blamed for leading the successful fights against Haynsworth and another southern jurist, Harrold Carswell, nominated by Nixon to fill seats on the Supreme Court. Below these "liberals" West was pictured and, lest anyone miss the point, the advertisement added that West had supported all these men, while South Carolina had rejected them. In the right column Richard Nixon, Spiro Agnew, Barry Goldwater, and Strom Thurmond, all popular figures in the state, were pictured above Watson.[37]

West responded in kind, running an ad of the same format with different pictures. Popular Democrats such as South Carolina Congressman Mendel Rivers, Representative Wilbur Mills, and Senators Richard Russell and Sam Ervin were pictured above West. On the other side were photographs of New York Republican Senator Jacob Javits, said to have an "anti-South bias"; former Supreme Court Chief Justice Earl Warren, widely blamed in the South for his role in the *Brown* decision; Robert Finch, the HEW secretary "who helped kill freedom of choice in the South"; and Jerris Leonard, the assistant attorney general for civil rights, who openly declared "freedom of choice is dead." Albert Watson was pictured below these men above the caption "Yes, indeed! Which man will best represent you as Governor? Elect a good man governor—John West."[38]

The West advertisement sought to parry the Watson thrust by appealing to the same type of voter; it also served to point out the inconsistency of Watson's and Thurmond's claims that they and the Republicans had done anything to turn back the assault on the South and southern desegregation progress. Incongruity, however, also lurked in the Democratic message. By favoring the discounted freedom-of-choice plans and continuing to claim adherence to the law, Democrats participated in a type of hypocrisy of their own. One member of the strategy committee warned of this danger: "To hold the liberal-moderate-black vote and chase the right-wing vote too is . . . a paradox that will only result in confusion among your loyal supporters and the blacks which could end in an apathy and antagonism that may cost you the election."[39]

By July, however, many Democrats had tired of Republican efforts to blame them for desegregation. Some of West's advisors believed that Watson had picked up momentum by taking advantage of the school integration issue and that the Democratic candidate must enter the fray. Prior to July, West had attempted to deliver a positive message emphasizing the importance of maintaining quality education rather than criticizing desegregation. West's public relations firm questioned this tact after seeing the results of an early survey. "As we all suspected the dominant issue in South Carolina remains race. The biggest single factor, of course, being school integration," the PR men wrote in a campaign memo. "God help us in November but for now we seem saddled with our predetermined decision to ignore the issue publicly."[40]

Although the Democratic prospects for victory depended on the black vote, many advisors came to believe that West must take a firmer stand against unpopular desegregation measures. A forceful defense would help to revitalize West's indecisive image among the electorate, steal Watson's thunder, and entice conservative white voters. A West campaign position paper on desegregation pointed to the issue as one that Republicans used "to rile the people" because they felt that West "could not gamble on the loss of the Negro vote." The author of the paper believed the Republican assumption false. "The Negro voter is going to vote Democratic no matter who the candidate is." The author went on to contend that West could take an even stronger stand against the courts and HEW than the Republicans and "would not alienate a single Negro voter." West apparently took this advice to heart. He hedged some of his statements and even attacked the Department of Health, Education and Welfare for "social experimentation." The state "must fight," West declared, "to prevent the massive disruption of our public school system threatened by the actions of the federal government." West and his campaign advisors now believed that he must make his opposition clear and place the responsibility for the recent spate of school desegregation rulings on the Republicans. Thus Democrats began to take advantage of the Nixon administration's enforcement of integration in the state. HEW had recently filed suits against ten South Carolina school districts. The state Democratic chairman, Harry Lightsey, pointed out that Republicans had failed to come through with promises to slow down federal encroachment on local school systems. The Republicans responded by claiming that HEW took these actions because radicals from previous Democratic administrations dominated the agency.[41]

Governor McNair defended his administration's record of opposing federal efforts to impose racial integration on South Carolina's public schools. When Greenville and Darlington school districts faced "instant" desegregation in January 1970 and McNair had made his statement that the state had run out of courts and run out of time, the governor asserted that further resistance would have invited the courts to extend an "instant" order statewide. McNair claimed that Republicans had "intentionally misled" the people of the state by promising that the Nixon administration would slow desegregation. "Freedom of choice prevailed," Mc-Nair reminded South Carolinians, "until this administration came into office."[42]

West also got into the act of pointing out the failure of Republicans to deliver on their promises. Several citizens from around the state wrote to the lieutenant governor protesting busing plans. West responded to several of these letters by sharing his opposition to the busing of schoolchildren to achieve racial balances. As to further actions these irate citizens should take, the candidate replied with a tongue-in-cheek response: "I suggest you immediately wire or contact Senator Thurmond and President Nixon, both of whom, in the campaign of 1968, pledged to preserve freedom of choice." West sought to claim the middle ground on the issue. The Nixon administration and state Republicans had extended false hopes. If elected he would resist federal pressure to integrate schools, but West would not guarantee ultimate success, promising only to obey the law. "We have succeeded in gradually adjusting to what was forced upon us in a way that did not divide our people or destroy their respect for law and order," West said. He accused the Nixon administration of extending false hope by promising freedom of choice. The so-called southern strategy, West asserted, consisted of "soft words and hard deeds," meaning "massive integration of every facet of our education system this year so all the broken promises will be forgotten by 1972."[43]

West and the Democrats gleefully reminded South Carolinians of Senator Thurmond's "broken promises" in television advertisements. These commercials replayed speeches of Senator Thurmond campaigning for Nixon in 1968, promising that the state would have a sympathetic ear concerning desegregation pressures in Washington. The advertising ploy reminded voters that Thurmond and the Republicans had made commitments that they did not keep and demonstrated the futility of resisting federal desegregation pressures. Thurmond vented his anger by threatening that the Federal Communications Commission would revoke the licenses of the television stations that ran the ads.[44]

The broken promises theme rang true. The actions of some in the Nixon administration created political havoc for South Carolina Republicans. Officials in HEW and the Justice Department charged with implementing desegregation had targeted South Carolina, as well as other southern states that had not fully complied with federal mandates. This posed problems for those South Carolinians who hoped to make the gubernatorial campaign a test of the so-called southern strategy of the

Nixon administration. Senator Thurmond wrote to the president on April 30, 1970, complaining that Jerris Leonard, the assistant attorney general for civil rights, had visited South Carolina to inform school officials of the "ramifications" of a lawsuit being threatened against the state by the Justice Department. Thurmond related that he had called half a dozen people in the administration who oversaw desegregation matters and advised them that the trip was ill-advised and that it would "be detrimental to the Republican cause in South Carolina." The visit, as Thurmond predicted, generated unfavorable publicity. One school board chairman told Leonard that in the 1968 campaign Nixon had given them the impression that the state would have freedom of choice. "That was a political statement," Leonard responded, according to Thurmond. Then Leonard went on to make a point of saying that freedom of choice was dead. "This undercutting was not only harmful to you, it also hurts Congressman Watson, who is running for Governor," Thurmond complained. "The repercussions of this visit and to these statements have been severe and will be difficult to overcome between now and election day."[45]

Vice President Spiro Agnew also let the president know that the administration's actions might jeopardize the South Carolina political races. "Therefore we should have HEW and Justice do everything possible to settle these school negotiations in a very reasonable manner," said Agnew. "The Party leaders, Congressman Watson and Senator Thurmond feel that the school superintendents have the impression there has been no change at HEW. They say they are having difficulty getting proper cooperation at HEW."[46]

Watson also pleaded with the administration concerning the backlash to Leonard's visit. Writing directly to the president, Watson quoted extensively from a columnist identified as "an experienced, astute, highly respected and usually conservative writer." The article described Watson as being stabbed in the back by presumed friends. The columnist contended that Jerris Leonard and Robert Mardian, executive director of the vice president's task force on school desegregation, had delivered the blows as they "alternately bullied and cajoled" school leaders in the state to "knuckle under to 'unitary' integrated classrooms by September 1 or face a statewide desegregation suit." The decision was "a monumental blunder that may rob Nixon of the southern votes he will need for a second term and Watson of any real chance to win the governor's office. . . . With such 'friends,' the hapless Watson has no need of any enemies." The article suggested that Watson's only hope for political survival would be to disavow and disassociate himself from Nixon and his administration. Watson assured the president that "such a suggestion is both abhorrent and shocking to me, but even the public suggestion by a responsible columnist should disturb us all." Watson warned the president that, "unless help is forthcoming, the political harvest for 1970 and '72 will be mighty lean."[47]

An open rebellion among state and national Republicans had erupted over federal desegregation pressures. On July 17, 1970, CBS led off the evening news with coverage of Senator Thurmond publicly criticizing the Nixon administration's handling of school desegregation. Nixon's "breach of faith," warned Thurmond, could cost the president the election in 1972. Two moves by the administration had spurred these criticisms. One involved the reversal of the IRS policy of extending tax exemptions for private academies that were springing up around the South to avoid integration; the other was the "proposed invasion of one hundred carpet-bagging Justice Department lawyers" ordered south to monitor school desegregation. "I condemn these actions," Thurmond said. "I strongly condemn them; without end I condemn them. They are wrong as social policy, and they are wrong as law. This is the sort of program we would expect to get from a Democratic administration. They are a breach of faith with the people of the South." Nixon's southern point man, Harry Dent, went to work smoothing the feathers of Thurmond, his former boss. But just as Dent believed he and the president had gotten Senator Thurmond back on their team, an HEW official leaked a story that Thurmond had in effect helped to integrate South Carolina schools for the purpose of avoiding a statewide lawsuit that would hurt him politically. Although Thurmond publicly called the story "absolutely false," he blasted Dent and demanded to know who leaked the information. Dent sent a memo to Bob Haldeman, Nixon's chief of staff, asking that someone be "properly chastised." The disclosure would be used, Dent explained, to "hurt Thurmond and the Watson for Governor campaign effort." The pressure from Thurmond compelled Nixon to backtrack. On the last day of July he announced that southern desegregation would not be forced, and that Justice Department desegregation monitors would be sent into the South only upon request. Justice Department officials, responsible for implementing the policy, admitted confusion as to exactly what the current administration position demanded or allowed.[48]

The administration's actions and the president's vacillations had rendered Nixon so unpopular in the South, said Thurmond, that he would not want the president campaigning for him in South Carolina. Neither did Watson. The president's popularity, according to a prominent member of the Watson campaign, had declined in the state due to the school situation. The gubernatorial candidate did, however, arrange for Vice President Spiro Agnew to make several stops in the state. Agnew visited Greenville in October and denied that the Nixon administration had raised false hopes with its opposition to busing. "I don't think there's much doubt in the minds of the people of the South how Judge Haynsworth or Judge Carswell would have felt about compulsory busing," Agnew said. "If we are given a Senate where the Republicans have a majority," he continued, "we should be able to get a southern strict constructionist on the Supreme Court."[49]

Despite unpopular actions by members of the Nixon administration and the Republican fratricide over school integration in South Carolina, West would not take full advantage of the issue. The midsummer decision to move closer to the Watson position on race relations made West feel uncomfortable; years later he would call this the low point of his campaign. A Methodist minister from Cheraw, South Carolina, wrote to West expressing confusion and disappointment concerning his criticism of the Justice Department's efforts to eliminate dual school systems in the state. The minister told West that those statements sounded similar to the ones voiced by Watson at Lamar and "seemed to be designed to use the school situation for political appeal." If the campaign "turned on the loudest demagogic appeal," the minister asked, "what difference will it make if the demagogue is to be named Albert or John?" The minister ended with a heartfelt appeal to West that many people had been counting on him to lead the state "into an era of reason, sound judgement, fair dealing with all citizens, the elimination of basic discrimination against helpless people. Don't let us down now." The letter apparently touched a raw nerve in West. He responded that it had caused him to stop and take stock of a situation filled with problems and tensions. "I hope that I can show you . . . that I have no intention of being a party to any demagogic action which results in unfairness to any one." Some of West's advisors also believed that the candidate should not continue down this rightward path. Ike McLeese told West in a memo that they had outflanked Watson on the school issue and thereby created some problems for themselves. Having established his position, McLeese advised West that he "should now cool it." Another aide gave more specific strategy advice. "Always emphasize past performance. You have appeared too hot over the issue of integration lately. Stay away from it. Let others try to fulfill their impossible promises. If you must take a stand, take a moderate one and always be consistent . . . Watson wins conservative votes because of his anti-integration sentiments. Fight this approach by showing that his promises are never fulfilled."[50]

West willingly took the advice. Shortly after his descent from the high road West issued marching orders to his campaign strategy committee. "As you have undoubtedly sensed, I have been concerned in the last ten days about the course of the campaign and especially the role which political necessities seem to have dictated that I take. Again as you have probably sensed, I have not been completely happy in this role." West then set his campaign on a course he could comfortably follow. "I cannot project the image of a die-hard segregationist who will 'require federal marshals and court orders.'" Nor, West conceded, could he gain political charisma by changing his personality in the remaining three months of the campaign, "even if it means the failure to attain the goal which we all seek." The veteran of sixteen years in elective office, however, maintained "an abiding confidence in the good sense and good judgement of the electorate." West would emphasize a positive "build South Carolina" theme. The Democratic Party could continue to remind the public of the Republican broken promises but he, and members of his campaign, would eliminate all criticisms of his opponent.[51]

While West and his advisors recognized the inconsistency of moving closer to Watson, the Democratic candidate received criticism from both ends of the political spectrum. State Republican chairman Ray Harris called West's "sudden switch to a pseudo-segregationist stance" the actions of a "political phony." Watson accused West of making a "180 degree turn" and coming over to his position, for which both West and McNair had criticized Watson. On the other end of the political spectrum, the state NAACP field representative, Isaac Williams, believed that West had "torn his pants" with black voters. West's statement attacking desegregation seemed "designed to appease white bigots and racists," said Williams, reminding the candidate that black voters made up a quarter of the electorate in the state. Williams' warnings did not fall on deaf ears. One member of the West campaign advised the candidate: "I do not think we will get the massive turnout we must have of black voters, nor the heavy percentages, if we pursue a segregationist viewpoint in an attempt to woo right-wing voters." Apparently thousands of African Americans agreed. According to surveys conducted by his own campaign, West's committed vote among black voters dropped 33 percent between June and September.[52]

The uncertainty of black support created tremendous distress within the West campaign. Their polling demonstrated that the Democratic candidate would not win without massive black support. Even before the survey results, West, his advisors, and Democratic strategy groups had emphasized the importance of black backing. As election day neared, the Democratic Party put out an organizational paper on the status and development of the 1970 race. The paper discussed meetings with the Voter Education Project and a large number of black leaders. "The problem of splinter groups is being handled with some success and the major problem seems to be to stimulate enthusiasm for a large turnout." Two black attorneys provide an example of these efforts. The attorneys, from Sumter, South Carolina, sent West samples of "Get out the Negro vote" pamphlets. One member of the strategy committee wrote to West that he saw a danger in "slipping off the razor's edge in either direction on racial matters. I cannot yet see any weakness in your hold on black voters in view of the nature of your two opponents. You must guard, of course, against the danger of any of the blacks going fishing in November and somehow capitalize on their fear of Albert and Red to bring them to the polls." (The two opponents referred to were Watson and A. W. "Red" Bethea, who ran under George Wallace's American Independent Party banner.) All of the attention to the black vote was something new in South Carolina politics. Several local politicos wrote to West advising him of potential votes in their areas. In these assessments many included the names of local power brokers in the black community whom West should contact. West himself wrote personal letters to black leaders, including one to Bishop William Ball asking him to "write or contact the ministers in the A.M.E. [African Methodist Episcopal Church] and say a word in our behalf."[53]

The black segment of the electorate also drew the attention of the GOP. Since Republicans had attempted to exploit white resentments concerning desegregation, they did not expect to garner any of the black vote and for that reason began to identify this group as a "bloc vote." The master of southern political efficacy, George Wallace, had recently saved his career in a tight gubernatorial campaign by using this ploy. In 1970 other southern candidates who could not count on the black vote followed Wallace's example and sought to demonize it. The state *Republican Newsletter* wrote of a bloc vote in South Carolina that would support the Democrats: "Don't let any 3rd or 4th party effort fool you. Both are a hoax. . . . In the final analysis, 90% of the Negro voters in this state will remain 'political slaves' . . . All of these bloc voters will be told how to vote Sunday night prior to the general election on November 3." In an effort to counteract this so-called bloc vote's going to West, the Republicans encouraged a fledgling black-oriented third party. West's campaign strategy had placed him in a precarious position. While he desperately needed black votes as part of a winning coalition, he feared that aligning himself too closely with black voters would alienate the white majority in the state. Although black leaders criticized West's hedging statements, they also realized the pragmatism of supporting him. Not to do so would guarantee a governor opposed to the interests of black citizens. And so the same black leaders who had publicly criticized West quietly went about the state convincing black voters that supporting Republican-inspired third-party efforts would elect Watson by draining off support from John West.[54]

Any fears West may have held concerning the loss of black support vanished in September. In that month Watson ran a five-minute television commercial in which he narrated over footage of black rioters. "Are we going to be ruled by the bloc?" asked Watson. "Look what it did in Watts . . . in the nation's capital," he said as film clips showed clashes between police and black rioters. These ads drew widespread criticism, but Watson refused to "label" the commercial, saying that the people of the state could decide for themselves if his campaign was "racist." The usually conservative *Greenville News* clearly expressed its decision in an editorial that said, "the Republican campaign has to be regarded as racist to a disturbing degree." The Republican mayor of Greenville, South Carolina, R. Cooper White, Jr., also made up his mind when he accused Watson of conducting a campaign that was "polarizing the races" and refused to greet Watson and Vice President Agnew during a campaign stop in his city. In the midst of the controversy Senator Thurmond recorded a radio and television spot in support of the Republican candidate. "Albert Watson will stand up and fight for the people," said Thurmond. "The South is under attack and we need a man who will exert positive leadership in this time of crisis." And in an interview Thurmond rejected charges of racism in Watson's campaign. "I know of nothing Watson has said that he could be accused of being a racist," said Thurmond. "But the Democrats down here have tried to accuse him of that. Some of the liberal press has. It is purely expedient politics to do that. But I'm confident he has not done or said anything which would make him guilty of racism."[55]

The South Carolina *Republican Newsletter* blamed the injection of race into the campaign on the opposition. "Democratic leaders in this state will stop at nothing to win this election . . . even to the point of calling our candidate a racist," asserted the newsletter in October. The opposition party had "used, abused, and manipulated the Negroes in this state for their own personal political and economic gain. Every knowledgeable person is aware of this."[56]

The Greenville *Piedmont* condemned Watson's concentration on the bloc vote in the campaign and his commercial question: "Are we going to be ruled by the bloc?" The paper asked voters if they would want a person in a position of statewide power "who would make such a prurient TV appeal to racism?"[57]

Harry Dent circulated an internal memo at the White House (for Bryce Harlow) refuting accusations of racist intent in Watson's campaign. Dent criticized a feature article in the *Los Angeles Times* on the South Carolina gubernatorial campaign as badly slanted against Watson. The reporter even tried to portray the Republican candidate as further to the right on the race question than George Wallace, complained Dent. "This is simply not so." Dent said that the writer had taken Watson's comments concerning racism out of context and included a transcript of Watson being questioned on a South Carolina telecast. While alluding to the five-minute television program that concentrated on a bloc vote in the state, Dent claimed that it had been "done in haste" and without the candidate's "prior review as I understand it," and Dent pointed out that it had been pulled off the air almost immediately.[58]

The candidate himself, however, remained unrepentant. When accused of racist campaign tactics Watson replied: "If they're calling me 'racist' then they're calling the majority of the people of this state 'racist' . . . I'll stand with the people." Watson believed that the Democrats were "trying the same liberal trick against me that is daily used against our courageous Vice President, who continues, as I am doing, to tell it like it is. Just as his liberal critics have not silenced Vice President Agnew, I will not be silenced by mine." Watson's rhetoric of resistance spoke to the frustration of many whites in the state. And Watson did little to discourage this identification. "Only thing folks are talking about is if the colored are gonna run our schools or if we are," one white South Carolina truck driver told the *New York Times*. "For my money only one man is standing up for white folks, and that's Albert Watson." Indeed Watson's approach seemed effective among some South Carolinians. In October the 1968

George Wallace campaign leadership in the state endorsed Watson. This endorsement came despite the fact that "Red" Bethea, the candidate running for governor under Wallace's own American Independent Party, had claimed George Wallace's unannounced support.[59]

In October, Watson called for a probe into school disruptions after a racial fight erupted at A. C. Flora High School near Columbia while two of his aides happened to be there with a cameraman. Watson called an "emergency" news conference at which he strongly urged the state legislature to pass an anti-busing bill. Senator Thurmond praised Watson for "doing his duty" in speaking out about school trouble in Columbia. David Eisenhower, son of one former Republican president and son-in-law of the current one, visiting South Carolina at the time, added his praise for Watson as one who recognized that "law and order is not a code word for racism but a legitimate demand for every American citizen."[60]

Governor McNair angrily accused Watson of inciting the incident and exploiting racial trouble at the high school. So too did the Columbia police department. The mayor of Forest Acres, the town where A. C. Flora High School was located, issued a press release: "I feel the time has come to end the kind of political activity that has as its goal the division of the people of our community and state." The mayor said that a Watson staff member "who had no known business in the vicinity began taking pictures and greatly aggravated the minor incident into one of a much more serious nature." John West made no direct mention of Watson but issued a statement calling the "safety and future of children" too important for partisan politics. A confidential campaign memo concerning West's final television program advised the candidate to "tell it like it is." The memo pointed to "evidence of political meddling in Flora's troubles . . . by Watson's aides. . . . There should be no reluctance to join this issue which was raised by the opponent. The public is entitled to the facts."[61]

While Watson's rhetoric and actions suggested that if elected he would do something about unpopular methods of mixing the races, West made no promises. "False promises and political rhetoric," said West, "have complicated problems in newly integrated schools." And busing, according to West, was a "phony issue. We are all against busing." Earlier that year the largely Democratic state legislature had passed a law that forbade the assignment of children to schools to meet racial quotas. "It is not in the scope of your governor to do any more than has now been done." Only the Supreme Court or Congress could decide the issue and regardless of what they decided, West maintained, "we've got to provide quality education for every black and white child despite the disenchantment, disappointment, and frustration. We can't afford to withdraw one iota of our support of public education. The future of South Carolina depends on it."[62]

In an effort to offset Watson's "image and appeal" and to overcome West's "insufficient exposure and relatively colorless image" by showing him "as a firm, dignified, sincere and direct speaking candidate," the campaign employed a series of five-minute television shows, and a scripted thirty-minute television program that provided questions for three average citizens to ask the candidate. Tootsie, a housewife, asked: "How about education, Mister West? With all the changes now taking place, and all the trouble and confusion in our schools, what will happen to education in South Carolina? And more specifically what is going to be done about busing?" West's opening and closing monologue and answers to all the questions were not scripted but given in short outline form. For Tootsie's questions, West's points were: "(1) Purpose of our schools is education. (2) State will keep order. (3) Opposed to busing." And in a statewide mailing West wrote: "Right now, our state has no greater challenge than the preservation and defense of our public school system. There are no easy solutions and politicians who promise them only compound the problems by deluding the people."[63]

Relying on survey data gathered shortly before the election, Republicans believed that their candidate led among those committed voters but that more than 30 percent of the voters had not made up their minds as to how they would vote in the upcoming governor's race. "This is an unusually high percentage of undecided voters at this stage." During the first two weeks of October, the Republicans commissioned pollsters to ask the opinions of 480 white voters in twenty-eight counties and forty-six precincts that had voted within a few percentage points of the way the entire state had voted in previous elections. When asked about problems facing the state, 39 percent responded that racial problems concerned them most while 29 percent believed that education and school problems (presumably meaning recent integration orders) topped the list. When asked what they thought about recent large-scale public school integration, 64 percent characterized these actions as bad while only 18 percent called them good. But when asked the results of the integration measures, 38 percent said things had gone better than they expected while only 9 percent said it had been worse than they thought it would be.[64]

Indeed, integration had gone quite well in South Carolina's ninety-three school districts. Even Strom Thurmond High School in Edgefield County had been desegregated. M. Hayes Mizell, a white civil rights activist, contended that the school districts had done "pretty much what they're supposed to do . . . I get no feedback from blacks of chicanery." James E. Clyburn, head of the state's Commission for Farm Workers and the state's first Human Affairs commissioner, believed the revulsion to the violence at Lamar in March had contributed to the peaceful school integration that fall. "The sight on national television of parents overturning a bus was too much for South Carolinians," said Clyburn. "They were determined not to let it happen again." Robert S. Davis, head of the state's Education Advisory Committee set up by the Nixon administration to help smooth the desegregation process, believed that businessmen were largely responsible. "We sold the business community on the idea that if public education goes down the drain, then business goes down the drain," said Davis. "We didn't tell them desegregation was right or humane or Christian."[65]

Rather than applauding the success of South Carolinians for gracefully acquiescing to a difficult situation, Albert Watson sought to stir up feelings of resentment resulting from school integration. Watson wrapped up his campaign by concentrating on the three largest cities of the state, which happened to be those areas hardest hit by desegregation: Columbia, Charleston, and Greenville. He boiled his message down into a neatly packaged twenty-minute talk stressing school discipline and crime. Watson tied frictions between students at integrated schools and lawlessness together and then proclaimed this "the issue in the campaign."[66]

In an editorial, the *State* took Watson to task for commandeering the school integration issue. The candidate had perhaps struck "political oil," but the editorial warned of explosive gases, that is, human emotions. "Mr. Watson is a polished political performer with a keen appreciation of what people want to hear." The editorial pointed out that Watson had supported freedom of choice, anti-busing legislation, and stronger discipline in schools and that these matters had struck responsive chords among most citizens. But the newspaper pointed out that freedom of choice had been ruled out by the Supreme Court and that unless it changed or Congress and the states approved a Constitutional amendment, the state could do nothing to restore freedom-of-choice integration plans. On the issue of busing to achieve racial balance the paper pointed out that the Supreme Court had the issue under consideration and that the South Carolina legislature could do nothing to influence the outcome. The *State* expressed the hope that in the emotional atmosphere surrounding these issues Watson and all other candidates would "guard against letting exploitation develop into explosion."[67]

With more than 220,000 registered black voters among the state's total of almost 900,000, John West was counting on a coalition of white and black voters to seat him in the governor's chair. West, stumping the state in the last week of the election, outlined the progress the state had made under Democratic rule and proclaimed that "the real issue" in the election was "whether we continue our progress of recent years or stop, change directions and turn back the clock."[68]

Most newspapers in South Carolina endorsed John West. The largest daily newspaper, the *State*, did so even though William Workman, the editor of the newspaper, had run for the United States Senate as a Republican in 1962, and the paper had endorsed Richard Nixon in 1968. After the election West called to thank the editor, as did Senator "Fritz" Hollings, who believed that the *State* and other newspaper endorsements helped turned the tide in West's favor. Readers of the *State* contributed their own opinions to the newspaper concerning the candidates a few days before the election. "I am particularly impressed with the calm, reasonable manner in which Mr. West has approached the problems in our schools," said one reader from Blythewood. "His refusal to resort to emotional appeals, but to firmly stand up for quality education and law and order has captured my respect. I agree with his opposition to busing to achieve racial equality and his support of the neighborhood school concept." Noting the recent visit by Spiro Agnew to the state, a man from Blackville believed that voters would demand a governor who "can offer more than an echo of the rhetoric of the Vice President. . . . Let us not fool ourselves. There are no simple answers to the problems that confront our state and nation. . . . The issue, then, is one of leadership versus destructive and reckless rhetoric."[69]

Robert McNair, the outgoing governor, also feared what a Watson victory could bring. "I can see all the good we've done in handling the school situation, under adverse conditions, just being lost." McNair need not have worried—his lieutenant governor won over 52 percent of the vote. Watson received almost 46 percent, and "Red" Bethea of Wallace's American Independent party received only 2 percent of the vote. West garnered over 90 percent of the black vote, accounting for 56 percent of his total. That made him the first South Carolina governor to receive more black votes than white. But he also pulled support from both Nixon and Wallace voters. For example, in the upper-middle-class suburban Arcadia precinct near Columbia, Nixon in 1968 had received 667 votes, compared with 132 for Humphrey and 69 for Wallace. Watson won this precinct, but only by 23 votes out of 843 votes cast. Wallace had carried Anderson County in 1968 with a majority of 6,419 votes, while Nixon and Humphrey had achieved a combined total of 5,043. West defeated Watson in Anderson County by almost a two to one margin, 10,532 to 5,362. In Columbia's Ward Nine, where all but 24 of the 1,904 registered voters were black, it was West 1,006 and Watson 19. Even Nixon voters reacted against Watson's raucous rhetoric of resistance, and Wallace voters, many of them traditional Democrats, saw little improvement in the Nixon administration. And the influence of Strom Thurmond was greatly diminished by the actions of the Nixon administration and the airing of the "broken promises" commercials by the West campaign.[70]

There was no shortage of Republicans offering evaluations of Watson's loss. Arthur Ravenel wrote to Harry Dent after the election with harsh words for the GOP in the state. "The idiocy of this 'the Party will not change direction' is astounding. The only direction we need to change is not from conservative to liberal, as Harris implies [Ray Harris, state party chairman], but from negative, which Watson proved bankrupt, to positive."[71]

Harry Dent summed up the election from his vantage point in Washington. "Obviously, the entire school problem was of great concern, but to my knowledge," Dent said, "it was never determined exactly what the average voter wanted done—or not done—about it." Dent maintained that the Watson campaign was labeled as racist because of the television ads and the last-minute appeal for school discipline. "Carefully considered, however, these, in themselves, could not be considered 'racist.'" The Watson campaign suffered the onus of racism, Dent believed, because of its inability to define any other issue. "We did not hit long enough on the right to be creditable, nor were we . . . palatable to the center. Although the incumbent Administration was attacked for its wrongs, we offered virtually no positive programs to offset these wrongs. . . . To my knowledge, there was no conscious development or study of issues, but rather reaction to isolated events."[72]

The South Carolina *Republican Newsletter* claimed unrepentantly that Democratic accusations of racism leveled at their party for mentioning the "bloc vote" had cost them the election. "Yet, during the final days of the campaign, the news media consistently reported on the importance of the Negro vote in John West's campaign. What Republicans were accused of promoting became a fact of life in the end. . . . The news media reported that 97 percent of the Negro vote went for the Democrat ticket. It wasn't the 'silent majority' that elected Mr. West as he claimed, but rather a *vocal minority*." Moderate white voters "who in previous elections voted Republican gave support this year to the Democrat ticket," claimed the newsletter. "This can be credited to two things: a) the unfounded 'racism' charges against Republicans; and b) unfair treatment by the news media. Democrats exploited the 'racism' charge, and the news media gave them all the support they needed."[73]

One prominent Republican pointed the finger of blame at his own party. James Duffy evaluated Republican efforts bluntly in a letter to Harry Dent. "The campaign was lost because our party ran a stupid race. All other reasons, or excuses, stem from this one base. . . . We will not immediately gain the black vote. . . . If we never are positive, and we certainly have not been, we will never take the first step. Better to lose an election by appealing to all and then win the next election then [sic] to never make an appeal and never win." In another letter to a political consultant who had worked with the Ravenel campaign, Duffy said that the state GOP "managed to take a certain winner and blow the election. . . . The story is a long one but essentially it was racist oriented and that would not wash with too many non-party Republicans who would not vote for what they considered to be the Wallace image." And in a letter to the failed Republican lieutenant gubernatorial candidate, Duffy wrote: "No one suggests making a deal for any votes, bloc or otherwise. But by the same token it is absolutely necessary that we counteract the negative image some of our leadership is burdened with."[74]

Another Republican intimately involved in the race gave his own assessment of the campaign. On election night Senator Thurmond put his arm around the defeated candidate and said: "Well, Albert, this proves we can't win elections any more by cussin' Nigras." Not long after the Republican defeat Strom Thurmond began to develop a new image. In February 1971, Harry Dent discussed plans in an interview with a South Carolina newspaper to build a new image for the senator. "We've got to get him on the high ground of fairness on the race question," Dent said. "We've got to get him in a position where he can't be attacked like Watson was attacked by liberals as being a racist." Shortly thereafter Thurmond took his former aide's advice and hired a black staff member, former Voter Education Project official Thomas Moss, to help coordinate race relations between the senator and his state's electorate. Others in the Republican Party also saw the need for change. The new state GOP chairman said that the party would seek to attract black voters by convincing them that conservative principles will provide the best government for all the people. And in a memo from the Republican executive committee to GOP officers at all levels around the state was this advice: "We shouldn't talk about seeking black votes and vice versa we should stop talking about block votes. . . . As Republicans we should offer all voters the same—the opportunity to participate. That's all—no more, no less. As Republicans, we should make no special public plea—just let everybody know this party is open."[75]

Assessments of the campaign victory by Democrats did not differ significantly from those of their GOP counterparts. Senator "Fritz" Hollings believed that West's victory came "despite the worst run campaign" he ever saw because the people had reacted against "Watson's emphasis on the race issue." A Charleston attorney wrote to congratulate West and praised the state's electorate, "who obviously refused to accept the most degrading of all human characteristics, that of racism." A state representative from McCormick County also praised the people, "who demonstrated to the Nation that we are an intelligent electorate, now free of bigotry and united for the broad, general progress of our beloved State." And an attorney from Hartsville, South Carolina, hoped that West's election would "once and for all remove the racial issue from our politics."[76]

By running a campaign that catered to racial fears in 1970, Watson made sure that West would receive the black vote with very little effort or accommodation. Although West veered to the right in the course of the campaign, he could always answer the wild rhetoric of Watson with calm and dignified assurances that he would resist federal desegregation pressures while maintaining law and order and providing quality education for all the state's children. This position played well on television. West drove home the futility of defiance, advocated by the Republicans, with an effective television advertising campaign that pointed to the broken promises of the Nixon administration and Senator Thurmond in slowing the pace of desegregation. While Watson's fiery speeches and the resulting mob violence embarrassed South Carolinians and reminded them of the turbulent disruptions of the previous decade, West urged voters to "Elect A Good Man Governor." After he won the election West demonstrated that he meant to live up to his slogan with statements promising an end to racial politics. "We in the South have too long been concerned with the problem of race," said the new governor. "For the last 30 years it has been the burning issue in political campaigns. It has taken most of the thoughts and energies of candidates. . . . I would hope last fall's campaign would be the last time race will be the issue in the governor's race." In his inaugural address West signaled a change in his state. "The politics of race and divisiveness fortunately have been soundly repudiated in South Carolina," West said. "We pledge to minority groups no special status other than full-fledged responsibility in a government that is totally color-blind."[77]

6

Georgia

The state seal proclaims wisdom, justice, and moderation as the virtues that guide Georgia. A Deep South state that had often served as a bellwether for the region as a whole, Georgia reflected the ambivalence of the South. The state had more difficulty with race relations than many of the peripheral states of the region, but seldom demonstrated the defiance of the other Deep South states.

The desire to avoid racial disturbances sprang from economic considerations rooted in the city of Atlanta. The process of urbanization and its concomitant adjustments contributed to white acceptance of integration in many states of the old Confederacy, but none more so than Georgia. These big-city changes had ramifications that went beyond the state. "If anything good spills over into the South," said Helen Bullard, a legendary figure in Atlanta politics, "it comes from Atlanta." A long-standing tradition of civic boosterism existed in the Georgia capital. For decades, businessmen and civic leaders had sought to grow the town's economy by promoting northern investments. Between 1926 and 1929 the Forward Atlanta Commission promoted the city nationwide in an effort to lure commerce and industry from outside the region. The business recruiting campaign drew 679 new factories, warehouses, and sales offices to the city, along with seventeen thousand employees and payrolls that totaled more than $30 million.[1]

These ongoing promotion efforts dovetailed with economic and demographic changes in the region and gradually shifted the balance of power in the state away from plantation county elites, who played on poor rural whites' fears of economic competition from blacks, to the urban and suburban leaders who mostly supported segregation but who would not compromise their commitment to economic vitality.

During the 1920s while the urban-economic elite promoted the For-

ward Atlanta campaign, approximately half of the state's population resided on rural farms and agriculture still dominated the labor market. A
decade after the Forward Atlanta Commission completed its efforts,
Georgia remained largely rural; little more than a third of the population
lived in communities classified by the census as urban and fewer than
three in ten resided in metropolitan areas. By 1960 more than 55 percent
were urbanite and 45 percent were metropolitan. These demographic
changes increased the numbers of urban and suburban voters as well as
the power of the leaders of those areas.[2]

As the influence of Atlanta's leaders grew, so too did their ambitions for
the city. Ivan Allen, the co-chairman of the Atlanta Forward Commission,
promoted the city as a regional distribution center. Thirty years later his
son, Ivan Allen, Jr., as president of the Atlanta Chamber of Commerce,
envisioned Atlanta as a national city. During the 1950s, Atlanta's five-
county metropolitan population grew 40 percent and became the twenty-
second largest metropolitan area in the nation with over a million people.[3]

The *Brown* decision, the subsequent civil rights movement, and the
federal assault on segregation would test the dreams of Atlanta's leadership. Mayor William Hartsfield, who took office as a segregationist in the
late thirties, guided Atlanta throughout the decades of the 1940s and
1950s. Hartsfield came to believe that the racial strife occurring throughout much of the South during that decade would tarnish Atlanta's image as
a modern, prosperous metropolis and hinder its ability to draw commerce
and industry. In 1955 he engineered the peaceful integration of the city's
golf courses. Shortly after the Montgomery bus boycott in 1957 he quietly worked to help blacks challenge the city's segregated seating policy on
buses. With these successes and with other avoidances of disruption the
mayor heralded Atlanta as the "city too busy to hate."[4]

School desegregation would challenge Georgia's ability to maintain
racial peace and continue its economic growth. In the wake of the *Brown*
decision, the Atlanta Board of Education took measures to reduce severe
overcrowding of black schools. The school board began by simply making
schools that had previously been used by whites available for black students. In 1956 the city planned, for the first time, to spend more on black
school construction than on schools for whites. The school board sought
to bring equality of facilities to a school system that had long been separate. The board, however, would not pursue desegregation until ordered
to do so by the courts. Still, compared to many other southern cities, Atlanta represented an island of moderation in a state controlled by anti-

urban, rural county legislators. In 1958 Ernest Vandiver had been elected governor, vowing that "No, not one!" black child would attend school with whites. The Georgia legislature endorsed the governor's threat by passing massive resistance laws that not only cut off state funds to integrated schools but also required an entire school district to close if any one of its schools swayed from strict segregation. In June 1959, in response to a class action suit against the Atlanta Board of Education, U.S. district judge Frank Hooper ordered Atlanta to prepare a school desegregation plan by the end of the year. The board filed its plan by the required deadline, and the court approved an amended version in January, but state laws prohibiting integration delayed implementation of the plan. The prospect of widespread school closings in the Georgia capital terrified Atlanta's business and civic leaders, who exerted considerable pressure to resist massive resistance. They, along with parents, teachers, ministers, and organizations such as Help Our Public Education (HOPE), which sprang up in direct response to the crisis, demonstrated strong public support to keep schools open. Atlanta's newspapers, the *Journal* and especially the *Constitution*, edited for decades by Ralph McGill, a powerful advocate for racial justice, made sure the rest of the world knew the sentiments of the many moderate Atlantans and warned others in the city of dire economic consequences in the event of school closings. Twenty-five members of Atlanta's economic elite, including chamber of commerce president Ivan Allen, Jr., pleaded to keep schools open, warning politicians that "next to our children, the Georgia business community has the most at stake in the present school crisis." Mayor Hartsfield added his voice to the growing consensus that economic progress could not be sustained if schools closed to resist integration. "It will do little good to bring about more brick, stone and concrete," Hartsfield insisted, "while a shocked and amazed world looks at a hundred thousand innocent children roaming the streets."[5]

The effort to compromise on integration prompted public indignation from political leaders who relied on rural support. The state's Association of County Commissioners opposed "any race mixing in any Georgia schools anywhere, at any time, under any circumstances." Governor Vandiver accused Atlanta moderates of running up "the flag of surrender over our capital city" and displaying "a defeatist spirit." Even though the rhetoric of resistance echoed through the hills and valleys of Georgia's rural landscape, the state's most powerful leaders such as Governor Vandiver and Senator Herman Talmadge could hear the voices of increased numbers of urban dwellers and the sounds of progress and economic prosperity that accompanied urbanization. They realized that desegregation was inevitable and would be much more palatable if implemented in a peaceful manner.[6]

During the uncertainty and delay that accompanied Atlanta's court-ordered desegregation plan, Governor Vandiver's chief of staff, Griffin Bell, who would later serve as U.S. attorney general, asked John Sibley, a seventy-one-year-old lawyer, banker, and prominent member of the Atlanta business establishment, to hold statewide hearings to determine if Georgians wanted to close public schools and set up private schools with state-funded tuition grants, or continue public education even if districts in Atlanta and elsewhere were integrated. Sibley was a segregationist, but according to Governor Vandiver, "he was a fair, impartial man who had tremendous respect." The Sibley Commission recommended a local option policy that would preclude action by the state and allow local communities to respond to desegregation as they chose. In January 1961, the legislature adopted the Sibley committee's local option recommendations and altered state law to allow integration of Georgia schools.[7]

Atlanta's leadership had guided the state toward a more moderate stance regarding race relations. The process of urbanization and the accompanying adjustments required to attract business had created a consensus that valued economic interests over maintaining the traditional caste system. The school desegregation crisis signaled the growing influence and authority of urban elites over important political decisions and marked the death knell of the established rural-plantation county power structure that had ruled the state for generations. These small rural counties had maintained power by means of the county unit electoral system, which assigned no fewer than two and no more than six unit votes to each county. In this system three tiny counties equaled the vastly larger and more populated Atlanta/Fulton County area. Even though Atlanta moderates had averted disruptions, they saw the potential for economic disaster in the recent school desegregation crisis. For this reason, in 1962 civic and business leaders in Atlanta supported a court suit that challenged the state's archaic election process. The results proved timely, as a gubernatorial campaign had just begun. One of the candidates was former governor Marvin Griffin, a colorful demagogue who played on rural prejudices. Griffin threatened to "brain" integrationists with a "blackjack sapling" and urged the white people of the state to vote for him because his opponent had "the unqualified support and backing of Ralph McGill, Martin

Luther King, and the Atlanta political machine." Carl Sanders, the opponent that Griffin lambasted, sprang from Augusta, the second largest city
in the state, and would have had little chance of success under the old
voting scheme. The end of the county unit system, however, allowed
Sanders to gain victory as the first man elected from a city since the
1920s.[8]

In 1970 Georgia, like the other southern states discussed in this work,
chose a young, moderate, forward-looking governor. But the methods of
the campaign in Georgia differed from those in other states. In Arkansas,
Florida, and South Carolina, the successful candidates spoke in the quiet
tones of moderation and assiduously avoided giving voice to the rhetoric
of desegregation defiance, while their noisy opponents, all of whom either
represented the demagogic past or at least its tactics, proved that blatant
racial politics no longer appealed to the bulk of white voters. In Georgia a
figure from the past who as governor had introduced the tactics of political moderation in the early 1960s sought to reclaim the governor's chair.
But the successful candidate would master new techniques for binding a
diverse and dubious coalition by tapping into class resentments that included race antagonisms without calling direct attention to race.

By 1970, Georgia's political landscape displayed certain prominent fea-
tures. On the one hand, Georgia was going to have the first black candidate for governor in its history, and black voters constituted 20 percent of
the electorate. On the other hand, 1970 would be the first gubernatorial
election since George Wallace carried Georgia in his 1968 bid for the
presidency, and the state's electorate remained highly receptive to his
brand of antiestablishment, anti-integration rhetoric. To complicate matters further, the Republican Party, for the first time since Reconstruction,
had a good chance of capturing Georgia's governorship. In 1966 the Republican candidate had actually received a plurality of the votes in the
general election but had lost when a write-in candidate prevented a majority for any candidate and threw the election into the heavily Democratic state legislature. The outcome of that decision placed Lester
Maddox in the governor's chair, who before entering politics had gained
national notoriety by using ax handles to prevent blacks from entering the
Atlanta chicken restaurant he owned.

In other words, Georgia would be standing at a crossroads in 1970. In
which direction would it go? Did Lester Maddox's election in 1966 indi-
cate a trend, or was it just a fluke? If the Georgia political scene just prior
to Maddox's election was any indication, the state had stumbled off its

path and would probably resume its previous course of economic progress and moderate race relations. The state's governor from 1963 to 1967, Carl Sanders, had been one of the first southern politicians to stake out and hold to a moderate position on racial matters. Sanders promised to use "every legal means to preserve segregation of the races in Georgia," but he also vowed that he would govern with dignity. "I won't cause you and your state to be spread across headlines all over the nation, and cause you embarrassment." According to the *Christian Science Monitor*, Sanders was "one of the South's most moderate, progressive chief executives." An important campaign promise was to keep public schools open even if it meant integrating them, and as governor, he stuck to his promise. When racial confrontations arose, Sanders defused them and compiled a modest record of progress in civil rights. He appointed the first blacks to the Georgia state patrol as well as the first black members to the Georgia delegation to the Democratic national convention. Sanders also employed the moderate racial climate to encourage many businesses to relocate in the Peach State and was instrumental in bringing major league baseball, basketball, and football to Georgia—the first state in the South to acquire professional sports franchises. Georgians welcomed his emphasis on the future rather than the past and his calm assurances of peace and progress during the turbulent sixties. At the end of his term Sanders remained immensely popular; had Georgia law not prevented successive gubernatorial terms, he would almost certainly have been reelected in 1966. During his four years out of office Sanders continued to have strong political and financial support; virtually all political observers considered him the odds-on favorite to win in 1970. Sanders' popularity and strong support suggested that Georgia in 1970 would resume her moderate-liberal course, after a four-year Maddox aberration.[9]

On the other hand, the enormous popularity Maddox had gained during his four years in office could not be ignored. Some Georgians had wildly applauded his branding of integration as "un-American, un-Godly and even criminal" and had responded to his criticism of busing with a zeal not seen in the state for many years. Maddox's popularity, taken in conjunction with the 1968 Wallace-for-president vote in the state, could well be read as an indication that in 1970, Georgia was destined for another Maddox-like Democrat or even a like-minded Republican.[10]

With Maddox prevented by constitutional provision from succeeding himself and with no fiery segregationist of prominence, Carl Sanders would be the man to beat. William Hamilton, a Washington pollster hired by another candidate, Jimmy Carter, conducted five polls between September 1969 and October 1970. The first of these surveys confirmed what most political observers already suspected: 84 percent of Georgia voters had a favorable view of Sanders' governorship, and 20 percent rated him "excellent." Hamilton noted in his report to Carter that "this is one of the best job ratings I have ever seen given a former governor after three years out of office." If the election were held immediately, Hamilton's poll indicated, Sanders would get 53 percent of the vote and Carter only 21 percent. But the report also pointed out that no one had started "shooting at" Sanders yet and that Carter had plenty of time to build a "favorable image" among voters who did not yet know him.[11]

Moreover, Hamilton's report stressed, there were a few chinks in Sanders' armor. From 20 to 25 percent of Sanders' support was "soft," meaning there was something about him that his supporters did not like: his affluence since leaving the governor's office, his ties to the "Atlanta bigwigs," his closeness to Washington. The poll echoed a 1968 memo to an aide scribbled by Carter: "Some images to be projected regarding Carl Sanders . . . refuses to let Georgia Democrats have a voice in the Democratic party . . . Atlanta-oriented . . . pretty . . . nouveau riche . . . excluded George Wallace from state . . . right now we just need to collect all these rough ideas we can. Later we can start driving a wedge between me and him." Hamilton's poll, therefore, confirmed Carter's earlier assessment of Sanders and convinced Carter to portray Sanders as a rich "brash, young, eager man who doesn't deserve to be governor" and himself as a humble country boy who was "not going to let him be."[12]

A country boy indeed. Jimmy Carter came from a family that had farmed in America since the 1630s, first in Virginia, then North Carolina, and finally Georgia a century and a half later. As a child, Jimmy Carter seldom wore shoes between April and October. He fished for catfish and eels in the creeks of his south Georgia home and often, because of his size and agility, would climb to shake down treed possums and raccoons. Inspired by his mother and one of his Plains teachers, Jimmy came to love reading and employed literature as a way of escaping the isolation of his small-town home. Perhaps the desire to see the world motivated Carter's early decision to pursue a career in the navy. Carter entered the U.S. Naval Academy during World War II and graduated fifty-ninth in his class the year after the war ended; he served in submarines and traveled extensively. In 1952, Carter entered the elite new group of officers assembled by Admiral Hyman Rickover to develop nuclear submarines. Carter thrived in the challenges of the nuclear program, and the technical nature of the work suited his detail-oriented mind. When his father died in 1953, however, Jimmy resigned his commission in the navy and returned to Plains to run the family peanut business. He expanded the business, became involved in community service organizations, and won a seat in the state senate in 1962.[13]

The 1970 race was not Carter's first try for Georgia's governorship. He had run four years earlier. Carter did not like being positioned on the left or right of the political spectrum, saying, "I believe that I'm a more complicated person than that." But in 1966 Carter appealed to moderate-liberal voters and conducted a gentlemanly, nonracist campaign. Bruce Galphin of the *Atlanta Constitution* wrote at the time that it was hard to meet Jimmy Carter and hear him talk without "admiring his integrity." Carter, Galphin went on to say, was a breed of politician new to Georgia, subdued, frank even about his deficiencies, and unwilling "to torture the traditional whipping boys." In 1966, race was still Georgia's most readily exploitable political issue. But Jimmy Carter had refused to use it. He was not a racist.[14]

Carter's background, however, mirrored that of many rural Georgians raised in a segregated society. Perhaps more than any other politician running for office in 1970, Carter exemplified the moral ambivalence of white southerners. James Earl Carter, Jr. was born on October 1, 1924, only hours before the governor of Georgia delivered the keynote address to the annual convention of the Ku Klux Klan. Shortly before Jimmy's fourth birthday the family moved three miles west of their Plains home to Archery, Georgia. Only one other white family resided there alongside thirty or so impoverished black families. Jimmy grew up with black children as playmates. When these children came home with Jimmy, his mother, Lillian, unlike other whites, allowed the boys to eat in her kitchen. Jimmy's father, Earl, had very different views on race than his wife. Like most every other white in that time and place, Earl adamantly believed in segregation. Although they seldom argued about race relations, the Carters held to their differing views by ignoring each other's actions. When Lillian would receive blacks in her house or attend black funerals, Earl would conveniently disappear. And yet, Earl harbored no animosity toward blacks. Indeed, many blacks in and around Archery and Plains counted on "Mr. Earl," as well as "Miss Lillian," for all sorts of help and support. With no doctor in Webster County, Lillian, a nurse, served both black and white, and on many occasions Earl paid for medicines of indigent patients of both races.[15]

In 1953, when Earl Carter was diagnosed with advanced pancreatic cancer, Jimmy returned home to spend time with his father. The two differed on several issues, including that of race. Prior to Earl's illness, after Jimmy proudly related an incident in which he and his submarine crew had refused an invitation to a social function because their one black shipmate had been excluded, Earl expressed his view that the separation of the races was altogether appropriate. This had strained their relationship and led Jimmy to think of his father as uncaring and unjust. But during Earl's dying days, Jimmy discovered many of the acts of kindness and anonymous aid extended to dozens of poor black families. At Mr. Earl's funeral Jimmy was astonished at the hundreds of people, both black and white, who came to express sympathy and relate stories of his father's generosity over the years. Jimmy came to appreciate his father's actions and believe that perhaps this was a man that was not racist but a product of his times.[16]

When Carter returned to live in Plains he joined many World War II veterans who had returned to the South and recognized the basic inequities of the social caste system that they had never questioned growing up. They realized that change would come, but wanted the change to come in an orderly fashion. In reality, a white southerner could do very little in those days of strict segregation. Jimmy and Rosalynn felt strongly about the injustices blacks were forced to endure. Jimmy, as his father before him, performed acts of personal charity and generosity, but he also worked hard to make his business a success and that meant not being an outspoken defender of the *Brown* decision. "You just knew where Jimmy stood," said Warren Fortson, a Plains attorney, of Carter's view on racial matters. "You knew that Jimmy also was a person who had no truck with that kind of stuff." At times, however, Jimmy showed his true colors. Carter refused, in the face of considerable pressure, to join the White Citizens Council, and in a heated congregational squabble he made an impassioned speech in favor of allowing blacks to worship in his church. As a state senator, he made one of his first speeches in opposition to Georgia's infamous "thirty questions" law used to disqualify black voters.[17]

Though Jimmy Carter finished a surprisingly close third in the 1966 race, Lester Maddox's victory convinced Carter that the racial issue, like it or not, could not be ignored. After his 1966 loss, therefore, Carter began some hard thinking and decided two things. One, he would run again in 1970. That surprised no one who knew him or had watched him closely. As one journalist observed, "to go out and make nice speeches and lose is not Jimmy Carter's style." The other thing Carter decided was, as he later wrote in his autobiography, that he "did not intend to lose again." That meant he was going to have to make a third decision.[18]

Eight years earlier, George Wallace, like Jimmy Carter, had lost his 1958 bid for Alabama's governorship because he was perceived as more moderate than his race-baiting opponent, John Patterson. As a result, Wallace had decided, and declared, that he would never be "out-nigguhed again." Carter was going to have to decide if he would go in the same direction, and if so, how far. Before he made that decision, he waited to see how the Georgia political situation would shape up in 1970.[19]

Not surprisingly, Carl Sanders' candidacy dominated the political landscape. His reputation as a politician who avoided racial demagoguery, coupled with his record of progressive governance, garnered widespread support in Georgia's increasingly moderate electorate and made Sanders the man to beat. If a candidate expected to be successful, his strategy must cut into Sanders' appeal. Carter realized this instinctively and looked toward another candidate to assist him in that task. One contender in the Democratic primary who might cut into Sanders' constituency was the black candidate, C. B. King. King was an Albany lawyer (one of only three black attorneys in the state outside Atlanta in the early 1960s) who had played a prominent role in the Southern Christian Leadership Conference's Albany movement in 1962. King's candidacy, it should be noted, was legitimate and had no connection with Carter's machinations. Some black leaders and political organizations endorsed King, but most of the others, believing that he could not win even if he made the Democratic runoff election, supported Sanders. Few black voters supported the largely unknown Carter. But for Carter that was a blessing. King could not possibly make the runoff, but he might draw enough black voters to keep Sanders from winning on the first ballot, giving Carter a good chance of being in a runoff with Sanders.[20]

But where would Carter get enough votes to make it into a runoff? With his natural constituency of moderates, liberals, and blacks preempted by Sanders and King, Carter's only hope lay with the Maddox-Wallace camp. Getting their votes would be tricky. He would need to make himself attractive to Georgia's "lower status whites" as Numan Bartley called them in his *From Thurmond to Wallace*, the state's "most politically conservative people . . . racist in social attitudes, fundamentalist in religion, provincial in outlook." At the same time, Carter could not make himself so attractive to the Maddox and Wallace people as to permanently alienate Georgia's moderate, liberal, and black voters. If he managed to win the Democratic nomination, he would need their support in the general election, in which he would face a Republican. The GOP had revealed its character by inviting Lester Maddox to join its ranks and by opening remarks in the state convention assuring newsmen that C. B. King would not be welcome in the Republican primary.[21]

Carter's plan to paint Sanders as a smug, citified dandy would sell well in poor rural Georgia. It always had. Sanders would be an easy target, for after his term expired he had remained in Atlanta to become a rich lawyer. Looking back on the campaign twenty years later, Carl Sanders admitted that Carter succeeded in drawing "more of a class distinction than a race distinction. I think he postured himself as a peanut farmer from outside of Atlanta and . . . he pictured me as a corporate lawyer in Atlanta who had capitalized on being governor and who was now representing the fat cats and he was out there representing the average citizen. That's a pretty tough thing to overcome." Indeed it was. Carter even criticized Sanders' wife, claiming that while his own wife shook hands with factory workers, Mrs. Sanders attended a fashion show. The actions of the wives were, Carter suggested, "symbolic" of the interests of the candidates: "high society versus the working man." Caricaturing Sanders and his wife, however, would not be enough. Carter would also have to appeal to the Maddox-Wallace people on issues. In the memo he dictated in 1966, Carter had noted that he might need to portray Sanders as too liberal for Georgia voters; "more liberal" was his exact phrase. And William Hamilton's poll of 1969 had confirmed that hunch. Hamilton noted that Sanders had "a slight problem with his liberal image."[22]

Carter decided that to win the support of the Maddox-Wallace followers, he was going to have to place himself to the right of Sanders. Although Carter was, in fact, the more liberal of the two, his record was not as well known as Sanders.' That fact made the scheme possible. As a first step in portraying himself as more conservative than Sanders, Carter made his cousin, Hugh Carter, his campaign manager. Hugh Carter was a good-old-boy politician with solid conservative credentials. His job was to reassure conservatives in the state that "Jimmy Carter was a safe man." Jimmy Carter could easily combine his planned portrayal of Sanders as too rich to understand the average man, too citified, too sophisticated, and too liberal for Georgians, with attacks on his ties to "big government," to "the power elite," and to "the Washington establishment," all phrases George Wallace had made popular. In short, Carter would make Sanders into a "limousine liberal."[23]

But even that would not be enough. While it was true, as Reg Murphy and Hal Gulliver pointed out in *The Southern Strategy*, that "liberal" and "conservative" were racial code words in the South, "liberal" meaning integrationist and "conservative" meaning segregationist, such code words alone would not convince the Maddox-Wallace camp. As much as he may have wished to, Jimmy Carter could not escape dealing with the integration issue. According to one poll, public sentiment that integration was moving too fast rose from 35 percent in March 1968 to 54 percent in April 1970. As Jim Gillis, Jr., a county commissioner and son of Georgia's powerful highway department director, said at the time: "The school thing is like a funeral. The family knows you can't bring the body back to life, but they want you there holding their hands." Although Jimmy Carter never heard Gillis's analogy, he understood it well, and he determined to be there, holding the hands of Georgia's segregationists.[24]

At the same time he was holding hands with conservatives and segregationists, Jimmy Carter had to reach out to liberal and black voters. This was an awkward posture, to say the least, but one Carter found necessary both to assuage his conscience and to insure liberal and black support against the Republican nominee in the later general election. In effect, Carter's campaign plan called for a two-faceted—his critics would say a two-faced—campaign: one facet designed to appeal to segregationists and the other to give heart to liberals and blacks.

To obscure the inconsistencies in his two-faceted strategy and to excuse his personal attacks on Sanders, Carter cloaked the whole of his campaign in the guise of "populism." According to one of the early polls Hamilton did for Carter, 81 percent of the Georgia electorate felt alienated from government. In addition to integration coming too fast, they were most concerned about high taxes and the welfare system, "the issues of Nixon's forgotten man, middle America." Political pragmatism dictated that Carter must appeal to racist elements in Georgia's electorate, but he would run a "redneck" campaign, emphasizing class rather than race distinctions. He would embrace all workers in the rhetoric of populism, while carefully avoiding any overt appeal to racism. That way he could perhaps deflate the race issues. "Jimmy is a populist," asserted Charles Kirbo, a longtime Carter friend and political advisor. "Jimmy can and does appeal to the Wallace voter, but not on the racial thing."[25]

There was nothing unusual, much less unique, about Jimmy Carter's appeal to "populism." What James Perry of the *National Observer* called a "new populism" was sweeping the South in 1970. New faces in the Democratic Party were winning elections to governors' and senators' seats by refocusing their party objectives in terms of the common man. "More important for the Democrats than specific issues was the successful selling of the populist symbols," wrote James Clotfelter and William Hamilton (Carter's pollster) in *South Today*. "The common ingredient was voters believing the candidate cared about what they cared about, that he was one of their own and would not forget them."[26]

When Carter announced his candidacy in early April 1970, he mapped out his strategy for Steve Ball, political editor of the *Atlanta Journal*. He would aim his campaign at a coalition of Georgians in the middle- and low-income brackets. This included Nixon's silent majority, the poor, both black and white, and the conservative Georgians who had voted for Lester Maddox in 1966 and for George Wallace in 1968. His appeal, he went on to say, would be to "average working people" who wanted "someone in the governor's office who understands their problems."[27]

Jimmy Carter succeeded, but his success proved to be both gruesomely hard and soul-taxing. The only easy part was adopting, adapting, and inventing his own brand of "populism." In the minds of rural and urban blue-collar Georgia voters, nothing better represented the wealth and power of the establishment than the Atlanta press. "The people in the state," said one longtime politico, "whatever the Atlanta newspapers are for, they're against." Successful Georgia politicians had been haranguing "those lying Atlanta newspapers" since the campaigns of Eugene Talmadge in the 1930s. Carter simply continued the tradition. He did not want, he insisted, the support of "the big-shots that own the Atlanta newspapers." He charged that the *Atlanta Constitution* made a "major editorial commitment" to smear him, particularly in its political cartoons. Carter's press aide, Bill Pope, said after the campaign: "We loved all those scurrilous cartoons. We just didn't want it to stop." Bill Shipp was right when he later wrote that Carter had "calculatedly incurred the wrath of the big city daily press."[28]

At the same time, Jimmy Carter made himself look as ordinary and colorless as he could, or at least his political image packager, Gerald Rafshoon, did. Billboards and brochures carried the ugliest photograph of Carter his staff could find. "It made Jimmy look like an average working man," a Carter campaign aide said. The picture made him look like "he had a little fear in him . . . a little wary perhaps." That Carter made sure he looked like a populist was significant because, in the words of his own pollster, William Hamilton, Carter was a "stylistic populist" whose success derived not from changing specific policies, but from "personal campaign style."[29]

More uniquely his own was Jimmy Carter's ability at personal campaigning. He traveled the state on the civic club speech-making circuit; kept active in the Baptist church, farm organizations, business groups, and the Lions Club; and had himself made state chairman of the March of Dimes. By the time he announced his candidacy Jimmy Carter had visited more than 400 towns, made more than 1,800 speeches, and met 600,000 Georgians. Once the campaign began in earnest, he shook thousands of hands in factory shift lines at five A.M. and again at midnight. Eighteen-hour days of nonstop campaigning were typical. In many small counties a visit from someone running for governor was rare. Carter visited most of the small counties not once but two or three times, and shook every hand he could find. Numerous observers noted the effectiveness of this person-to-person campaigning: "It is a peculiar thing, involving human warmth, and not relating at all to issues," wrote the *Atlanta Journal*'s Steve Ball. "It works for him everywhere." Even Reg Murphy, editor of the *Atlanta Constitution* and one of Carter's severest critics, admitted that "one-on-one, he's probably as convincing as anybody I've ever seen."[30]

Carter found the personal campaigning natural, did not mind the toning down of his looks, and managed the populist rhetoric easily because, in his heart, he believed it. But Carter would also have to draw sharp class distinctions between himself and Carl Sanders. Carter's polls indicated that average voters watched television but did not read newspapers, which dictated a TV crusade against Sanders. That crusade focused on portraying Jimmy Carter as the candidate of the working man and Carl Sanders as the candidate of the ultra-rich. One commercial showed Carter harvesting peanuts. The voice-over asked, "Can you imagine any of the other candidates for governor working in the hot August sun? Isn't it time someone spoke up for you?" Carter's fund-raising ads said other candidates were supported by "big money asking for big favors," but that

"Jimmy Carter made it the hard way." Perhaps Carter's most effective commercial opened with the camera panning in on a closed door. Voice-over: "This is the door to an exclusive country club where the big-money boys play cards, drink cocktails, and raise money for their candidate, Carl Sanders." Country club door swings open; close-up of man writing check. Voice-over: "People like us aren't invited. We're too busy working for a living." Footage of Carter talking with an "average man." Voice-over: "That's why our votes are going for Jimmy Carter. Vote for Jimmy Carter, our kind of man, our kind of governor."[31]

"Carter used television effectively," remembered Bill Shipp, "with Gerry Rafshoon doing a whole series of some of the best negative advertising I've ever seen aimed at Sanders. And Sanders' own advertising played right into their hands." Sanders' advertising campaign actually benefited Carter. His ads were expensive, slick, and elitist. Sanders was pictured jogging, boating, and flying his plane. Sanders avoided appealing to the common man and portrayed himself as prosperous and prestigious. Even the Sanders campaign slogan did not sit well with many Georgians: "Carl Sanders ought to be governor again." Two of Sanders' own campaign aides later admitted that the slogan sounded like Sanders had a right to be governor, as if it were a "monarchial privilege."[32]

Carter saw his opportunity and made the most of it. He immediately began portraying Sanders as a king who had robbed his subjects. In one of Carter's televised spots Sanders, whom Carter always called "Cuff Links Carl," was shown boarding a Lear jet; then the camera quickly cut to a close-up of a man's hand taking hold of a briefcase full of money. At the wrists were huge cuff links. Throughout the campaign Carter harped on the theme that Sanders had "used secret information to get rich." Over and over, Carter proclaimed that "Georgians never again want a governor who will use the tremendous power and prestige of office for his own personal wealth." And once, while campaigning at a bank, Carter stuck his head into a vault and quipped: "Looks like Carl Sanders' basement." When Sanders retorted by calling Carter a penny-ante politician, Carter again bested him. Yes, he said, "my campaign is based on peanuts, pennies, and people. That's better than one based on bucks, banks, and boondoggles."[33]

In fact, Carl Sanders' administration had not had a hint of scandal about it. And Carter's own polling information indicated that only 1 percent of the electorate believed Sanders had used the governor's office for personal gain. But Jimmy Carter would make sure that by election day a great many more voters believed it. Carter attacked Sanders daily and promised the press that he had proof of Sanders' misdeeds that he would release in due course. At the same time, Carter put Sanders on the defensive by repeatedly calling for public disclosure of his personal finances. Sanders lamely protested that his personal finances were not part of the campaign.[34]

Two weeks before the primary Carter released his long awaited "proof" that Carl Sanders had abused the powers of the governor's office. He charged that Sanders, while governor, had used his influence with the Federal Communications Commission to help a friend and business associate acquire several television and radio stations. Carter handed out copies of papers filed with the FCC. The documents listed Sanders as secretary of his friend's firm, gave his occupation as governor of Georgia, and listed his address as the governor's mansion. But the documents also showed that Sanders owned no stock in the company.[35]

Carter's bombshell had proven a dud, and the newspapers had a field day. Carter had, in the words of the *Macon Telegraph*, "over-promised and under-delivered." The *Macon News* labeled Carter "a classic example of a good man whose high standards have been undermined by political ambition." And the *Atlanta Constitution* wrote that Carter had gone at Sanders with a "vengeance." While Jimmy Carter admitted that there was no proof of illegality, he insisted that the facts showed "a consistent pattern of combining political and business interests on behalf of Mr. Sanders." The weakness of the response did not matter, for the damage to Sanders had been done. The dirty trick had worked. But discrediting Sanders amounted to blackening the former governor's character, and Carter was beginning to pay the price of conscience. According to Phil Gardner, editor of the *Atlanta Journal*, Jimmy Carter, at the time, agonized over "whether he should have used the tactic in the first place."[36]

But Carter played far more and dirtier tricks on Sanders. Early in the summer the Carter campaign put out a series of anonymous pamphlets and "fact-sheets" that hit Sanders from all sides. One of the most effective was a photograph of Carl Sanders being doused with champagne by a black Atlanta Hawks basketball player during a victory celebration. The picture became known as the "champagne shampoo." Copies were mailed to small-town barbershops, rural churches, service stations, and country stores, and were passed out at Ku Klux Klan rallies. Sanders was part owner of the Atlanta Hawks, and the photograph originally had run on the sports page of the *Atlanta Constitution*. But as a political flyer it reminded people that Sanders was rich and associated him with high living and alcohol, both still bugaboos in puritanical and teetotaling rural Georgia.[37]

Most important, the photograph associated Sanders, in a close personal way, with blacks. That association was carried further by "factsheets" that said or implied that Sanders was a close ally of the controversial black state representative Julian Bond (actually the two detested each other), that Sanders had attended the funeral of Martin Luther King, Jr. (which, in fact, he had), and that as governor Sanders had conspired to keep George Wallace out of Georgia (Sanders did). Bill Pope, Carter's press secretary, prepared the leaflets, and Carter's top campaign aide, Hamilton Jordan, directed their mailing. Such tactics were all part of an operation Carter campaign workers called the "stink tank."[38]

In order to win the Democratic nomination, Jimmy Carter needed to draw as much black support away from Sanders as possible. But at the same time, he needed to string black voters along, for he would need their support in the general election in which he would face a Republican. The two-faceted campaign was again in play.

The "stink tank" was once again put to work. The Carter campaign created a fictitious "Black Concern Committee." The "committee" sent pamphlets that charged Sanders had not kept his 1962 campaign promises to black voters and even implied that Sanders had been responsible for the death of a black prison inmate. These sheets were mailed to black barber shops, funeral homes, and pool halls. Simultaneously, the Rafshoon agency, in order to draw black voters away from Sanders, prepared and paid for radio spots for C. B. King. At the same time Carter consistently asserted that he had "excellent support from the NAACP and Negro churchmen across the state," and he told black Atlanta leader Vernon Jordan, "You won't like my campaign, but you will like my administration."[39]

Carter also went directly to black voters. Although Carter's staff advised against it, he was the only white candidate to campaign openly in black communities. "I've been to see 'em in their filling stations, in their churches," Carter would be able to say. "I've been to see 'em in their drugstores and in their homes." On one occasion, for example, Carter walked to the back of a small-town drugstore to shake hands with a black janitor whom he could easily have ignored, while three whites he had just been talking to looked on disapprovingly. Carter promised to appoint black citizens to high-level state offices and constitutional boards: "the state ought to set the example in its employment," he explained.[40]

In stringing black voters along even as he appealed to Georgia's segregationists, Carter employed dual-purpose rhetoric with acumen. While he never outright said he was a segregationist, he managed to leave that impression with a great many voters. Hamilton Jordan told the *Atlanta Journal* that in some counties the Carter campaign actually set up two organizations, one designed to cultivate the backing of Wallace-Maddox supporters and the other to appeal to more moderate voters. Similarly, Republican candidate Hal Suit said that Carter had one brochure for use in extreme segregationist-minded areas of south Georgia, and another one for distribution in the rest of the state. And during the campaign Carter, on several occasions, gave different answers to the same questions, depending on where and to whom he was speaking. On one occasion Carter had said he was against giving a "single dime" to private schools; on another occasion and in a different place—this time at one of the many private schools being established in order to avoid integration—he told an audience, "you can rest assured I'll do everything I can for private schools." More often and more typically when asked about forced integration, he sidestepped the question with responses such as "I don't like being pushed around."[41]

Throughout the primary Carter sought to identify himself with George Wallace, even incorporating Wallace's campaign slogan, "our kind of man," into his own advertising. He said he expected "to have particularly strong support from the people who voted for George Wallace for President and the ones who voted for Lester Maddox." And he repeatedly promised he would invite George Wallace to Georgia to right the slight done the Alabama governor by Sanders, who had refused to allow Wallace to speak to the Georgia state legislature. ABC-TV's fact-book on the election concluded that Carter largely "confined his campaign promises to one issue—if elected governor he would invite George Wallace to Georgia."[42]

Five days before the primary Carter visited the Augusta police station in order to show support for two policemen charged in the shooting of two blacks during riots in Augusta. There he made a tough law-and-order speech. "The main thing I want you to know," Carter told the assembled police force, "is that when I am governor of Georgia, you need not ever fear I will pull the rug out from under you when you try to enforce the law against any sort of rioters or lawbreakers. I'll back you up one hundred percent." Press Secretary Bill Pope summed it all up after the election when he told the *Washington Post* that he had run a "nigger campaign" for Carter.[43]

In the Democratic primary on September 9, Carter won handily, with 388,280 votes or 48.6 percent of the total. Sanders came in second with 301,179 votes, or 37.7 percent. Carter had missed winning without a run-off by only 10,000 votes. Carter's strategy had worked. He had swept the rural areas and small towns and left Sanders only urban and black voters to draw from. In the counties where Lester Maddox did well, Carter also did well. Maddox, running for lieutenant governor, was the only Democrat in a multicandidate race to win without a runoff. In 1966 Jimmy Carter's liberal image served him well in the city and in the state's northern, generally liberal to moderate counties. In 1970 these were Carter's weakest areas of support.[44]

Carter still faced a runoff election with Sanders. But Carter's unexpectedly large, 87,000-vote margin called for a change in tactics. In the runoff Carter would no longer attack Sanders, who, no longer forced to be defensive, would probably take the offensive and start attacking. Carter would then play the part of the "little man" being put upon by the rich and powerful Sanders.

As expected, Sanders came out swinging. Two days after the primary, he called a press conference and launched into the first of a series of attacks on Carter as a liar, a "smiling hypocrite," an oppressor of tenant farmers, and an ultra-liberal who was trying to pass himself off as a hard-working farmer. "The last time Carter worked in the fields in the hot August sun," Sanders shouted, "was when his slick advertising agency took the pictures you see on television every day." Carter had worked to delete the word "God" from the Georgia constitution, had voted against old and disabled persons, and had sided with organized crime, Sanders charged. Carter was an "unprincipled grinning chameleon." Carter responded by labeling Sanders "an embittered and desperate man . . . waging a smear campaign."[45]

In spite of repeated challenges by Sanders, Carter ruled out a debate with such a "bad loser." "My strength is with the people," he said, "and I intend to spend my time with them." In desperation Sanders had a television debate anyway, with an empty chair. But Carter one-upped him again. "Some folks," he quipped, "said the chair was ahead."[46]

C. B. King, the black candidate who placed third in the Democratic primary, accused both Sanders and Carter of running racist campaigns. Asked for comment, Carter replied in a typical two-faceted statement, that he would appreciate any Negro votes, but added, "I can win this election without a single black vote." One day later Carter met with Roy Harris, the former chairman of Georgia's White Citizens Council, George Wallace's 1968 Georgia campaign director, and editor of the racist *Augusta Courier*. At the end of the private but much speculated upon meeting, Carter emerged with an endorsement from Harris. The Sanders camp was delighted. They immediately distributed a flyer featuring a cartoon of Carter climbing into bed with Roy Harris and saying: ". . . move over, Roy. You're right! Who needs black votes." Shortly afterward, the Sanders people released another flyer that had pictures of run-down tenant houses on Carter's farm, captioned with a slightly altered version of the Carter campaign slogan: "Isn't it time someone spoke up for these people?"[47]

Carter immediately fired off memos to all his county campaign chairmen telling them to get the word out that Sanders was mailing "smear sheets" that attacked him personally and stirred up racial hatreds. He was right. During the final days of the runoff the Sanders campaign launched what amounted to a massive "smear sheet airlift." But Carter again outmaneuvered Carl Sanders. Local Carter campaign people simply met the incoming planes, posed as Sanders' campaign workers, picked up the "smear sheets," and had bonfires.[48]

On election day Sanders got his old supporters back to the polls, plus most of C. B. King's, who gave him 93 percent of the black vote. But Carter won three out of every four white votes and carried 135 of 159 counties for a 60 percent win. In rural counties he had routinely triumphed with three-to-one margins.[49]

Almost as good news for the Carter camp as the victory was that the Republican nominee was Hal Suit. If Suit's nomination surprised virtually everyone in the state, it delighted Carter and his people. Like everyone else, they had expected the Republicans to run James Bentley, and they dreaded the prospect. State Comptroller Jimmy Bentley was the Georgia GOP's most able politician and one of the most conservative political figures in the state. Elected as a Democrat, Bentley switched parties in 1968.

Bentley had sent out $1,600 worth of telegrams to public officials warning that Earth Day was also Lenin's birthday and suggesting that the observances were somehow Communist-affiliated. Like Carter, he saw that the Maddox-Wallace vote in Georgia would be the deciding factor in the 1970 governor's race. Three months before the Republican primary Bill Shipp had written that Bentley was already "taking a campaign cue from George Wallace's victory in Alabama and is taking a hard, perhaps even vicious turn to the right." Bentley had begun running a television commercial that opened with the camera focused on an oncoming school bus. Voice-over: "This year this bus and the laws that drive it threaten to change the life of your child." The bus roared closer and closer and loomed larger and larger until the screen was filled, then obliterated, by its front bumper and radiator grill. Carter had placed Sanders to his left with little difficulty, but it would be impossible to move to the right of Jimmy Bentley.[50]

Hal Suit, on the other hand, an Atlanta broadcaster virtually unknown outside the urban area, was a political novice. More important from the Carter camp's point of view, he had no established, much less well-known, reputation as a hard-liner on segregation. And as Newt Gingrich, then a history professor at West Georgia College, wrote: "Suit had only about one-fourth as much money as Carter, and about one-tenth as much organization."[51] Compared to Bentley, Suit would be a pushover. But even that would require careful planning and a lot of work. Carter would need to continue to portray himself as "conservative" and brand Suit a "liberal." That meant continued courting of the Maddox-Wallace vote. But at the same time, Carter wanted to appeal to moderate, urban, and black voters.

Suit recognized the importance of a conservative label as well as Carter did but, in fact, there were few issues on which the two candidates really differed. So the two candidates hurled accusations of "ultra-liberal" and "counterfeit conservative" at each other. "The big issue in the lackluster contest," the *Atlanta Journal* observed, "boiled down to who is the 'liberal.'"[52]

In the liberal-hurling contest, Suit proved no match for Carter. For example, although Suit knew of Carter's voting for the integration of his own church in Plains, he considered it irrelevant to the campaign and did not mention it. In retrospect he realized he should have. The problem, as Newt Gingrich wrote, was that Suit "lacked the experience to tear away at the phony image and reveal the liberal heart under the blue collar picture."[53]

At the same time, Carter began to cut into Suit's urban constituency by shifting his target from the Atlanta establishment to the Washington power structure and the Republican Party, which was, he repeatedly charged, "controlled by a handful of big-shots." Instead of going to the Georgia voters for support, Suit had, Carter said, "snuck off to Washington" for help from President Nixon. But all Suit got, he added, was "a ballpoint pen and an autographed golf ball."[54]

Even though Hal Suit was not the staunch segregationist he had expected to face in the general election, Carter followed his original plan of trying to retrieve the black support he had relinquished to Sanders in the primary. He began to soften his segregationist image and talk again in terms, however vague, of a colorblind "populist" coalition: "I got the vote of a lot of segregationists and integrationists" in the primary, Carter maintained, and "I never did ask their philosophy when I sought their vote." To a group of farmers in Abraham, Georgia, as in other towns around the state, he began saying that conservatism no longer meant, "hatred of another person because he is different from us." Nor did it mean "a lack of passion or foresight, but simply an insistence that individuals be left alone as much as possible to guide their own destinies."[55]

Despite his new moderation, Jimmy Carter's earlier courtship with segregationists paid off big in late September. Lester Maddox at that point endorsed him and praised him for "running a Maddox-type campaign." And Maddox kept up his support; two weeks later, at a state Democratic meeting, he promised that as lieutenant governor he would be watching to make sure Carter kept his campaign promises. "When I put my money into a peanut machine, I don't expect to get bubble gum, and neither do the people." Carter at the same meeting swallowed his pride and praised Maddox: "He has brought a standard of forthright expression and personal honesty to the governor's office and I hope to measure up to this standard." And on the last day of the campaign Carter announced he was going to vote for Maddox as lieutenant governor.[56]

In Las Vegas, Jimmy the Greek set the odds for the Georgia election: Carter to win at two-and-a-half to one. The Greek was right. On November 3, 1970, Carter won 62 percent of the vote and became the seventy-sixth governor of Georgia.[57]

The 1970 election represented a watershed in Georgia's history, but the fact that Jimmy Carter won it did not. Even if Carl Sanders won, it would have been a major turning point in the state's political history because both he and Carter were a new breed of political leaders emerging in the South at the time. Race as a campaign issue, at least as a public campaign issue, would have ended with a Sanders victory as surely as it did with Carter's victory.

For any newcomer to stand a chance of winning, he would have had to steal Maddox's thunder and make himself the candidate of the state's segregationist camp. At the same time, because Sanders' record was unassailable, any newcomer would have had to bring the former governor down by tarring him with personal attacks.

The newcomer in this case was, of course, the personally honorable and politically liberal and integrationist-minded Jimmy Carter. No one but Jimmy Carter knew then, or knows now, how hard it was for him to decide to do what was necessary to win. But what is clear is that actually doing what he decided to do caused him great personal suffering. It was immediately obvious to others that Jimmy Carter had not run a campaign he could be proud of. Shortly after the election, state senator Leroy Johnson, Sanders' black campaign leader for the Atlanta area, made a poignant observation: "I understand why he ran that kind of ultra-conservative campaign . . . you have to do that to win. And that's the main thing."[58]

But Carter had far more trouble justifying his actions to himself. After the election, Carter was distraught. He immediately telephoned Carl Sanders to apologize for the personal attacks and began confiding to close friends that he "felt bad" about some of the things he had said and done. He confessed "to the Lord" and "prayed for forgiveness," and told Rosalynn that he would never go through such a campaign again. When he began his campaign for the presidency in 1976 he employed the slogan, "I'll never lie to you."[59]

In his famous 1976 *Playboy* interview Carter said that when he looked on women with lust he was committing adultery in his heart. For born-again Jimmy Carter, the thought was equivalent to the action. Although he convinced himself that the subterfuge of his campaign did not make him a racist, Carter's personal anguish over the campaign of 1970 had profound consequences for the politics of the South. Upon winning his election he immediately began to build bridges to black citizens with his inaugural address. "I say to you quite frankly that the time for racial discrimination is over," he declared. "Our people have already made this major and difficult decision. No poor, rural, weak or black person should ever have to bear the additional burden of being deprived of the opportunity for an education, a job, or simple justice."[60] This pronouncement by a Deep South governor that racism was dead created front-page news in the national media. Carter's speech and the campaigns and speeches of the other moderate southern governors signaled an end to racial politics and allowed the region to rejoin the nation in a way heretofore impossible since the Civil War. The fact that Carter found it necessary to conduct a campaign that was less than forthright affected him not only as a politician, but as a moral, religious man who believed in the powers of redemption. Carter believed that his campaign and his experience as a southerner could heal the racial divide.

7

Conclusion

The four 1970 gubernatorial campaigns discussed in this work reveal a great deal about the men who won them, the southern body politic, and the changing politics of race. Each campaign, of course, exhibited distinctive characteristics, shaped by history, issues, and political developments peculiar to each different state. Republican incumbents dominated the political contests in Arkansas and Florida, while in the other two states no incumbent was eligible to run. In Arkansas and Georgia, the toughest test came from a former governor in the Democratic primary. In South Carolina, neither party held primary contests. These differences dictated candidates' strategies and tactics as they marshaled their forces according to the strength and number of their opponents.

Nevertheless, Bumpers, Askew, West, and Carter took several common characteristics into the campaign. All of these white men sprang from rural areas and modest backgrounds. Each of the candidates actively participated in their Protestant churches. All four had served in the military; two of them, West and Carter, attended military academies. All had been raised during the Great Depression of the 1930s but had come of age during a time of prosperity and optimism. They represented a new generation of white southerners who longed to escape the adverse effects that racism had inflicted upon the region.

These four men pursued office with an attitude of personal confidence and idealism. They believed that if given the chance, they could accomplish great things. They campaigned, therefore, emphasizing their personal qualities rather than focusing on issues. All four of the successful gubernatorial candidates in 1970 avoided controversial topics. All sought to portray themselves as good men whom voters could trust. A powerful new tool in politics facilitated this approach. Television offered the perfect tool for avoiding contentious issues and presenting personal qualities. Image replaced substance.

The power of images benefited all four of these men. Bumpers effectively employed television in presenting himself as a leader the people could trust. Even though Askew could not afford an extensive television advertising campaign, he made the most of the coverage he received. His single most important asset in the 1970 campaign, according to a *New York Times Magazine* feature article, was "the ability to project the image of complete sincerity over television." Askew also benefited indirectly from negative media coverage of Governor Kirk's seizure of a school district in defiance of court orders. John West profited as well from the television coverage of violent crowds overturning school buses after a speech by his opponent seemed to support extreme measures of resistance. And West employed an effective advertising campaign pointing out the futility of defiance by playing back Republican Senator Strom Thurmond's "broken promises" to ease federal desegregation pressure. Jimmy Carter employed pictures that cast his opponent as a rich, corrupt politician who could not understand the problems of common folk while portraying himself as a man of the people.[1]

Television allowed the successful candidates of 1970 to emphasize their personal qualities without dwelling on the issues. The candidates knew, however, that they must seek favor from a diverse, ambivalent, and changing electorate. The civil rights movement had convinced many white southerners that the abuses heaped upon blacks in the past must cease. Others did not like integration, but came to tolerate it; to do otherwise, they realized, would only invite more stringent desegregation remedies and federal intrusion. This acceptance juxtaposed against the turbulence of the previous decade compelled many to embrace those candidates who seemed sincere in their efforts to find solutions that would avoid undue disruptions.

One issue that threatened the resilience of this newfound moderation, however, was busing. While many southerners had come to accept integration, an even greater number believed that uprooting children out of their neighborhood schools in order to achieve some seemingly arbitrary racial balance represented a misguided effort that went beyond correcting past injustices. In every campaign in 1970, at least one candidate sought to play on the racial misgivings of southern whites. The efforts of these candidates failed. The rejection of political pandering to racial antagonisms takes on added significance when one considers the tumult over busing in the South, as well as elsewhere in the nation. To their credit, the successful candidates did not try to exploit the issue. Roundly opposed by a wide spectrum of voters, busing offered tremendous political appeal. Bumpers, Askew, West, and Carter did a great service to the South by not pandering to these widespread resentments at a critical time in the South's political and racial development. Growing racial moderation among the people of the region could have deteriorated into the racial intolerance of old, especially with an issue as unpopular as busing. The men who would ultimately represent the New South, however, refused to encourage the furor over this court-ordered remedy.

While Arkansas's Orval Faubus ranted that his opposition to this objectionable measure qualified him to represent the state as governor, Dale Bumpers calmly pointed out that all the candidates opposed busing, but that until the Supreme Court ruled none of them could do anything about it. Bumpers expressed the sentiments of many in the southern electorate in his willingness to abide by the law. He also assured voters that they could trust him to do the right thing, without ever saying exactly what that might be.

Florida's Reubin Askew refused to compete in the busing melee initiated by Governor Claude Kirk. While conceding that Kirk may have voiced the sentiments of the majority of the people concerning busing, he emphasized that Kirk's goal was to garner headlines rather than solve the dilemmas of desegregation. Askew later explained his actions by contending that he could not allow "the emotions of the hour to become the legacy of a generation." Askew disapproved of busing, even though he, more than any other southern governor, would defend the necessity of busing. Governor Askew would later tell parents of his state: "Nobody really wants [busing] . . . yet the law demands, and rightly so, that we put an end to segregation in our society. We must demonstrate good faith in doing just that . . . we must stop inviting, by our own intransigence, devices which are repugnant to us. In this way and this way only will we stop massive busing . . . only in this way will we put the divisive and self-defeating issue of race behind us once and for all. And only in this way can we redirect our energies to our real quest—that of providing an equal opportunity for quality education to all of our children."[2]

During the campaign, however, Askew spoke very little about racial problems facing the state. Like Bumpers, he said only that he would work for solutions and not cause more problems.

In South Carolina, Albert Watson, a political protégé of Strom Thurmond, sought to test the limits of the Republican southern strategy. Watson called on the electorate to reject the more moderate stance of the recent Democratic administration. Like candidates in the other southern states, Watson chose busing as an issue through which to exploit the ambivalence of many whites over the pace of integration. An impassioned anti-busing speech by Watson led to violence. Pictures broadcast around the world of a white mob overturning buses that had carried black schoolchildren allowed John West to portray himself as someone who sought peaceful solutions to the integration problems without really offering what those solutions might be. Calling busing a "phony issue," West conceded that "we are all against busing," but he reminded voters that only the Supreme Court or Congress, and not the governor, could decide the issue. West promised that whatever was decided, his administration would not take any action that might harm public schools. West's approach reflected the sentiments of an electorate opposed to busing but committed to education.[3]

In Georgia, Jimmy Carter did not want to become embroiled in the busing debate. Because of the political realities he faced in that campaign Carter had to speak to the current fears of the segregationists without calling the racial shibboleths of the past out by name. He focused on resentments of class and avoided blatant racial appeals. In political forums when other candidates concentrated on busing, Carter pointed to estrangement of the common man from government decisions. He subtly appealed to the rancor of those whose wishes were ignored in racial matters, without alienating the growing moderate body of voters who saw the necessity for integration. The two-faceted campaign cost the moral-minded Jimmy Carter. But Carter, like the other New South candidates, knew he did not hold racist views and would, if elected, right many of the wrongs done to black citizens. Carter may have eased his moral dilemma by taking refuge in Reinhold Niebuhr's argument that in democracies perfection is never possible and that a moral man must content himself with accepting a necessary amount of compromise. Carter opened his 1975 autobiography, *Why Not the Best?*, with a quotation from Niebuhr: "The sad duty of politics is to establish justice in a sinful world."[4]

All of the South's successful gubernatorial candidates, in sum, refused to exploit the busing issue in 1970 and then delivered inaugural speeches announcing an end to state-sponsored racism. National ambitions shared by these young politicians militated against pandering to racial politics.

Their elections helped sustain the improving image of the South and thereby improved their own national political prospects. The success of these four New South governors also demonstrated the durability of moderation in the region. And finally, the elections signaled an end to the politics of persecution and defiance.

And yet, none of these men took firm stands on racial justice as candidates. Never publicly acknowledging racial antagonisms during their campaigns, all the successful southern gubernatorial candidates of 1970 tacitly acknowledged those fears by neglecting to reach out to black voters and by avoiding racially charged issues. The candidates realized that they could not alienate the large number of white voters who held reservations about busing and that the issue could destroy the region's newfound moderation. Although good intentions may have lain behind dodging issues such as busing, the avoidance also precluded any real effort to incorporate racial justice into their platforms. After examining the successful campaigns of 1970, one might applaud the transformation of southern politics, or one might come away saddened by the missed opportunity to end racial politics. These men realized they must first achieve electoral success before they could implement the benefits of the growing moderation of their states. And it must be remembered that all these men issued a repudiation of racial injustice in their inaugural addresses. It is difficult to lay blame on the shoulders of these men who did so much in office, but at least some of their campaigns set a precedent of evasion that future politicians followed nationwide. Real racial progress missed its chance. Renunciation of revived attempts to unite the white electorate in the name of resistance to integration succumbed to equivocation. In the future, electoral success would lie in subliminal appeals.

Rather than reaching out in an effort to unite, the representatives of the New South had finessed the issues and rested their appeal on their image. They called on voters to elect them because they could be trusted to do the right thing without ever asserting what the right thing might be. Different voters had different right things in mind. One of the losing candidates who sought to challenge the busing issue may have been prescient in his observations. Years after Reubin Askew unseated Florida's incumbent governor, Claude Kirk called Askew a "middle-of-the-road, don't-do-anything individual." Kirk asserted that the smiling "trust me" image that proved so successful for Askew, and the other New South candidates of 1970, masked an avoidance of controversy and damaged democracy. Askew, according to Kirk, "went in with [Jimmy] Carter—another smiling, 'Trust me' type of character. One shouldn't have been governor. The other shouldn't have been president. . . . Anytime you just sit around, eat hamburgers, and act like a good guy, you are letting cancers grow. . . . If you stand around and watch a bank robbery, you're not going to jail, but you ought to be ashamed of not picking up the telephone."

Kirk's mixed metaphor rings true. Perhaps malignancies were growing undetected within the body politic of the South. Maybe the voters were being robbed of the value that comes out of facing up to responsibility while these new politicians stood by silently. The days of the yelling southern demagogic race-baiter had ended. White southerners wanted to shed the image of noisy, violent resistance. The soft, smooth medium of television had changed the nature of politics. After 1970, when political operatives focused on these campaigns they saw the practical benefits of evasion. Subtle avoidance of racially charged issues appealed to an electorate that had grown weary of upheaval. In the long run, the new trend of political avoidance of race, of trying to mollify a moderate electorate that would accept integration as long as it did not lead to disruptions, may have encouraged attractive candidates with soothing voices to say nothing and exacerbate racial harmony by smoothing over festering problems.[5]

This work began with the words of a retired Georgia farmer. "Always before, you could tell right easy how somebody stood on the nigras," said the farmer, puzzled by the racial stance of the gubernatorial candidates during the 1970 campaign. "I don't say it isn't a good thing, but it does make for a mighty peculiar election." The farmer's statement reflected not only the ambivalence of the region in regard to racial moderation, but also the obfuscation of the politicians who sought to manipulate that ambivalence. Mighty peculiar elections indeed.

Notes

Chapter 1. Mighty Peculiar Elections

1. *New York Times*, October 15, 1970, 52.

2. Bartley and Graham, *Southern Politics and the Second Reconstruction*, 153.

3. *Louisville Courier-Journal*, January 23, 1971, A4.

4. Wicker, "New Mood in the South," sec. 4, p. 15; *Time*, May 31, 1971, 19, which is also the issue with Carter on the cover; *New York Times*, January 22, 1971, 39; Yoder, "Southern Governors," 161. For changes in the South as reflected by the elections of this new type of governor see also: Tyson, "'Politics of Fear,'" 9B; James Perry, "Jimmy Carter and a Changing South," 5; Murphy, "Southern Governors Speak Out," 4; Lindsay, "Southern Leaders Cool," 1; *Life*, January 29, 1971, 30–31; *Time*, May 31, 1971, 14–20; "Hope for a New South," 8.

5. *Arkansas Gazette*, January 13, 1971, 10A.

6. *Washington Post*, January 27, 1971, A18.

7. *New York Times*, January 20, 1971, 1/17.

8. *New York Times*, January 13, 1971, 1.

9. *Time*, May 31, 1971, 16; Clotfelter and Hamilton, "Beyond Race Politics," 156.

10. Kerner et al., *Report of the National Advisory Commission*, 1.

11. For a fuller explanation of southern politics in the decades leading up to 1970 see Lamis, *The Two Party South*; Black and Black, *Politics and Society in the South*; Bass and DeVries, *The Transformation of Southern Politics*; Bartley, *The New South*; Bartley and Graham, *Southern Politics and the Second Reconstruction*; and Havard, *The Changing Politics of the South*.

Chapter 2. The Other

1. *New York Times*, April 25, 1971, sec. 4, p. 15; "White Voices of the South," 164; *Time*, May 31, 1971, 16.

2. Gaston, *The New South Creed*, 7; Tindall, *The Emergence of the New South*, 70, 731.

3. Bevier, "Dear Dixie," 67; *New York Times*, October 25, 1970, sec. 4, p. 2; *Wall*

Street Journal, November 10, 1972, 1, 16; *U.S. News & World Report*, February 26, 1973, 53–55; *New York Times*, August 16, 1970, 1, 54; *New York Times*, July 4, 1972, 17; Bevier, "Dear Dixie," 64–67; Goldfield, *Black, White and Southern*, 171.

4. Reichley, *Conservatives in an Age of Change*, 183; Watters, "Southern Integrationists," 104.

5. *New York Times*, November 10, 1969, 39; *Arkansas Democrat*, August 19, 1979, 7A.

6. Cobb, *The Selling of the South*, 123, 129–30.

7. Rustin, "From Protest to Politics," 25; Jacoway, "Civil Rights and the Changing South," 1–14; Mathews and Prothro, *Negroes and the New South Politics*, 361–66.

8. *Time*, May 31, 1971, 16–17; Hornsby, "City Too Busy to Hate," 120–36; Brownell and Goldfield, *The City in Southern History*, 8.

9. *New York Times*, January 11, 1971, 19.

10. "White Voices of the South," 165–66.

11. Bass and DeVries, *The Transformation of Southern Politics*, 15; *New York Times*, May 9, 1971, sec. 4, p. 13; Broom and Glenn, "Negro-White Differences," 187.

12. *New York Times*, September 2, 1970, 36; *National Observer*, April 5, 1970, 5; *New York Times*, May 9, 1971, sec. 4, p. 13.

13. *New York Times*, October 25, 1970, sec. 4, p. 2.

14. Goldfield, *Promised Land*, 122; *New York Times*, June 3, 1970, 24; *New York Times*, November 10, 1969, 39.

15. *Florida Times Union*, January 15, 1970, B2.

16. Hall, *Oxford Companion to the Supreme Court*, 347.

17. *Facts on File*, 1969, 524.

18. *Facts on File*, 1969, 735; Bartley, *Creation of Modern Georgia*, 179.

19. *Tallahassee Democrat*, January 29, 1970, 4.

20. *Facts on File*, 1970, 69, 39.

21. Rilling, "Desegregation: The South *Is* Different," 18. See also: Richard Gergel, "School Desegregation," 34–38.

22. Black and Black, *Politics and Society*, 206; *New York Times*, May 3, 1970, 53; Smith, *Myth, Media and the Southern Mind*, 55; *Boston Globe*, December 28, 1970.

23. Bartley, *Rise of Massive Resistance*, 342–43.

24. Black and Black, *Politics and Society*, 199.

25. *U.S. News & World Report*, September 14, 1970, 15–16, 121; *Winston-Salem Journal*, August 19, 1970, 16; *Birmingham News*, August 23, 1970, 12; *Charlotte Observer*, September 6, 1970, 19A; *Richmond Times-Dispatch*, August 27, 1970, 1; *Charleston News & Courier*, October 17, 1970, 1B.

26. *New York Times*, September 3, 1969, 34; ibid., September 5, 1969, 1, 21; ibid., September 7, 1969, sec. 4, p. 4; *Time*, September 14, 1970, 39; *Washington Post*, January 27, 1971, A18.

27. *New York Times*, October 11, 1970, 58; *Birmingham News*, August 23, 1970, 12; *Charlotte Observer*, September 6, 1970, 9A; *U.S. News & World Report*, September 14, 1970, 52; *Washington Post*, September 7, 1970, A8; *Winston-Salem Journal*, August 19, 1970, 16.

28. Reed and Black, "Blacks and Southerners," 116–17.

29. *Atlanta Constitution*, February 7, 1971, 14A; "Black Voices of the South," 53.

30. *New York Times*, March 4, 1971, 1; *New York Times*, October 25, 1970, sec. 4, p. 2.

31. *U.S. News & World Report*, February 26, 1973, 54.

32. *New York Times*, August 16, 1970, 1, 54; *Chicago Tribune Magazine*, February 13, 1972, 67; *Wall Street Journal*, November 10, 1972, 16.

33. *Wall Street Journal*, November 10, 1972, 16; *Chicago Tribune Magazine*, February 13, 1972, 67.

34. *Chicago Tribune Magazine*, February 13, 1972, 67; Gallup, *The Gallup Poll 1935–1971*, vol. 3, August 15, 1971.

35. Yoder, "Southern Governors," 164–65.

36. *Atlanta Constitution*, August 22, 1971, 1A, 16A; Sabato, "New South Governors," 194–213.

37. Havard, "Intransigence to Transition," 519.

38. *Congressional Quarterly Weekly Report* 28 (April 3, 1970): 921–22; *New York Times*, October 11, 1970, 58; *U.S. News & World Report*, March 29, 1971, 23; *Atlanta Constitution*, August 22, 1971, 16A.

39. *Time*, May 31, 1971, 16; Clotfelter and Hamilton, "Beyond Race Politics," 156.

40. Clotfelter, "Populism in Office," 56–61; Carlson, *Wallace and the Politics of Powerlessness*, 17; Clotfelter and Hamilton, "Electing a Governor in the Seventies," 32–39; Clotfelter, Hamilton, and Harkins, "In Search of Populism," 9.

41. Sale, *Power Shift*, 104.

42. *Newsweek*, May 4, 1970, 108; Goldfield, *Black, White and Southern*, 179.

43. Bass and DeVries, *Transformation of Southern Politics*, 96, 262; Clotfelter and Hamilton, "Electing a Governor," 32–39; Sanders, "Sad Duty of Politics," 619.

44. Sanders, "Sad Duty of Politics," 622.

45. Goldfield, *Promised Land*, 188–89.

46. Bruce Campbell, "Patterns of Change," 730–61; Tindall, *Disruption of the Solid South*, 60.

47. Pomper, "From Confusion to Clarity," 415–28; Beck, "Partisan Dealignment," 489.

48. Beck, "Partisan Dealignment," 494, 496.

49. Bruce Campbell, "Patterns of Change," 730–61; Wolfinger and Arseneau, "Partisan Change in the South," 179–210; *U.S. News & World Report*, March 29, 1971, 23.

50. *New York Post*, February 12, 1970; *New York Times*, April 25, 1971, sec. 4, p. 15.

51. *Miami Herald*, April 5, 1971, 9B; *National Observer*, April 5, 1970, 5.

52. Kerner et al., *Report of the National Advisory Commission on Civil Disorders*, 1.

53. "White Voices of the South," 164.

54. Goldfield, *Promised Land*, 132.

55. Goldfield, *Promised Land*, 128.

56. Dearmore, "First Angry Man," 32–33; memorandum from Richard Nixon to H. R. Haldeman, February 9, 1970, box 229, Haldeman files, Nixon Presidential Materials; Haldeman, *The Haldeman Diaries: Inside the Nixon White House*, 136, 151; Kirby, *Media Made Dixie*, 136; Gergel, "School Desegregation," 69; Malone, *Country Music, U.S.A.*, 317–19; Malone, "The Rural South Moves to the City," 115.

Chapter 3. Arkansas

1. Peirce, *The Deep South States of America*, 130; *New York Times*, December 15, 1994, 1, B21; Donovan, Gatewood, and Whayne, *The Governors of Arkansas*, 225–35.

2. *New York Times*, December 15, 1994, 1, B21; Donovan, Gatewood, and Whayne, *Governors of Arkansas*, 225–35.

3. *Arkansas Gazette*, August 2, 1956.

4. Havard, *Changing Politics of the South*, 271. For an interpretation of events that spreads the blame around, see Bartley, "Looking Back At Little Rock," 101–16. See also Freyer, *The Little Rock Crisis: A Constitutional Interpretation*.

5. Havard, *Changing Politics*, 271; Peirce, *Deep South*, 132.

6. Peirce, *Deep South*, 132.

7. Havard, *Changing Politics*, 272; Ranchino, *Faubus to Bumpers*, 29.

8. *New York Times*, December 15, 1994, B21.

9. Havard, *Changing Politics*, 273; Ward, *The Arkansas Rockefeller*, 160, 60.

10. Peirce, *Deep South*, 131, 133.

11. *Arkansas Gazette*, May 2, 1970, 1–2A.

12. *Arkansas Gazette*, May 2, 1970, 1–2A; Voter and Issue Research Associates, "1970 Issues Opinion Poll," series 5, subseries 8, box 89, folder 5, Orval Faubus Papers.

13. Oliver Quayle and Company, "A Survey of the Political Climate in Arkansas," October 1968, series 29, box 1002, folder ll, Faubus Papers.

14. *Arkansas Gazette*, May 2, 1970, 2A.

15. *Arkansas Gazette*, May 2, 1970, 1A–2A; *New York Times*, May 21, 1970, 40.

16. *Arkansas Gazette*, August 16, 1970, 10A–11A.

17. *New York Times*, July 28, 1970, 10; ibid., August 26, 1970, 1.

18. Faubus campaign flyer, series 5, subseries 8, box 84, folder 3, Faubus Papers.

19. *Arkansas Gazette*, August 19, 1970, 13A.

20. "The Arkansas Press: Editorial Comment at End of Campaigns," *Arkansas Gazette*, August 23, 1970, 3E.

21. Donovan, Gatewood, and Whayne, *Governors of Arkansas*, 246–47.

22. Donovan, Gatewood, and Whayne, *Governors of Arkansas*, 247.

23. *Arkansas Gazette*, May 22, 1970, 2A; Dale Bumpers, interview by author; *Arkansas Gazette*, June 13, 1970, 3A; ibid., July 19, 1970, 3A; ibid., August 5, 1970, 2A; ibid., August 16, 1970, 10A.

24. Douglass Bradley to Orval Faubus, August 28, 1970, series 5, subseries 8, box 87, folder 9, Faubus Papers.

25. Donovan, Gatewood, and Whayne, *Governors of Arkansas*, 248; *Arkansas Gazette*, May 22, 1970, 2A; ibid., June 13, 1970, 3A; ibid., July 19, 1970, 3A; ibid., August 5, 1970, 2A; ibid., August 16, 1970, 10A.

26. Dale Bumpers, interview by author; Deloss Walker, interview by author; Ernie Dumas, interview by author; Archie Schaffer, interview by author; *Arkansas Gazette*, September 4, 1970, 1B.

27. Dale Bumpers, interview by author; *New York Times*, September 10, 1970, 38; Peirce, *Deep South*, 134.

28. Dale Bumpers, interview by author; Deloss Walker, interview by author; *Arkansas Gazette*, August 16, 1970, 10A.

29. *Arkansas Gazette*, August 20, 1970, 1A; Ernie Dumas, interview by author.

30. *Arkansas Gazette*, August 20, 1970, 1A; Ernie Dumas, interview by author; *Arkansas Gazette*, August 16, 1970, 10A.

31. *Arkansas Gazette*, August 20, 1970, 1A.

32. *Arkansas Gazette*, August 21, 1970, 6A.

33. Deloss Walker, interview by author; Ranchino, *Faubus to Bumpers*, 67; group IV, box 82, file 4, Winthrop Rockefeller Papers.

34. *Arkansas Gazette*, November 14, 1970, 3A; Ranchino, *Faubus to Bumpers*, 67; *Arkansas Gazette*, August 30, 1970, 2A; Dale Bumpers, interview by author.

35. *Arkansas Gazette*, August 27, 1970, 2A; Dale Bumpers, interview by author; *Arkansas Gazette*, September 6,1970, 2D.

36. *Arkansas Gazette*, August 28, 1970, 1A; ibid., September 5, 1970, 1A; text of Faubus television speech in series 5, subseries 8, box 91, folder 1, Faubus Papers; *Arkansas Gazette*, August 30, 1970, 2E.

37. *Arkansas Gazette*, August 28, 1970, 1A; letter to Faubus, August 21, 1970, series 5, subseries 8, box 87, folder 8, Faubus Papers; *Arkansas Gazette*, August 30, 1970, 2A; ibid., August 28, 1970, 2A.

38. *Arkansas Gazette*, August 30, 1970, 3E; Dale Bumpers, interview by author; *Arkansas Gazette*, August 27, 1970, 2A.

39. *Arkansas Gazette*, August 30, 1970, 1A; Citizens Council questionnaire, series 5, subseries 8, box 84, folder 2, Faubus Papers.

40. *Arkansas Gazette*, September 4, 1970, 1A; ibid., August 30, 1970, 1A, 2A, 3E; ibid., August 31, 1970, 4A.

41. *Arkansas Gazette*, August 31, 1970, 1A, 2A; ibid., August 30, 1970, 2A, 5A; ibid., September 13, 1970, 6A; ibid., August 31, 1970, 1A, 2A; ibid., September 3, 1970, 1A; ibid., September 8, 1970, 1A.

42. Faubus advertisement in series 5, subseries 8, box 84, folder 3, Faubus Papers; *Arkansas Gazette*, September 7, 1970, 1A, 2A.

43. *Arkansas Gazette*, September 1, 1970, 1A.

44. *Arkansas Gazette*, August 29, 1970, 4A; ibid., September 4, 1970, 1B; ibid., August 30, 1970, 2A, 3E; *McGehee Times*, September 2, 1970; *Arkansas Gazette*, August 31, 1970, 4A; *Helena-West Helena World*, September 2, 1970; *Eagle Democrat* (Warren, Arkansas), September 2, 1970; *Times* (North Little Rock), September 3, 1970.

45. *Arkansas Gazette*, September 7, 1970, 1A.

46. *Arkansas Gazette*, September 1, 1970, 1A; ibid., September 2, 1970, 1A; *Commercial Appeal*, September 6, 1970.

47. Faubus to Carter Jenkins, September 28, 1970, series 5, subseries 8, box 88, Faubus Papers; *Arkansas Gazette*, September 9, 1970, 1A.

48. *Time*, September 21, 1970, 16; *Arkansas Gazette*, September 10, 1970, 6A.

49. Dale Bumpers, interview by author.

50. *Conway Democrat*, September 10, 1970, 12; series 5, subseries 8, box 88, folder 1–2, Faubus Papers; *Arkansas Gazette*, September 9, 1970, 1A; Ray Curtis to Orval Faubus, September 10, 1970, series 5, subseries 8, box 88, folder 1, Faubus Papers; Donovan, Gatewood, and Whayne, *Governors of Arkansas*, 248.

51. *New York Times*, September 10, 1970, 38; *Arkansas Gazette*, September 11, 1970, 1A; ibid., September 10, 1970, 1A, 12A.

52. *Arkansas Gazette*, September 16, 1970, 6A; ibid., September 18, 1970, 6A; September 20, 1970, 3E; *New York Times*, September 11, 1970, 40.

53. Peirce, *Deep South*, 134–36.

54. *New York Times*, December 6, 1970, 36; Peirce, *Deep South*, 136–37.

55. Urwin, *Agenda for Reform*, 32–42, 47; Donovan, Gatewood, and Whayne, *Governors of Arkansas*, 240; James Perry, *The New Politics*, 139–40.

56. Urwin, *Agenda for Reform*, 48–49; Peirce, *Deep South*, 139.

57. Ward, *Arkansas Rockefeller*, 48–49.

58. Urwin, *Agenda for Reform*, 49.

59. Ranchino, *Faubus to Bumpers*, 37–38; Peirce, *Deep South*, 139; Urwin, *Agenda for Reform*, 48, 53.

60. *Ripon Forum*, July-August 1970, 23, MSS 158, box 5, folder 180, Harry Dent Papers, Clemson University; Donovan, Gatewood, and Whayne, *Governors of Arkansas*, 240–41.

61. Ward, *Arkansas Rockefeller*, 49, 55–60.

62. Peirce, *Deep South*, 139; Ranchino, *Faubus to Bumpers*, 41–43; Ward, *Arkansas Rockefeller*, 55–60. See also Lisenby, "Winthrop Rockefeller and the Arkansas Image," 143–52.

63. Urwin, *Agenda for Reform*, 56.

64. Peirce, *Deep South*, 140–41.

65. "A Survey of the Political Climate of Arkansas," October 1968, Oliver Quayle poll for Democratic Committee of Arkansas, series 29, box 1002, Faubus Papers; Urwin, *Agenda for Reform*, 110–11; Ward, *Arkansas Rockefeller*, 117.

66. Urwin, *Agenda for Reform*, 111, 234 note 90; Ward, *Arkansas Rockefeller*, 126–28; Ranchino, *Faubus to Bumpers*, 49–51.

67. *Ripon Forum*, July-August 1970, 25, MSS 158, box 5, folder 180, Dent Papers, Clemson University; Ranchino, *Faubus to Bumpers*, 50–51.

68. Peirce, *Deep South*, 141.

69. Ward, *Arkansas Rockefeller*, 132–33.

70. Donovan, Gatewood, and Whayne, *Governors of Arkansas*, 244.

71. Ward, *Arkansas Rockefeller*, 179–80; Urwin, *Agenda for Reform*, 174–75.

72. Urwin, *Agenda for Reform*, 175; Ward, *Arkansas Rockefeller*, 182–83.

73. Memorandum for the Vice President from Harry Dent, October 6, 1970, MSS 158, box 4, folder 106, Dent Papers, Clemson University; Mid-South Opinion Surveys, September 13, 1970, Record Group IV, box 82, Rockefeller Papers.

74. *Arkansas Gazette*, September 11, 1970, 1A.

75. Mid-South Opinion Surveys, October 1–3, 1970, Record Group IV, box 82, Rockefeller Papers.

76. Mid-South Opinion Surveys, October 1–3, 1970, and October 13–15, 1970, Record Group IV, box 82, Rockefeller Papers.

77. Ranchino, *Faubus to Bumpers*, 69–70.

78. *Arkansas Gazette*, September 21, 1970, 1A; ibid., September 27, 1970, 3E.

79. *Washington Post*, November 1, 1970, 1, 14; *Arkansas Gazette*, October 29, 1970, 1–2A; ibid., October 31, 1970, 1A; Donovan, Gatewood, and Whayne, *Governors of Arkansas*, 249; *Commercial Appeal*, January 1, 1971.

80. *Arkansas Gazette*, October 13, 1970, 6A.

81. *Arkansas Gazette*, October 8, 1970, 6A; ibid., September 30, 1970, 6A.

82. Ward, *Arkansas Rockefeller*, 165–67.

83. McGraw, Stockley, and Williams, "We Speak for Ourselves," 40–43; *Arkansas Gazette*, August 20, 1969, 6A; Ward, *Arkansas Rockefeller*, 170–74; *Arkansas Gazette*, October 23, 1970, 6A. See also "Mob Rule in Forrest City," 84; *Washington Post*, October 12, 1969, C1, C5.

84. Winthrop Rockefeller to Jerris Leonard, April 3, 1970, Record Group III, box 521, folder 1, Rockefeller Papers; *Arkansas Gazette*, April 4, 1970; *New York Times*, June 28, 1969, 12.

85. *New York Times*, September 18, 1969, 50; Ward, *Arkansas Rockefeller*, 176; *Arkansas Gazette*, January 24, 1970; Rockefeller statement on busing, February 21, 1970, Record Group IV, box 165, folder 4, Rockefeller Papers; *Pine Bluff Commercial*, February 24, 1970; memo from Harry Dent to Larry Higby in White House, box 7, folder 212, Dent Papers, Clemson University; *Arkansas Gazette*, September 30, 1970, 2A.

86. Peirce, *Deep South*, 142; *Arkansas Gazette*, October 25, 1970, 3E.

87. *Arkansas Gazette*, October 7, 1970, 1B; ibid., October 22, 1970, 23A.

88. *Arkansas Gazette*, October 27, 1970, 1A, 4A; ibid., October 29, 1970, 2A.

89. Hammons, "Campaign Communication Strategies," 68; *Arkansas Gazette*, October 29, 1970, 2A; ibid., November 1, 1970, 4A; ibid., October 29, 1970, 2A.

90. *Arkansas Gazette*, October 27, 1970, 1A, 4A; ibid., October 25, 1970, 3E.

91. *Arkansas Gazette*, November 5, 1970, 1A, 2A; ibid., November 15, 1970, 14A; Ranchino, *Faubus to Bumpers*, 71.

92. *Arkansas Gazette*, November 14, 1970, 3A; *Washington Post*, November 1, 1970, 1, 14; *Arkansas Gazette*, November 8, 1970, 3E.

93. Ranchino, *Faubus to Bumpers*, 71; *Arkansas Gazette*, November 15, 1970, 14A; *Washington Post*, August 4, 1971, A1, A11.

94. Peirce, *Deep South*, 147.

Chapter 4. Florida

1. Key, *Southern Politics in State and Nation*, 83; Bass and DeVries, *Transformation of Southern Politics*, 109, 503; Cobb, *Selling of the South*, 180; Bass and DeVries, *Transformation of Southern Politics*, 108; Tebeau, *A History of Florida*, 431.

2. Bass and DeVries, *Transformation of Southern Politics*, 108–9, 503; Tebeau, *A History of Florida*, 449, 434–35.

3. Colburn and Scher, *Florida's Gubernatorial Politics*, 225.

4. Tebeau, *A History of Florida*, 449; *Tallahassee Democrat*, January 12, 1970, 10.

5. Klingman, *Neither Dies nor Surrenders*, 168–69.

6. Klingman, *Neither Dies nor Surrenders*, 172–74.

7. *Florida Times Union*, April 11, 1970, B4.

8. Klingman, *Neither Dies nor Surrenders*, 175–76.

9. Kallina, *Politics of Confrontation*, 186–87; *Ripon Forum*, July-August 1970, 33.

10. Kallina, *Politics of Confrontation*, 190–91; *Tallahassee Democrat*, April 21, 1970, 1, 8.

11. *Tallahassee Democrat*, April 21, 1970, 1, 8.

12. *Tallahassee Democrat*, April 21, 1970, 1; ibid., April 23, 1970, 27; ibid., April 27, 1970, 1.

13. *St. Petersburg Times*, April 21, 1970, 1A, 4A; *Tallahassee Democrat*, April 21, 1970, 20; *St. Petersburg Times*, April 21, 1970, 1A, 4A, 6A; *Tallahassee Democrat*, April 21, 1970, 8.

14. *St. Petersburg Times*, April 21, 1970, 1A.

15. Harry Dent, memo to Bob Haldeman, March 5, 1970, MSS 158, box 4, folder 130, Dent Papers, Clemson University; *St. Petersburg Times*, April 24, 1970, 1A, 6A; ibid., April 25, 1970, 7A; ibid., April 26, 1970, 5B.

16. *St. Petersburg Times*, April 24, 1970, 1A, 6A; *Tallahassee Democrat*, April 24, 1970, 1.

17. *Tallahassee Democrat*, April 26, 1970, 8A.

18. *Tallahassee Democrat*, January 14, 1970, 17; *Florida Times Union*, January 15, 1970, B2; *Tallahassee Democrat*, January 11, 1970, 1C; ibid., January 17, 1970, 4.

19. *Ripon Forum*, July-August 1970, 32; *Tallahassee Democrat*, January 25, 1970, 1A; Reubin Askew, interview by author; Tindall, *Disruption of the Solid South*, 60.

20. *Miami Herald*, January 14, 1970, 1, 4A; *Tallahassee Democrat*, January 14, 1970, 1, 8.

21. *Tallahassee Democrat*, January 14, 1970, 9; ibid., January 16, 1970, 4.

22. *Miami Herald*, January 15, 1970, 24A; *Florida Times Union*, January 15, 1970, B2.

23. *Tallahassee Democrat*, January 15, 1970, 1, 8; ibid., January 21, 1970, 9.

24. *Tallahassee Democrat*, January 15, 1970, 15; ibid., January 16, 1970, 4.

25. *Florida Times Union*, January 15, 1970, B2.

26. Claude Kirk, "A Desegregation Plan for the Manatee County Public Schools," January 1970, Manatee County 1970 folder, box 78, series 923, Claude Kirk Papers; Reubin Askew, interview by author; *Tallahassee Democrat*, January 19, 1970, 1; *Florida Times Union*, January 20, 1970, B2; *Tallahassee Democrat*, January 20, 1970, 1, 10.

27. *Tallahassee Democrat*, January 20, 1970 2, 5.

28. *Tallahassee Democrat*, January 20, 1970, 11; ibid., January 21, 1970, 2; *Florida Times Union*, January 22,1970, A1; *Tallahassee Democrat*, January 21, 1970, 9.

29. *Tallahassee Democrat*, January 21, 1970, 9; *Florida Times Union*, January 24, 1970, A1; *Tallahassee Democrat*, January 22, 1970, 15; ibid., January 24, 1970, 1.

30. *St. Petersburg Times*, January 24, 1970, 1A, 10A; ibid., January 25, 1970, 1B.

31. *Tallahassee Democrat*, January 25, 1970, 1A; *Florida Times Union*, February 1, 1970, C1.

32. *St. Petersburg Times*, January 24, 1970, 10A.

33. *Florida Times Union*, January 27, 1970, B2; *Tallahassee Democrat*, January 27, 1970, 4; *Florida Times Union*, January 29, 1970, B2.

34. *Florida Times Union*, February 2, 1970, B2; ibid., February 3, 1970, A1, B2; ibid., February 4, 1970, A1, A2.

35. *Florida Times Union*, February 15, 1970, C2; ibid., March 2, 1970, B2; ibid., February 15, 1970, C2.

36. *Tallahassee Democrat*, April 7, 1970, 1; Floyd Christian to Claude Kirk, April 2, 1970, Record Group 102, series 926, box 2, Kirk Papers. See also *New York Times*, April 6–14, 1970; *Television News Index and Abstracts*, April 6–14, 1970; *Time*, April 6, 13, 20, 27, 1970; *Newsweek*, April 6, 13, 20, 27, 1970.

37. *St. Petersburg Times*, April 6, 1970, 1B, 3B; *New York Times*, April 8, 1970, 1; ibid., April 6, 1970, 1, 23; "Executive Order," April 5, 1970, series 926, box 3, Kirk Papers.

38. *Florida Times Union*, April 7, 1970, A1, B5; *Tallahassee Democrat*, April 7, 1970, 1.

39. *St. Petersburg Times*, April 12, 1970, 1B; *Florida Times Union*, April 12, 1970, B3; *St. Petersburg Times*, April 10, 1970, 1B; *Tallahassee Democrat*, April 10, 1970, 1.

40. *St. Petersburg Times*, April 12, 1970, 1B, 2B, 3B; ibid., April 7, 1970, 1A, 9A 14A; *Tallahassee Democrat*, April 7, 1970, 1.

41. *Florida Times Union*, April 7, 1970, B1, B5; Reubin Askew, interview by author.

42. *New York Times*, April 7, 1970, 1, 28; *Florida Times Union*, April 10, 1970, B3; *St. Petersburg Times*, April 14, 1970, 8A.

43. *New York Times*, April 8, 1970, 1, 24; Manatee County Emergency Proclamation, April 9, 1970, series 926, box 3, Kirk Papers; *New York Times*, April 9, 1970, 1, 33; *Tallahassee Democrat*, April 9, 1970, 1; *New York Times*, April 10, 1970, 1, 18; *Florida Times Union*, April 10, 1970, A1; *Time*, April 20, 1970, 16.

44. *St. Petersburg Times*, April 10, 1970, 1A, 9A; *New York Times*, April 9, 1970, 1, 33; *Florida Times Union*, April 10, 1970, A1.

45. *New York Times*, April 11, 1970, 12; *Florida Times Union*, April 11, 1970, A1.

46. Judge Ben Krentzman, Order to hold Claude Kirk in civil contempt and fined $10,000 per day, April 11, 1970, series 926, box 3, Kirk Papers; *Florida Times Union*, April 12, 1970, A1; *New York Times*, April 13, 1970, 30.

47. Certificate from Gerald Mager, legal counsel, to Governor Kirk, complying with Judge Krentzman's order, April 13, 1970, series 926, box 3, Kirk Papers; *New York Times*, April 12, 1970, 1, 31; ibid., April 13, 1970, 1, 30.

48. *New York Times*, April 14, 1970, 37; *St. Petersburg Times*, April 14, 1970, 1A, 4A.

49. *Florida Times Union*, April 11, 1970, B2; *St. Petersburg Times*, April 11, 1970, 15A; ibid., April 10, 1970, 18A; *Florida Times Union*, April 11, 1970, A8; ibid., April 14, 1970, A4.

50. Harry Dent, memo to Richard Nixon, May 1, 1970, MSS 155, box 4, folder 130, Dent Papers, Clemson University. To illustrate the preponderance of out-of-state support for Kirk in the letters to the governor, one folder contained thirty-seven letters from outside the state favoring Kirk's anti-busing stance with only one from Florida. Another folder contained forty-seven letters. Twenty-four of these letters favored Kirk, with only one of those from inside the state. In the same folder twenty-three Floridians expressed disapproval. "Correspondence on Busing Incoming," Record Group 102, series 923, boxes 14–16, Kirk Papers; *Tallahassee Democrat*, April 13, 1970, 4.

51. *St. Petersburg Times*, April 17, 1970, 3B; *Tallahassee Democrat*, April 17, 1970, 9.

52. *Florida Times Union*, April 15, 1970, B2; *St. Petersburg Times*, April 15, 1970, 1B; *Tallahassee Democrat*, April 19, 1970, 2C.

53. *Florida Times Union*, April 21, 1970, 1A; ibid., September 5, 1970, B3; ibid., October 16, 1970, B1; ibid., October 17, 1970, B2; ibid., October 24, 1970, B1; ibid., October 23, 1970, B4; *Tallahassee Democrat*, July 28, 1970, 1; ibid., July 19, 1970, 12A; ibid., July 5, 1970, 3B; ibid., July 17, 1970, 2; *Florida Times Union*, July 25, 1970, B2; ibid., August 20, 1970, B4.

54. *Florida Times Union*, July 24, 1970, C14; ibid., August 1, 1970, B2; ibid., August 7, 1970, B2; *Tallahassee Democrat*, July 3, 1970, 1, 9.

55. *Florida Times Union*, August 23, 1970, B3; *Tallahassee Democrat*, July 26, 1970, 11A; ibid., July 29, 1970, 16.

56. *Florida Times Union,* February 12, 1970, B3.

57. Nordheimer, "'Supersquare,'" 11, 52–54; Reubin Askew, interview by author; *Florida Times Union,* February 15, 1970, C3.

58. Reubin Askew, interview by author; Nordheimer, "'Supersquare,'" 52–53.

59. *Florida Times Union,* August 3, 1970, B2; *St. Petersburg Times,* April 27, 1970, 1B; *Florida Times Union,* August 1, 1970, B2; ibid., August 20, 1970, B4; ibid., August 23, 1970, B3; Reubin Askew, interview by author.

60. "Florida Report," June 18, 1970, MSS 158, box 4, folder 130, Dent Papers, Clemson University; *Florida Times Union,* November 4, 1970, B2; "Press Releases Askew-Adams 1970 Campaign," Record Group 9000, series 849, box 5, Askew Papers.

61. Colburn and Scher, *Florida's Gubernatorial Politics,* 85; Reubin Askew, interview by author; *St. Petersburg Times,* September 14, 1970, 1B; *Florida Times Union,* August 22, 1970, B2; *Miami Herald,* September 17, 1970, 1.

62. Press release, Askew speaking in Sarasota, Florida, October 14, 1970, "Askew-Adams 1970 Campaign," Record Group 103, series 849, box 5, Askew Papers; *Florida Times Union,* August 22, 1970, B2; ibid., September 21, 1970, B2; ibid., August 20, 1970, B4; ibid., August 29, 1970, B2; ibid., October 21, 1970, B3; *St. Petersburg Times,* September 10, 1970, 18A.

63. "Press Releases: Askew-Adams 1970 Campaign," Record Group 90000, series 849, box 5, Askew Papers.

64. Kallina, *Politics of Confrontation,* 187–88.

65. *St. Petersburg Times,* September 10, 1970, 1A, 11A.

66. *Florida Times Union,* September 13, 1970, B2; ibid., September 12, 1970, B2.

67. *Florida Times Union,* September 24, 1970, B3; ibid., September 20, 1970, B3.

68. Bartley and Graham, *Southern Elections,* 60.

69. *Tallahassee Democrat,* July 15, 1970, 1, 8; ibid., July 17, 1970, 8; *Florida Times Union,* August 9, 1970, D4.

70. *Florida Times Union,* November 3, 1970, B3; Kallina, *Politics of Confrontation,* 193.

71. *Florida Times Union,* October 1, 1970, 1.

72. *Florida Times Union,* October 4, 1970, B5; Colburn and Scher, *Florida's Gubernatorial Politics,* 81–83.

73. *Florida Times Union,* October 20, 1970, B3; ibid., October 25, 1970, B11; ibid., February 12, 1970, B3; *Atlanta Journal and Constitution,* August 22, 1971, 16A; Nordheimer, "'Supersquare,'" 11, 52–54; *Florida Times Union,* February 15, 1970, C3.

74. *Florida Times Union,* October 25, 1970, B11.

75. *Florida Times Union,* October 12, 1970, A1, A10.

76. *Florida Times Union,* October 28, 1970, C3; ibid., October 21, 1970, B3; ibid., October 17, 1970, B1; ibid., November 5, 1970, B4.

77. *Florida Times Union*, October 10, 1970, B3; ibid., October 25, 1970, B11; ibid., October 19, 1970, B2.

78. Reubin Askew, interview by author; *Florida Times Union*, October 22, 1970, B2; 1970 Campaign Pledges, "Askew Press & Public Relations," Record Group 90000, series 849, box 1, Askew Papers; *St. Petersburg Times*, November 1, 1970, 11A; *Florida Times Union*, October 20, 1970, B3; ibid., October 21, 1970, B3.

79. *Florida Times Union*, October 25, 1970, A1; ibid., October 26, 1970, B2; ibid., October 18, 1970, B6; ibid., October 27, 1970, B2.

80. *Florida Times Union*, October 19, 1970, B2; ibid., October 21, 1970, B3.

81. *Florida Times Union*, October 23, 1970, B4; ibid., October 28, 1970, C3; press release of Florida press editorials, no date, *Gainesville Sun*, "Press releases: Askew-Adams 1970 Campaign," Record Group 90000, series 849, box 5, Askew Papers; *St. Petersburg Times*, November 1, 1970, 11A; *Florida Times Union*, October 25, 1970, D3.

82. *Florida Times Union*, October 25, 1970, D4; ibid., October 27, 1970, B2; Kallina, *Politics of Confrontation*, 194.

83. *Florida Times Union*, November 5, 1970, B2.

84. *Florida Times Union*, November 4, 1970, B2; ibid., November 5, 1970, B4.

85. Kirk's concession that his loss was due to racial emphasis is in *Washington Post*, January 27, 1971, A18.

86. Reubin Askew, interview by author.

87. Reubin Askew, interview by author.

88. Ayers and Naylor, *You Can't Eat Magnolias*, 362; Nordheimer, "'Super-square,'" 57.

Chapter 5. South Carolina

1. Key, *Southern Politics in State and Nation*, 131.

2. Bass and DeVries, *Transformation of Southern Politics*, 258, 256.

3. *Florida Times Union*, January 24, 1970, A1, A11; Bass, *Porgy Comes Home*, 78; *Ripon Forum*, July-August 1970, 65.

4. *Facts on File*, 1970, 39, 54; Bass and DeVries, *Transformation of Southern Politics*, 260; Bass, *Porgy Comes Home*, 68–69; *Wall Street Journal*, October 28, 1970, 18.

5. Bass, *Porgy Comes Home*, 76, 71, 73.

6. Spivey and Voreis, "A Study of Voting Behavior of Laurens County," February 13, 1970, folder 136, James Duffy Papers.

7. John F. Kraft, Inc., "A Study of Attitudes of Voters in South Carolina," June 1970, Personal, 1970 Campaign Records, topical files, South Carolina Voter Attitudes, John West Papers.

8. *New York Times*, November 30, 1969, 111.

9. Watson congressional campaign flyer, n.d., series V, reel 31, Congress of Racial Equality Papers on microfilm, Amistad Research Center, Tulane University; flyer dated August 1970, "Citizens for Watson," folder 141, Duffy Papers;

New York Times, November 30, 1969, 111; *Piedmont*, November 19, 1969; *New York Times*, March 22, 1970, 44.

10. *New York Times*, November 30, 1970, 111; *Piedmont*, December 9, 1969, 2.

11. *Greenville News*, December 19, 1969; ibid., March 7, 1968; both in folder 143, Duffy Papers.

12. Arthur Ravenel to William B. DePass, Jr., December 23, 1969, folder 134, Duffy Papers; Arthur Ravenel to Harry Dent, January 13, 1970, box 6, folder 207, Dent Papers, Clemson University.

13. James Duffy to Harry Bandouvers, February 13, 1970, folder 136, Duffy Papers; James Duffy to Richard Hines, January 31, 1970, folder 135, Duffy Papers.

14. *Los Angeles Times*, October 11, 1970, 4A.

15. *Tiger*, February 20, 1970, folder 143, Duffy Papers.

16. Invitation letter from Dennis Moore, January 7, 1970, folder 135, Duffy Papers.

17. An open letter to the editor of the *State* by William Hunter, March 17, 1970, box 6, Campaigns, 1970, William Workman Papers; letters in folder 134–35, Duffy Papers.

18. Arthur Ravenel to Harry Dent, January 13, 1970, box 6, folder 207, Dent Papers, Clemson University.

19. James Duffy to Arthur Ravenel, February 27, 1970, folder 137, Duffy Papers; John West, interview by author; letters in box 23, folder labeled "political affairs—campaigns—April to December 1970," Strom Thurmond Papers.

20. Ike McLeese, undated memo to John West, "In regards to our strategy meeting scheduled for the 3rd of August . . ." Personal, 1970 Campaign Records, topical files, Organization: Strategy: Committee, West Papers.

21. John West, interview by author.

22. Bass and DeVries, *Transformation of Southern Politics*, 258; John F. Kraft, Inc., "A Study of Attitudes of Voters in South Carolina," June 1970, Personal, 1970 Campaign Records, topical files, South Carolina Voter Attitudes, West Papers.

23. Text of statement by Lt. Governor John West, Columbia Exchange Club, February 23, 1970, Personal, 1970 Campaign Records, West Press Releases, 1970: Issued February-June, West Papers; *New York Times*, February 24, 1970, 28; *Piedmont*, February 24, 1970, 7.

24. *Charlotte Observer*, February 23, 1970, and *Piedmont*, February 24, 1970, both articles in folder 143, Duffy Papers; Bass, *Porgy Comes Home*, 390.

25. James Duffy to Arthur Ravenel, February 25, 1970, folder 137, Duffy Papers.

26. Thurmond news release, March 5, 1970, box 6, folder 207, Dent Papers, Clemson University; *Washington Post*, March 7, 1970, A3.

27. *State*, March 4, 1970, 12A.

28. *Television News Index and Abstracts*, March 2–5, 1970.

29. *Washington Post*, March 7, 1970, A3; Thurmond news release, March 5, 1970, box 6, folder 207, Dent Papers, Clemson University. See also South Carolina

Republican Party press release, March 9, 1970, "Republican Party of S.C.: News Releases, 1970" folder, box 2, Workman Papers.

30. Typed letter with "Confidential" handwritten across top, from Llewellyn ? to Bill ?, March 2, 1970, folder 138, Duffy Papers.

31. Mary Daniel to James Duffy, March 12, 1970, folder 138, Duffy Papers.

32. Duffy, memo, March 12, 1970, folder 138, Duffy Papers; Duffy to Harry Bandouveris, March 25, 1970, folder 138, Duffy Papers.

33. Arthur Ravenel to Colonel C. A. Nelson, March 11, 1970, folder 138, Duffy Papers.

34. South Carolina Republican Party press release, October 1, 1970, "Republican Party of SC: News Releases, 1970" folder, box 2, Workman Papers; "Statement of Principles" adopted by South Carolina Republican Convention, March 21, 1970, folder 138, Duffy Papers.

35. Harry Dent to Albert Watson, April 27, 1970, box 6, folder 207, Dent Papers, Clemson University.

36. South Carolina *Republican Newsletter*, September 10, 1970, 2–3, folder 141, Duffy Papers; Cohodas, *Strom Thurmond*, 411; Hubert Humphrey to John West, February 24, 1970, Personal, 1970 Campaign Records: February folder, West Papers; West response to Humphrey, March 3, 1970, Personal, 1970 Campaign Records: March folder, West Papers; "Fact Sheet: Humphrey, Wilkins, and West," Personal, 1970 Campaign Records, topical files: Albert Watson, West Papers.

37. "Fact Sheet: Humphrey, Wilkins, and West," Personal, 1970 Campaign Records, topical files: Albert Watson, West Papers; Cohodas, *Strom Thurmond*, 411; *State*, November 1, 1970, 8A; ibid., October 31, 1970, 3A.

38. *State*, November 1, 1970, 8A; ibid., October 31, 1970, 3A.

39. "Confidential summary and analysis of responses for appraisal of the campaign," Personal, 1970 Campaign Records, topical files, Organization: Strategy Committee, West Papers.

40. Cook/Ruef & Associates memo, no date, Personal, 1970 Campaign Records, topical files, Organization: Strategy, West Papers; "Desegregation in South Carolina," March 19, 1970, Public, topical files: School Desegregation: March-April 1970, West Papers.

41. Cook/Ruef & Associates memo, no date, Personal, 1970 Campaign Records, topical files, Organization: Strategy, West Papers; "Desegregation in South Carolina," March 19, 1970, Public, topical files: School Desegregation: March-April 1970, West Papers; press release, July 10, 1970, Public, Lt. Gov. Press Releases, West Papers; *Charleston News & Courier*, July 11, 1970, 1; *Charlotte Observer*, July 12, 1970, 1C.

42. *Charleston News & Courier*, July 17, 1970, 1B.

43. Letters in Public, Lt. Governor, 1967–71: General Correspondence: Greenville County: January-March 1970, West Papers; and in 1970 West Campaign: 1968–69 folder, West Papers; John West, interview by author; Bass and DeVries, *Transformation*, 262; *Charleston News & Courier*, July 11, 1970, 1.

44. *State*, October 29, 1970, 1B.

45. Strom Thurmond to President Nixon, April 30, 1970, box 6, folder 202, Dent Papers, Clemson University.

46. Vice President Agnew to President Nixon, memorandum draft [c. 1970], box 6, folder 207, Dent Papers, Clemson University.

47. Albert Watson to President Nixon, May 5, 1970, box 6, folder 207, Dent Papers, Clemson University.

48. Harry Dent to Bob Haldeman, memo, July 31, 1970, box 6, folder 207, Dent Papers, Clemson University; *Washington Post*, July 18, 1970, A1; ibid., July 25, 1970, A2; *Television News Index and Abstracts*, July 17, July 31, and August 6, 1970.

49. *Washington Post*, July 25, 1970, A2; *Los Angeles Times*, October 11, 1970, 4A; *State*, October 28, 1970, 3B.

50. Ike McLeese, undated memo to John West, "In regards to our strategy meeting scheduled for the 3rd of August . . ." Personal, 1970 Campaign Records, topical files, South Carolina Voter Attitudes, West Papers; John West, interview by author; Reverend W. F. Harris to John West, July 11, 1970, and response by West, July 20, 1970, Personal, 1970 Campaign Records, topical files, July 1970 folder, West Papers; Confidential summary and analysis of responses for appraisal of campaign, Personal, 1970 Campaign Records, topical files, Organization: Strategy Committee, West Papers

51. John West to Crawford Cook, July 17, 1970, Personal, 1970 Campaign Records, topical files, West Papers.

52. Republican news release, July 10, 1970, box 2, Republican Party, News Releases 1970 folder, Workman Papers; *Charlotte Observer*, July 11, 1970, 1B; *Charleston News & Courier*, July 23, 1970, 5C; Fred R. Sheheen to John West, July 23, 1970, Personal, 1970 Campaign Records, topical files, Organization: Strategy Committee, West Papers; John F. Kraft, Inc. Survey conducted September 27, 1970, Personal, 1970 Campaign Records, topical files, South Carolina Voter Attitudes, West Papers. The drop in West's black committed voters can be explained, at least partly, by the formation of a black third party. The Kraft poll noted that they expected many of these voters to return to West.

53. "Status & Development of the Democratic Party for 1970 Campaign," no date, Personal, 1970 Campaign Records, topical files, Democratic Party, West Papers; Sampson & Sampson, black attorneys from Sumter, South Carolina, to John West, Personal, 1970 Campaign Records, topical files, "October 1970" folder, West Papers; John Cauthen to West, July 24, 1970, Personal, 1970 Campaign Records, topical files, Organization: Strategy Committee, West Papers. For examples of letters to West from local politicos advising on black leaders, see two letters from J. Franklin Spears, "1970 West Campaign: February" folder, and another from C. Hugh Hemphill in "1970 West Campaign: September" folder, both in Personal, 1970 Campaign Records, topical files, West Papers. John West to

Bishop William F. Ball, October 22, 1970, "October 1970" folder, Personal, 1970 Campaign Records, West Papers.

54. South Carolina *Republican Newsletter*, September 10, 1970, 2–3, in folder 141, Duffy Papers; John West, interview by author.

55. *New York Times*, October 4, 1970, 33; *Greenville News*, September 11, 1970, 4; *State*, October 7, 1970, 1B; ibid., October 3, 1970, 7A; *Washington Post*, October 30, 1970, A1, A7.

56. South Carolina *Republican Newsletter*, October 16, 1970, folder 142, Duffy Papers.

57. *Piedmont*, September 9, 1970, editorial page, in folder 143, Duffy Papers.

58. Harry Dent to Bryce Harlow, October 14, 1970, box 6, folder 207, Dent Papers, Clemson University.

59. *State*, October 25, 1970, 6B; *Los Angeles Times*, October 11, 1970, 4A; *Wall Street Journal*, October 28, 1970, 1; *New York Times*, October 24, 1970, 13; *State*, October 12, 1970, 1B.

60. *State*, October 16, 1970, 1A; ibid., October 18, 1970, 2B; *New York Times*, October 24, 1970, 13; *State*, October 28, 1970, 1B.

61. *State*, October 17, 1970, 1A; "City of Forrest Acres, S.C. - Albert H. Burts, Mayor" Press Release, no date, "Topical Files: Persons: Albert Watson" folder, box 17, West Papers; "Confidential memo, Re: West's final T.V. appeal," October 29, 1970, "1970 West Campaign: October" folder, West Papers.

62. *State*, November 1, 1970, 1A; ibid., October 28, 1970, 1B; ibid., October 29, 1970, 1B; ibid., October 20, 1970, 1B; *Wall Street Journal*, October 28, 1970, 1, 18.

63. "Confidential memo, Re: West's final TV appeal," October 29, 1970, West Papers; Letter to county leaders, August 21, 1970, "Organization: County Leaders" folder, West Papers; Cook/Ruef & Associates-Client: John West for Governor, Subject: 30 minute TV program, "Publicity: TV" folder, West Papers; John West to Mr. & Mrs. James Duffy, October 23, 1970, folder 142, Duffy Papers.

64. South Carolina *Republican Newsletter*, October 16, 1970, folder 142, Duffy Papers; "Voter Opinion Survey - S.C. - October 2–15, 1970," Central Surveys Incorporated, Shenandoah, Iowa, box 6, folder 181, Dent Papers, Clemson University.

65. *Cleveland Plain Dealer*, September 28, 1970, box 4, folder 104, Dent Papers, Clemson University.

66. *State*, November 1, 1970, 1A.

67. *State*, October 18, 1970, 2B.

68. *State*, October 18, 1970, 2B; *Atlanta Journal*, August 23, 1971, 4A; *State*, November 1, 1970, 1A.

69. *State*, October 30, 1970, 1B; West and Hollings phone calls to Workman in "Post election reaction," "John West" folder, box 23, Workman Papers; Bass, *Porgy Comes Home*, 39; *State*, October 31, 1970, 13A.

70. *Wall Street Journal*, October 28, 1970, 18; *Atlanta Journal*, August 23, 1971, 4A; Bass, *Porgy Comes Home*, 40.

71. Arthur Ravenel to Harry Dent, November 24, 1970, folder 142, Duffy Papers.

72. Undated document assessing Watson campaign by Harry Dent, box 6, folder 207, Dent Papers, Clemson University.

73. South Carolina *Republican Newsletter*, November 24, 1970, 2, in folder 142, Duffy Papers.

74. James Duffy to Harry Dent and James Duffy to Harry Bandouveris, both dated November 25, 1970, also James Duffy to James Henderson, November 9, 1970, all in folder 142, Duffy Papers.

75. Cohodas, *Strom Thurmond*, 412; *New York Times*, October 17, 1971, 46; *Charlotte Observer*, January 12, 1971, 1C; *Aiken Standard*, February 16, 1971; Peirce, *Deep South*, 402; memo from Dan Ross to GOP County, District and State officers, November 1970, 3, folder 142, Duffy Papers.

76. Ernest Hollings, call to William Workman in "Post-election Reaction," John West folder, box 23, Workman Papers; Joseph Mendelsohn to John West, November 4, 1970, Julius Baggert to John West, November 4, 1970, Edward Saleeby to John West, November 5, 1970, all three letters in "1970 West Campaign: 1–9 November" folder, Personal, 1970 Campaign Records, West Papers.

77. *Atlanta Journal*, August 23, 1971, 1A, 4A; *New York Times*, January 20, 1971, 1.

Chapter 6. Georgia

1. Pomerantz, *Where Peachtree Meets*, 273, 97–98.

2. Bartley, *Creation of Modern Georgia*, 192–93.

3. Pomerantz, *Where Peachtree Meets*, 223.

4. Cobb, *Selling of the South*, 127; Cobb, *Industrialization and Southern Society*, 112; Bartley, *Creation of Modern Georgia*, 194; Powledge, "Black Man, Go South," 74.

5. Bayor, *Race and the Shaping*, 222–23; Cobb, *Selling of the South*, 128; Bartley, *Creation of Modern Georgia*, 194.

6. Bartley, *Creation of Modern Georgia*, 195.

7. Pomerantz, *Where Peachtree Meets*, 256; Bartley, *Creation of Modern Georgia*, 195; Bayor, *Race and the Shaping*, 224.

8. Cobb, *Industrialization and Southern Society*, 102; Bartley, *Creation of Modern Georgia*, 195–96; Henderson and Roberts, *Georgia Governors in an Age of Change*, 171–73; Saye, "Revolution," 10–14.

9. Black, *Southern Governors and Civil Rights*, 178; *Christian Science Monitor*, January 16, 1970, 15; Henderson and Roberts, *Georgia Governors*, 172, 179.

10. Henderson and Roberts, *Georgia Governors*, 295.

11. *Atlanta Constitution*, November 8, 1970, 2A.

12. Glad, *Jimmy Carter: In Search*, 127; Clotfelter and Hamilton, "Electing a Governor in the Seventies," 35; *Atlanta Journal*, April 7, 1970, 2A.

13. Bourne, *Jimmy Carter*, 9, 25, 43–48, 64–66, 72–79, 101–2, 113–20. For a fuller discussion of Carter's 1962 Georgia senate race see Jimmy Carter, *Turning Point*.

14. Bruce Galphin, "Jimmy Carter—A New Breed," *Atlanta Constitution*, July 2, 1966, 4.

15. Bourne, *Jimmy Carter*, 20–30.

16. Bourne, *Jimmy Carter*, 71–78.

17. Bourne, *Jimmy Carter*, 93, 99; Wheeler, *Jimmy Who?*, 35.

18. Miller, *Yankee from Georgia*, 109; Jimmy Carter, *Why Not the Best?*, 112.

19. Frady, *Wallace*, 127.

20. The best account of C. B. King's role in the Albany movement is found in Branch, *Parting the Waters*, 524–31.

21. Bartley, *From Thurmond to Wallace*, 140; *Ripon Forum*, July-August 1970, 43. Several good accounts of Carter's 1970 campaign exist. Carter's autobiographical *Why Not the Best?* contains a short but revealing chapter on 1970. The most detailed accounts of the campaign appear in the following works: Sanders, "The Sad Duty of Politics," 612–38; Wheeler, *Jimmy Who?*, 45–61; Murphy and Gulliver, *The Southern Strategy*, 173–97; and Glad, *Jimmy Carter: In Search*, 123–40. Bill Shipp, political editor of the *Atlanta Constitution* in 1970, had contacts within the Carter campaign and wrote a revealing account that ran in the *Atlanta Constitution* as a four-part series, November 8–11, 1970, entitled "How He Won It." For an illuminating insight into Carter's strategy, see Clotfelter and Hamilton, "Electing a Governor," 32–39. Two campaign aides from the Sanders campaign provide an insider's account in Coram and Tyson, "The Loser Who Won," 41–99. See also Lyons, "A Comparison of Carl Sanders' Gubernatorial Campaigns: 1962 and 1970." For interviews with participants and observers of the 1970 campaign, see Georgia Government Documentation Project.

22. Carl Sanders, interview by author; *Atlanta Constitution*, August 21, 1970, 14A; *Atlanta Constitution*, November 8, 1970, 2A.

23. Glad, *Jimmy Carter: In Search*, 126; Clotfelter and Hamilton, "Electing a Governor," 35.

24. Murphy and Gulliver, *The Southern Strategy*, 182–83; Coram and Tyson, "Loser Who Won," 66, 43.

25. Clotfelter and Hamilton, "Electing a Governor," 34–36; Lamis, *Two Party South*, 98.

26. *National Observer*, April 7, 1971, 5; Clotfelter and Hamilton, "But Which Southern Strategy?" 7.

27. *Atlanta Journal*, April 7, 1970, 2A.

28. Peirce, *Deep South*, 320; Havard, *Changing Politics of the South*, 303; *Atlanta Constitution*, September 4, 1970, 1, 22A; ibid., August 26, 1971, 18A; ibid., November 11, 1970, 14A.

29. *Atlanta Constitution*, November 11, 1970, 14A; Clotfelter and Hamilton, "Electing a Governor," 34.

30. Peirce, *Deep South*, 320; *Atlanta Constitution*, November 8, 1970, 2A; Steve Ball, *Atlanta Journal-Constitution*, August 23, 1970, 7A; Reg Murphy quote in Mazlish and Diamond, *Jimmy Carter*, 181.

31. Clotfelter and Hamilton, "Electing a Governor," 36; ibid., 34.

32. Bill Shipp, interview by Cliff Kuhn, April 22, 1987, Georgia Government Documentation Project; Coram and Tyson, "Loser," 41.

33. *Atlanta Constitution*, July 21, 1970, 6A; *Atlanta Journal*, July 28, 1970, 1; *Atlanta Constitution*, April 4, 1970, 4A; ibid., April 11, 1970, 15A; ibid., August 28, 1970, 1.

34. *Atlanta Constitution*, November 11, 1970, 1, 11A; Coram and Tyson, "Loser," 96.

35. *Atlanta Constitution*, August 27, 1970, 1.

36. *Macon Telegraph*, August 28, 1970, 4A; *Macon News* editorial reprinted in *Atlanta Constitution*, September 3, 1970, 5A; *Atlanta Constitution*, August 27, 1970, 1; *Atlanta Journal*, July 20, 1970, 2A.

37. Bill Shipp reported on the anonymous pamphlet aimed at Sanders in *Atlanta Constitution*, June 14, 1970, 1. Stephen Brill contended that Carter campaign workers were responsible for the pamphlets in "Jimmy Carter's Pathetic Lies," 79–80. Jody Powell issued a twenty-two-page rebuttal to the Brill article prior to its publication; several newspapers ran excerpts from both the article and the rebuttal. See "Charges and Responses Relating to Carter," compiled by Bill Allen, 3/76 – 6/76, [CF,O/A 751], box 1, Press Office—Powell, Carter-Mondale Campaign Materials file, Jimmy Carter Presidential Library. Phil Stanford assessed the charges in the Brill article and Carter media coverage in general in "The most remarkable piece of fiction Jimmy Carter ever read," 16.

38. Coram and Tyson, "Loser," 95; Brill, "Carter's Pathetic Lies," 79.

39. Brill, "Carter's Pathetic Lies," 79–80; *Atlanta Constitution*, June 21, 1970, 14A; Miller, *Yankee from Georgia*, 107.

40. *Atlanta Journal*, April 7, 1970, 2A; incident of Carter shaking hands with black janitor in *Atlanta Journal-Constitution*, September 27, 1970, 7A; Carter quote on state employment in *Atlanta Journal*, July 28, 1970, 1. See also Murphy and Gulliver, *Southern Strategy*, 195.

41. *Atlanta Journal*, July 28, 1970, 4A; Hal Suit, interview by author; *Atlanta Journal*, July 27, 1970, 2A; *Atlanta Constitution*, August 19, 1970, 6A.

42. Coram and Tyson, "Loser," 95; Carter quote on his support in *Atlanta Constitution*, June 21, 1970, 14A; ABC-TV's fact book reported in *Atlanta Constitution*, November 1, 1970, 5A.

43. *Atlanta Journal*, September 4, 1970, 1, 6A; *Washington Post*, March 7, 1970, C3.

44. *Atlanta Constitution*, September 24, 1970, 12A; Bartley and Graham, *Southern Elections*, 94. For a fuller discussion of county voting tendencies in Georgia, see Havard, *Changing Politics*, 353–57.

45. Coram and Tyson, "Loser," 96; *Atlanta Constitution*, September 12, 1970, 1, 12A; ibid., September 13, 1970, 2A.

46. *Atlanta Constitution*, September 13, 1970, 2A; ibid., September 23, 1970, 15A.

47. *Atlanta Constitution*, September 16, 1970, 1, 15A; ibid., September 14, 1970, 3A; ibid., September 15, 1970, 1, 6A. There was speculation at the time of Carter's meeting with Harris that there may have been a quid pro quo discussion concerning Harris's reappointment to the state University Board of Regents. During the general election campaign, Carter flip-flopped on whether he would or would not reappoint Harris. As governor, Carter refused to reappoint Harris and replaced him with an African American. See *Atlanta Journal*, October 16, 1970, 2A; *Atlanta Constitution*, October 22, 1970, 8A; Henderson and Roberts, *Georgia Governors*, 15; campaign flyers in "Sanders material," Hal Suit Personal Collection.

48. *Atlanta Constitution*, September 21, 1970, 1, 5A; Coram and Tyson, "Loser," 98.

49. *Atlanta Constitution*, September 24, 1970, 1, 12A.

50. Tom Lias to Harry Dent, April 29, 1970, MSS 158, box 4, folder 132, "Georgia Politics February - November 1970," Dent Papers, Clemson University; *Atlanta Constitution*, November 10, 1970, 7A; Bill Shipp in ibid., June 15, 1970, 1; Bentley commercial reported by Bill Shipp in ibid., August 18, 1970, 6A.

51. Gingrich, "Toward A Real Two Party System in Georgia," 2, Hal Suit Personal Collection.

52. Murphy and Gulliver, *Southern Strategy*, 183–84; Hal Suit's debate notes, Hal Suit Personal Collection; *Atlanta Journal*, October 26, 1970, 1, 9A; ibid., November 2, 1970, 2A.

53. *Atlanta Journal*, August 26, 1971, 19A; Gingrich, "Toward a Two Party System," 4–5, Hal Suit Personal Collection.

54. *Atlanta Journal*, October 7, 1970, 18A.

55. *Atlanta Constitution*, September 17, 1970, 1 and 13A; *Atlanta Journal*, October 23, 1970, 1, 4A.

56. *Atlanta Constitution*, September 24, 1970, 1; ibid., October 7, 1970, 1, 8A; ibid., November 3, 1970, 6A.

57. *Atlanta Constitution*, November 3, 1970, 6A; ibid., November 4, 1970, 1.

58. *Atlanta Constitution*, January 7, 1971, 10A.

59. Norton and Slosser, *The Miracle of Jimmy Carter*, 74; Wooten, *Dasher: The Roots and Rising of Jimmy Carter*, 295–96.

60. Jimmy Carter, *A Government as Good as Its People*, 14.

Chapter 7. Conclusion

1. Nordheimer, "'Supersquare,'" 54.

2. Nordheimer, "'Supersquare,'" 55.

3. *Wall Street Journal*, October 28, 1970, 1, 18.

4. Scheer, "Jimmy We Hardly Know Y'all," 190. See also Carter interview by Scheer in *Playboy*, November 1976, 63–68; Davis and Good, *Reinhold Niebuhr on Politics*, 180–81.

5.Colburn and Scher, *Florida's Gubernatorial Politics*, 86; Kallina, *Politics of Confrontation*, 193, 237.

Bibliography

Manuscript Collections

Alabama Department of Archives and History, Montgomery, Alabama
George Wallace Gubernatorial Papers
Arthur Brewer Gubernatorial Papers

Amistad Research Center, Tulane University, New Orleans, Louisiana
Congress of Racial Equality Papers

Jimmy Carter Library, Atlanta, Georgia
Jimmy Carter Papers

Clemson University, Special Collections, Clemson, South Carolina
Harry Dent Papers
James Duffy Papers
Strom Thurmond Papers

Florida Department of Archives, Tallahassee, Florida
Tom Adams Papers
Reubin Askew Gubernatorial Papers
Claude Kirk Gubernatorial Papers

Hal Suit Personal Collection
Hal Suit 1970 Campaign Papers

Richard Nixon Presidential Materials, National Archives, College Park, Maryland
Harry Dent Files
John Ehrlichman Files
H. R. Haldeman Files
President's Office Files

President's "Personal" Files
White House Special Files
White House Subject Files

South Caroliniana Library, Modern Political Collections, University of South Carolina, Columbia, South Carolina

William Jennings Bryan Dorn Papers
South Carolina Democratic Party Papers
South Carolina Republican Party Papers
John C. West Papers
William Workman Papers

South Carolina Department of Archives, Columbia, South Carolina

Robert McNair Gubernatorial Papers
John West Gubernatorial Papers

University of Arkansas, Fayetteville, Arkansas

Orval Faubus Papers

University of Arkansas, Little Rock, Arkansas

Winthrop Rockefeller Papers

Virginia Department of Archives, Richmond, Virginia

Lynwood Holton Papers

Oral History Materials

Author's Interviews

Reubin Askew, March 29, 1999, Tallahassee, Florida.
Staige Blackford, June 20, 1994, Charlottesville, Virginia.
Dale Bumpers, December 18, 1996, Washington, D.C.
Ernie Dumas, December 16, 1994, Little Rock, Arkansas.
Lynwood Holton, June 23, 1994, Washington, D.C.
Carl Sanders, March 28, 1989, Atlanta, Georgia.
Archie Schaffer, December 20, 1994, Fayetteville, Arkansas.
Hal Suit, March 30, 1989, Atlanta, Georgia.
Deloss Walker, December 12, 1994, Memphis, Tennessee.
John West, July 5, 1994, Hilton Head, South Carolina.

Georgia Government Documentation Project, Interviews in Special Collections, Georgia State University

Carl Sanders Interview
Bill Shipp Interview

Newspapers, Magazines, and Journals

Agricultural History
Arkansas Democrat
Arkansas Gazette
Arkansas Historical Quarterly
American Historical Review
American Political Science Review
American Sociological Review
Atlanta Constitution
Atlanta Journal
Augusta Courier
Baltimore Afro-American
Birmingham News
Birmingham Post-Herald
Boston Globe
Business Week
Charleston News & Courier
Charlotte Observer
Chicago Tribune
Christian Science Monitor
Cleveland Plain Dealer
Columbia Journalism Review
Commentary
Commercial Appeal (Memphis, Tennessee)
Congressional Quarterly
Conway Democrat (Conway, Arkansas)
Eagle Democrat (Warren, Arkansas)
Ebony
Esquire
Florida Historical Quarterly
Florida Times Union (Jacksonville, Florida)
Georgia Historical Review
Greenville News (Greenville, South Carolina)
Harper's
Helena-West Helena World (Helena, Arkansas)
Journal of American History
Journal of Politics
Journal of Social Issues
Los Angeles Times
Louisiana History
Life
Macon Telegraph (Macon, Georgia)
McGehee Times (McGehee, Arkansas)

Miami Herald
National Observer
New South
Newsweek
New York Times
Phylon
Piedmont (Greenville, South Carolina)
Pine Bluff Commercial (Pine Bluff, Arkansas)
Population Bulletin
Progressive
Public Opinion Quarterly
Republican Newsletter (South Carolina)
Richmond Times-Dispatch
Ripon Forum
Social Forces
Sociology and Social Research
South Today
State (Columbia, South Carolina)
St. Petersburg Evening Independent
St. Petersburg Times
Tallahassee Democrat
Tiger (Clemson University)
Time
Times (North Little Rock, Arkansas)
U.S. News & World Report
Virginia Quarterly Review
Wall Street Journal
Washington Post
Western Political Quarterly
Winston-Salem Journal

Books, Articles, and Dissertations

Ambrose, Stephen A. *Nixon: The Triumph of a Politician, 1962–1972.* New York: Simon & Schuster, 1989.

Ayers, H. Bryant, and Thomas H. Naylor, eds. *You Can't Eat Magnolias.* New York: McGraw-Hill, 1972.

Bartley, Numan V. *The Creation of Modern Georgia.* Athens: University of Georgia Press, 1983.

———. *From Thurmond to Wallace.* Baltimore: Johns Hopkins University Press, 1970.

———."Looking Back at Little Rock." *Arkansas Historical Quarterly* 25 (Summer 1966): 101–16.

———. *The New South, 1945–1980.* Baton Rouge: Louisiana State University Press, 1995.

———. *The Rise of Massive Resistance: Race and Politics in the South during the 1950's.* Baton Rouge: Louisiana State University Press, 1969.

Bartley, Numan V., and Hugh D. Graham. *Southern Elections: County and Precinct Data, 1950–1972.* Baton Rouge: Louisiana State University Press, 1978.

———. *Southern Politics and the Second Reconstruction.* Baltimore: Johns Hopkins University Press, 1975.

Baskett, Tom, Jr., ed. *Persistence of the Spirit: The Black Experience in Arkansas.* Little Rock: Arkansas Endowment for the Humanities, 1986.

Bass, Jack. *Porgy Comes Home: South Carolina . . . After 300 Years.* Columbia, S.C.: R. L. Bryan Company, 1972.

Bass, Jack, and Walter DeVries. *The Transformation of Southern Politics: Social and Political Consequences since 1945.* New York: Basic Books, 1976.

Bayor, Ronald H. *Race and the Shaping of Twentieth Century Atlanta.* Chapel Hill: University of North Carolina Press, 1996.

Beck, Paul Allen. "The Partisan Dealignment in the Postwar South." *American Political Science Review* 71 (June 1977): 477–96.

Bevier, Thomas. "Dear Dixie: You're looking better every day." *Chicago Tribune Magazine,* February 13, 1972, 67.

Beyle, Thad, and J. Oliver Williams, eds. *American Governors in Behavioral Perspective.* New York: Harper & Row, 1972.

Bigger, Jeanne C. "The Sunning of America: Migration to the Sunbelt." *Population Bulletin* 34 (March 1979): 3–43.

Black, Earl. *Southern Governors and Civil Rights: Racial Segregation as a Campaign Issue in the Second Reconstruction.* Cambridge, Mass.: Harvard University Press, 1976.

Black, Earl, and Merle Black. *Politics and Society in the South.* Cambridge, Mass.: Harvard University Press, 1987.

"Black Voices of the South." *Ebony* 26 (August 1971): 50–54.

Bourne, Peter G. *Jimmy Carter: A Comprehensive Biography from Plains to Postpresidency.* New York: Scribner, 1997.

Branch, Taylor, *Parting the Waters: America in the King Years, 1954–1963.* New York: Simon & Schuster, 1988.

Brill, Stephen. "Jimmy Carter's Pathetic Lies." *Harper's,* March 1976, 77–88.

Broom, Leonard, and Norval Glenn. "Negro-White Differences in Reported Attitudes and Behavior." *Sociology and Social Research* 50 (January 1966): 187–200.

Brownell, Blaine, and David Goldfield, eds. *The City in Southern History: The Growth of Urban Civilization in the South.* Port Washington, N.Y.: Kennikat Press, 1977.

Campbell, Angus. *White Attitudes Toward Black People.* Ann Arbor, Mich.: Institute of Social Research, 1971.

Campbell, Bruce A. "Patterns of Change in the Partisan Loyalties of Native Southerners: 1952–1972." *Journal of Politics* 39 (August 1977): 730–61.

Campbell, David, and Joe R. Feagin. "Black Politics in the South: A Descriptive Analysis." *Journal of Politics* 37 (February 1975): 129–62.

Carlson, Jody. *George C. Wallace and the Politics of Powerlessness: The Wallace Campaigns for President, 1964–1976.* New Brunswick, N.J.: Transaction Press, 1981.

Carter, Dan. *The Politics of Rage: George Wallace, the Origins of the New Conservatism, and the Transformation of American Politics.* New York: Simon & Schuster, 1995.

Carter, Jimmy. *A Government as Good as Its People.* New York: Simon & Schuster, 1977.

———. *Turning Point: A Candidate, a State, and a Nation Come of Age.* New York: Times Books, 1992.

———. *Why Not the Best?* Nashville, Tenn.: Broadman Press, 1975.

Chester, Lewis, Godfrey Hodgson, and Bruce Page. *American Melodrama: The Presidential Campaign of 1968.* New York: Viking, 1969.

Clotfelter, James. "Populism in Office or, Whatever Happened to Huey Long?" *New South* 28 (Spring 1973): 56–61.

Clotfelter, James, and William R. Hamilton. "Beyond Race Politics: Electing Southern Populists in the 1970s." In *You Can't Eat Magnolias,* ed. H. Bryant Ayers and Thomas H. Naylor. New York: McGraw-Hill, 1972.

———. "But Which Southern Strategy?" *South Today* 2 (April 1971): 1, 6–7.

———. "Electing a Governor in the Seventies." In *American Governors in Behavioral Perspective,* ed. Thad Beyle and J. Oliver Williams. New York: Harper & Row, 1972.

Clotfelter, James, William R. Hamilton, and Peter B. Harkins. "In Search of Populism." *New South* 26 (Winter 1971): 6–15.

Cobb, James C. *Industrialization and Southern Society, 1877–1984.* Lexington: University Press of Kentucky, 1984.

———. *The Selling of the South: The Southern Crusade for Industrial Development, 1936–1990.* Urbana: University of Illinois Press, 1993.

Cohodas, Nadine. *Strom Thurmond and the Politics of Southern Change.* New York: Simon & Schuster, 1993.

Colburn, David R., and Richard K. Scher. *Florida's Gubernatorial Politics in the Twentieth Century.* Tallahassee: University of Florida Presses, 1980.

———. "Race Relations and Florida Gubernatorial Politics since the *Brown* Decision." *Florida Historical Quarterly* 55 (Winter 1976): 153–69.

Coram, Robert, and Remer Tyson. "The Loser Who Won." *Atlanta Magazine,* November 1970, 41–99.

Daniel, Pete. *Standing at the Crossroads: Southern Life in the Twentieth Century.* Baltimore: Johns Hopkins University Press, 1986.

———. "The Transformation of the Rural South 1930 to the Present." *Agricultural History* 55 (July 1981): 231–48.

Davis, Harry R., and Robert C. Good, eds. *Reinhold Niebuhr on Politics*. New York: Scribners, 1960.

Dearmore, Tom. "First Angry Man of Country Singers." *New York Times Magazine*, 21 September 1969, 32–58.

Dent, Harry. *The Prodigal South Returns to Power*. New York: John Wiley & Sons, 1978.

Donovan, Timothy P., William B. Gatewood, Jr., and Jeannie M. Whayne, eds. *The Governors of Arkansas: Essays in Political Biography*. Fayetteville: University of Arkansas Press, 1995.

Ehrlichman, John. *Witness to Power: The Nixon Years*. New York: Simon & Schuster, 1982.

Erikson, Robert S., and William James Zavoina. "Issues and Voters in the 1970 Florida Election." *Florida State University Governmental Research Bulletin*, November 1971, 1–4.

Facts on File. New York: Oxford University Press, published yearly.

Faubus, Orval. *Down from the Hills*. Vol. 2. Little Rock, Ark.: Democrat Printing, 1985.

Fink, Gary. *Prelude to the Presidency: The Political Character and Legislative Leadership Style of Governor Jimmy Carter*. Westport, Conn.: Greenwood Press, 1980.

Frady, Marshall. *Wallace*. New York: World Publishing, 1968.

Freyer, Tony. *The Little Rock Crisis: A Constitutional Interpretation*. Westport, Conn.: Greenwood Press, 1984.

Gallup, George H. *The Gallup Poll: Public Opinion, 1935–1971*. 3 vols. New York: Random House, 1971.

Galphin, Bruce. "Jimmy Carter—A New Breed." *Atlanta Constitution*, July 2, 1966.

Garrow, David. *Protest at Selma: Martin Luther King, Jr., and the Voting Rights Act of 1965*. New Haven, Conn.: Yale University Press, 1978.

Gaston, Paul. *The New South Creed: A Study in Southern Mythmaking*. New York: Alfred A. Knopf, 1970.

Gergel, Richard. "School Desegregation: A Student's View." *New South* 26 (Winter 1971): 34–38.

Gitlan, Todd. *The Sixties: Years of Hope, Days of Rage*. New York: Bantam Books, 1987.

Glad, Betty. *Jimmy Carter: In Search of the Great White House*. New York: W.W. Norton & Company, 1980.

Goldfield, David R. *Black, White and Southern: Race Relations and Southern Culture, 1940 to the Present*. Baton Rouge: Louisiana State University Press, 1990.

———. *Cotton Fields and Skyscrapers: Southern City and Region, 1607–1980*. Baton Rouge: Louisiana State University Press, 1982.

———. *Promised Land: The South since 1945*. Arlington Heights, Ill.: Harlan Davidson, 1987.

———. *Region, Race and Cities: Interpreting the Urban South*. Baton Rouge: Louisiana State University Press, 1997.

———. "The Urban South: A Regional Framework." *American Historical Review* 86 (October-December 1981): 1009–34.

Graham, Hugh Davis. *The Civil Rights Era: Origins and Development of National Policy.* New York: Oxford University Press, 1990.

Haldeman, H. R. *The Haldeman Diaries: Inside the Nixon White House.* New York: G.P. Putnam's Sons, 1994.

Hall, Kermit L., ed. *The Oxford Companion to the Supreme Court of the United States.* New York: Oxford University Press, 1992.

Hall, Kermit L., and James W. Ely, Jr. *An Uncertain Tradition: Constitutionalism and the History of the South.* Athens: University of Georgia Press, 1989.

Hammons, Lyle W. "Campaign Communication Strategies and Techniques of Winthrop Rockefeller, A Study in Persuasion." M.A. Thesis, University of Arkansas, Little Rock, 1985.

Havard, William C., ed. *The Changing Politics of the South.* Baton Rouge: Louisiana State University Press, 1972.

———. "Intransigence to Transition: Thirty Years of Southern Politics." *Virginia Quarterly Review* 51 (Autumn 1975): 497–521.

———. "Protest, Defection, and Realignment in Contemporary Southern Politics." *Virginia Quarterly Review* 48 (Spring 1972): 161–84.

Henderson, Harold P., and Gary L. Roberts, eds. *Georgia Governors in an Age of Change.* Athens: University of Georgia Press, 1988.

"Hope for a New South." *Progressive* 35 (March 1971): 8.

Hornsby, Alton, Jr. "A City That Was Too Busy to Hate." In *Southern Businessmen and Desegregation*, ed. Elizabeth Jacoway and David R. Colburn. Baton Rouge: Louisiana State University Press, 1982.

Hurt, R. Douglass, ed. *The Rural South since World War II.* Baton Rouge: Louisiana State University Press, 1998.

Jacoway, Elizabeth. "Civil Rights and the Changing South." In *Southern Businessmen and Desegregation*, ed. Elizabeth Jacoway and David R. Colburn. Baton Rouge: Louisiana State University Press, 1982.

———, and David R. Colburn, eds. *Southern Businessmen and Desegregation.* Baton Rouge: Louisiana State University Press, 1982.

Kallina, Edmund F., Jr. *Claude Kirk and the Politics of Confrontation.* Gainesville: University Press of Florida, 1993.

Kelly, Jonathan. "The Politics of Busing." *Public Opinion Quarterly* 38 (Spring 1974): 23–39.

Kerner, Otto, et al. *Report of the National Advisory Commission on Civil Disorders.* New York: Bantam Books, 1968.

Key, V. O., Jr. *Southern Politics in State and Nation.* New York: Alfred A. Knopf, 1949.

Killian, Lewis, and Charles Grigg. "Race Relations in an Urbanized South." *Journal of Social Issues* 22 (January 1966): 20–29.

Kirby, Jack Temple. *Media Made Dixie.* Athens: University of Georgia Press, 1986.

Klingman, Peter D. *Neither Dies nor Surrenders: A History of the Republican Party in Florida, 1867–1970.* Gainesville: University Press of Florida, 1984.

Lamis, Alexander P. *The Two Party South.* New York: Oxford University Press, 1984.

Lea, James F., ed. *Contemporary Southern Politics.* Baton Rouge: Louisiana State University Press, 1988.

Lesher, Stephan. *George Wallace: American Populist.* Reading, Mass.: Addison-Wesley Publishing Company, 1994.

Lindsay, Leon W. "Southern Leaders Cool Color Issue." *Christian Science Monitor,* January 22, 1971, 1.

Liner, E. Blaine, and Lawrence K. Lynch, eds. *The Economics of Southern Growth.* Durham, N.C.: Seeman Printery, 1977.

Lisenby, Foy. "Winthrop Rockefeller and the Arkansas Image." *Arkansas Historical Quarterly* 43 (Summer 1984): 143–52.

Lubell, Samuel. *The Hidden Crisis in American Politics.* New York: W.W. Norton & Company, 1970.

Lyons, Margaret Spears. "A Comparison of Carl Sanders' Gubernatorial Campaigns: 1962 and 1970." M.A. Thesis, University of Georgia, 1971.

Maisel, Louis, and Joseph Cooper, eds. *Political Parties: Development and Decay.* Beverly Hills, Calif.: Sage Publications, 1978.

Malone, Bill C. *Country Music, U.S.A.* Austin: University of Texas Press, 1985.

———. "The Rural South Moves to the City: Country Music since World War II." In *The Rural South since World War II,* ed. R. Douglas Hurt. Baton Rouge: Louisiana State University Press, 1998.

———. *Southern Music: American Music.* Lexington: University of Kentucky Press, 1979.

Mathews, Donald, and James Prothro. *Negroes and the New South Politics.* New York: Harcourt, Brace, 1966.

Matusow, Allen J. *The Unraveling of America: A History of Liberalism in the 1960s.* New York: Harper & Row, 1984.

Mazlish, Bruce, and Edwin Diamond. *Jimmy Carter: An Interpretative Biography.* New York: Simon & Schuster, 1979.

McGinniss, Joe. *The Selling of the President, 1968.* New York: Trident Press, 1969.

McGraw, Patricia Washington, Grif Stockley, and Nudie E. Williams. "We Speak for Ourselves: 1954 and After." In *Persistence of the Spirit: The Black Experience in Arkansas,* ed. Tom Baskett, Jr. Little Rock: Arkansas Endowment for the Humanities, 1986.

McKinney, John C., and Linda Brookover Bourque. "The Changing South: National Incorporation of a Region." *American Sociological Review* 36 (June 1971): 399–412.

Miller, William Lee. *Yankee from Georgia.* New York: New York Times Books, 1978.

"Mob Rule in Forrest City." *New South* 24 (Fall 1969): 84.

Morris, Kenneth E. *Jimmy Carter: American Moralist.* Athens: University of Georgia Press, 1996.

Murphy, Reg. "Southern Governors Speak Out." *Atlanta Constitution,* January 21, 1971, 4.

Murphy, Reg, and Hal Gulliver. *The Southern Strategy.* New York: Scribners, 1971.

Naylor, Thomas H., and James Clotfelter, eds. *Strategies for Change in the South.* Chapel Hill: University of North Carolina Press, 1975.

"The New Rich South: Frontier for Growth." *Business Week,* September 2, 1972, 30–37.

Nicholls, William H. *Southern Tradition and Regional Progress.* Westport, Conn.: Greenwood Press, 1960.

Nordheimer, Jon. "Florida's 'Supersquare'—A Man to Watch." *New York Times Magazine,* March 5, 1972, 11, 52–57.

Norton, Howard, and Bob Slosser. *The Miracle of Jimmy Carter.* Plainfield, N.J.: Logos International, 1976.

O'Neill, William L. *Coming Apart: An Informal History of America in the 1960's.* Chicago: Quadrangle Books, 1971.

Orum, Anthony M., and Edward W. McCrane. "Class, Tradition, and Partisan Alignments in a Southern Urban Electorate." *Journal of Politics* 32 (February 1970): 156–76.

Peirce, Neal R. *The Deep South States of America: People, Politics and Power in the Seven Deep South States.* New York: W.W. Norton & Company, 1974.

Perry, David C., and Alfred J. Watkins, eds. *The Rise of the Sunbelt Cities.* Beverly Hills, Calif.: Sage Publications, 1977.

Perry, James. "Jimmy Carter and a Changing South." *National Observer,* April 5, 1970, 5.

———. *The New Politics, The Expanding Technology of Political Manipulation.* New York: Clarkson N. Potter, 1968.

Pettigrew, Thomas F. *Racially Separate or Together?* New York: McGraw-Hill, 1971.

Phillips, Kevin. *The Emerging Republican Majority.* New Rochelle, N.Y.: Arlington House, 1969.

Pomerantz, Gary M. *Where Peachtree Meets Sweet Auburn: The Saga of Two Families and the Making of Atlanta.* New York: Scribner, 1996.

Pomper, Gerald. "From Confusion to Clarity: Issues and American Voters, 1956–1968." *American Political Science Review* 66 (June 1972): 415–28.

Powledge, Fred. "Black Man, Go South." *Esquire,* August 1965, 72–74, 120–21.

Ranchino, Jim. *Faubus to Bumpers: Arkansas Voters, 1960–1970.* Arkadelphia, Ark.: Action Research, 1972.

Reed, John Shelton. *One South: An Ethnic Approach to Regional Culture.* Baton Rouge: Louisiana State University Press, 1982.

Reed, John Shelton, and Merle Black. "Blacks and Southerners." In *One South: An Ethnic Approach to Regional Culture,* ed. John Shelton Reed. Baton Rouge: Louisiana State University Press, 1982.

Reichley, James A. *Conservatives in an Age of Change*. Washington, D.C.: Brookings Institute, 1981.

Reid, John D. "Black Urbanization of the South." *Phylon* 35 (September 1974): 259–67.

Reissman, Leonard. "Social Development and the American South." *Journal of Social Issues* 22 (January 1966): 101–16.

Rilling, Paul. "Desegregation: The South *Is* Different." *New Republic*, May 16, 1970, 18.

Roland, Charles P. "The South, America's Will-o'-the-Wisp Eden." *Louisiana History* 11 (Spring 1970): 101–19.

Roof, Wade Clark, Thomas Van Valey, and Daphne Spain. "Residential Segregation in Southern Cities: 1970." *Social Forces* 55 (September 1976): 59–71.

Rustin, Bayard. "From Protest to Politics: The Future of the Civil Rights Movement." *Commentary* 39 (February 1965): 25–31.

Sabato, Larry. "New South Governors and the Governorship." In *Contemporary Southern Politics*, ed. James F. Lea. Baton Rouge: Louisiana State University Press, 1988.

Sale, Kirkpatrick. *Power Shift: The Rise of the Southern Rim and Its Challenge to the Eastern Establishment*. New York: Random House, 1975.

Sanders, Randy. "'The Sad Duty of Politics': Jimmy Carter and the Issue of Race in His 1970 Gubernatorial Campaign." *Georgia Historical Quarterly* 76 (Fall 1992): 612–38.

———. "Rassling a Governor: Defiance, Desegregation, Claude Kirk and the Politics of Richard Nixon's Southern Strategy." *Florida Historical Quarterly* 80 (Winter 2002): 332–59.

Saye, Albert B. "Revolution by Judicial Action in Georgia." *Western Political Quarterly* 17 (March 1964): 10–14.

Scheer, Robert. "Jimmy We Hardly Know Y'all." *Playboy*, November 1976, 63–86.

Smith, Stephen A. *Myth, Media and the Southern Mind*. Fayetteville: University of Arkansas Press, 1985.

Stanford, Phil. "'The most remarkable piece of fiction' Jimmy Carter ever read." *Columbia Journalism Review*, July/August 1976, 13–17.

Tebeau, Charlton W. *A History of Florida*. Coral Gables, Fla.: University of Miami Press, 1971.

Television News Index and Abstracts. Nashville: Vanderbilt University Television News Archive, 1970.

Tindall, George Brown. *The Disruption of the Solid South*. Athens: University of Georgia Press, 1972.

———. *The Emergence of the New South, 1913–1945*. Baton Rouge: Louisiana State University Press, 1967.

Tyson, Remer. "'Politics of Fear' Is Ending in South." *Miami Herald*, April 5, 1971, 9B.

Urwin, Cathy. *Agenda for Reform: Winthrop Rockefeller as Governor of Arkansas, 1967–71*. Fayetteville: University of Arkansas Press, 1991.

Wadley, Janet K., and Everett S. Lee. "The Disappearance of the Black Farmer." *Phylon* 35 (September 1974): 276–83.

Ward, John L. *The Arkansas Rockefeller*. Baton Rouge: Louisiana State University Press, 1978.

Watters, Pat. "Southern Integrationists Feel Betrayed by North." *New York Times Magazine*, May 3, 1970, 26–29, 65–78.

Wheeler, Leslie. *Jimmy Who? An Examination of Presidential Candidate Jimmy Carter: The Man, His Career, His Stands on the Issues*. New York: Barron's Woodbury, 1976.

"White Voices of the South." *Ebony* 26 (August 1971): 164–67.

Wicker, Tom. "New Mood in the South." *New York Times*, April 25, 1971, sec. 4, p. 15.

Wolfinger, Raymond, and Robert B. Arseneau. "Partisan Change in the South, 1952–1976." In *Political Parties: Development and Decay*, ed. Louis Maisel and Joseph Cooper. Beverly Hills, Calif.: Sage Publications, 1978.

Wooten, James. *Dasher: The Roots and Rising of Jimmy Carter*. New York: Summit Books, 1978.

Yoder, Edwin. "Southern Governors and the New State Politics." In *You Can't Eat Magnolias*, ed. H. Bryant Ayers and Thomas H. Naylor. New York: McGraw-Hill, 1972.

Index

ABC, 163

A. C. Flora High School, 138

Adams, Tom, 104

AFL-CIO, 56

Agnew, Spiro, 35, 68–69, 97, 127, 128, 131, 133, 136, 137, 141

Ailes, Roger, 81

Allen, Ivan, Jr., 16, 147–48

Allen, Ivan, Sr., 147

Alsop, Stewart, 28

A.M.E. (African Methodist Episcopal) Church, 135

American Civil Liberties Union, 33

American Independent Party, 29, 53, 66, 75, 78, 135, 138, 141

Arkansas, 1, 4, 9, 29, 37–76, 150, 170–72; AFL-CIO Committee on Political Education in, 53; *Arkansas Democrat*, 63; Arkansas Election Research Council, 59; *Arkansas Gazette*, 39, 41, 47, 50, 51, 53, 55, 58, 64, 69, 70, 71, 72, 74, 75; Arkansas Industrial Development Corporation, 15, 59; Arkansas White Citizens Council, 62; *Blytheville Courier News*, 55; Bumpers as governor of, 1, 5; busing in, 42, 45, 51–52, 56–57, 71; Central High School, integration of (1957), 5, 39–41, 44, 45, 62; Citizen Council of Arkansas, 53; Committee for Two Parties in, 59; Democratic Party in, 5, 37–38, 42–45, 47–57, 63, 72–73; *De Queen Bee*, 74; *Dumas Clarion*, 75; *Eagle Democrat* (Warren), 45, 55; Faubus as governor

of, 5, 38–41, 60–62; *Fordyce News-Advocate*, 68; *Helena–West Helena World*, 55, 72; *Jacksonville News*, 45; *Marked Tree Tribune*, 55, 75; *McGehee Times*, 48, 55; New South born in, 76; Office of Economic Opportunity in, 72; *Paragould Daily Press*, 45, 55, 58; *Pine Bluff Commercial*, 71, 74; *Record*, 38; Republican Party in, 2, 57, 59, 60, 62, 64–65, 69, 72–73; Rockefeller as governor of, 2, 42–44, 63–66, 70–75; *Springdale News*, 55; *Stone County Leader*, 74; *Times* (North Little Rock), 52, 72, 75; *Twin City Tribune* (West Helena), 51; Women's Emergency Committee of Little Rock, 41

—gubernatorial election results in: 1964, 61; 1966, 62; 1968, 64; 1970, 75

Arkansas State University, 73

Arnall, Ellis, 2

Arnold, Lynwood, 84

Arseneau, Robert, 32

Ashmore, Harry, 39

Askew, Reubin, 1, 3, 6, 9, 11, 26, 29, 85, 100–112, 170–72, 174; background of, 99–100; and busing, 85, 93, 172; editorial opinions of, 5, 100–102, 104, 108–9; fair share tax plan, 102, 105, 107–8, 111; inaugural address of, 5, 112; polling on, 102–3, 110–11; as presidential candidate, 7; racial views of, 99–100, 111, 172; and television, 99, 101, 112, 171; voter opinions of, 53, 109

Atkins, Rev. Joel, 86–87

Jim Crow, 16
Jimmy the Greek, 167
Johnson, Jim, 38–40, 61–62
Johnson, Leroy, 168
Johnson, Lyndon, 7, 18, 105, 127
Johnson, Wally, 90
Jordan, Hamilton, 162, 163
Jordan, Vernon, 24, 162
Justice Department, 71, 94–95, 130–33

Karl, Frederick, 89
Kennedy, John F., 6–7, 18, 115, 127
Kentucky Fried Chicken, 35
Key, V. O., 77, 113
King, C. B., 155, 162, 165
King, Rev. Martin Luther, Jr., 70, 72, 149–50, 162
Kirbo, Charles, 158
Kirk, Claude, 20–21, 30, 100–101, 171, 172, 174–75; assessment of failed 1970 candidacy of, 110–12; background of, 79; and Carswell, 81–84; and Cramer, 81–84; editorial opinions of, 86, 88–89, 90, 92, 95, 104, 108–9; as governor of, 5, 79–98, 106, 108–9; and Krentzman, 91–94; and polling, 95, 110, 111; racial views of, 85–86, 105, 110; reelection candidacy of, 80–81, 97–98, 102–12; and school desegregation, 86, 89–94, 96–97, 103, 111; vice-presidential ambitions of, 79; voter opinions of, 86–87, 92, 95–96, 98, 109
Krentzman, Benjamin, 91–94, 96
KTHV (Little Rock), 41
Ku Klux Klan, 121, 153, 161

Lane, Daniel, 25
Lee, Robert, 107
Lenin, 166
Leonard, Jerris, 13, 128, 131
Lewis, Bill, 47
Lewis, John, 24
Lightsey, Harry, 129
Loeb, William, 80
Long, Huey, 98
Los Angeles Times, 137

Louisville Courier-Journal, 4
L.Q.C. Lamar Society, 18

Macon News, 161
Macon Telegraph, 161
Maddox, Lester, 85, 118, 156, 163, 168; election victory (1966) of, 150, 154, 158; endorses Jimmy Carter (1970), 167; as governor of Georgia, 6, 16–17, 19–22, 150–51; in lieutenant governor election (1970), 164
Mager, Gerald, 89
Manchester (N.H.) *Union-Leader*, 80
March of Dimes, 159
Mardian, Robert, 131
Mathews, John, 100, 102–3
Matthews, Charles, 58
McCarthy, Eugene, 105
McClerkin, Hayes, 38
McCord, Robert, 41
McGill, Ralph, 13, 148, 149
McKeithen, John, 20
McLeese, Ike, 120–21, 133
McMath, Sidney, 38
McNair, Robert, 2, 114, 116, 117, 123, 124, 126, 127, 129–30, 134, 138, 141
Meredith, James, 25
Mikva, Abner, 93
Mills, Wilbur, 128
Mitchell, John, 68, 94
Mizell, M. Hayes, 114, 140
Montgomery bus boycott, 147
Morgan, Charles, 33
Morton, Rogers, 82–83
Moss, Thomas, 143
Murfin, William, 81
Murphy, Reg, 157, 159
Muskie, Edmund, 127

NAACP (National Association for the Advancement of Colored People), 8, 13, 19, 86–88, 91, 117, 121, 124, 127, 134, 162
National Advisory Commission on Civil Disorders, 8, 33
National Observer, 158

Randy Sanders is assistant professor of history at Southeastern Louisiana University.